JEANNETTE'S SECRET RECIPES

By the same author

SOUPS

JEANNETTE'S SECRET RECIPES

SIMPLIFYING THE ART OF FRENCH COOKING

JEANNETTE SEAVER

ILLUSTRATED BY
NATALIE SEAVER

Seaver Books
New York

Copyright © 1981 by Jeannette Seaver
All Rights Reserved
No part of this book may be reproduced, for any reason, by any means, including any method of photographic reproduction, without the permission of the publisher.

First published as a Borzoi Book in 1975 by Alfred A. Knopf, Inc. under the title Jeannette's Secrets of Everyday Good Cooking.
2nd Printing—July 1975
3rd Printing—December 1975
Book-of-the-Month Club edition published February 1975.
Reprinted in 1976 by Bantam Books

First Trade Paperbound Edition 1981
First Printing 1981
ISBN: 0-394-17845-9
Seaver Books ISBN: 0-86579-017-5
Library of Congress Catalog Card Number: 81-51528

Jacket design and illustrations by Natalie Seaver
Manufactured in the United States of America
Distributed by Grove Press, Inc., New York
Seaver Books, 333 Central Park West, New York, N.Y. 10025

To Dick,
*whose love inspired my cooking
and this book*

CONTENTS

THE FUN OF COOKING
AND THE CEREMONY OF EATING
1

GOOD COOKING BEGINS WITH
GOOD MANAGEMENT
11

BASIC DOUGHS, BASIC SAUCES,
ABOUT SALADS, HERBS AND SPICES
33

FAMILY DINNERS
61

SMALL DINNER PARTIES
(*Up to Eight*)
125

LARGE DINNER PARTIES AND BASHES
185

LEFTOVERS (*The Squirrel Complex*)
197

WINE TIPS
299

Index *follows page 310*

THE FUN OF COOKING AND THE CEREMONY OF EATING

Fine cooking is an art, and a great art. Like the other arts, it has a long history and tradition and requires three basic elements: the artist, the audience, and knowledge on the part of both.

Far too often, however, this culinary knowledge, history, and tradition have been looked upon as a closely guarded treasure, the province of the "happy few." This applies not only to the past but is still true to a large extent today: far too many cookbooks and guides, I have found, by their complexity, sheer volume, and terminology, tend to perpetuate the myth that good cooking is difficult . . . and lengthy.

Having been born and brought up in France, I grew up with fine cooking. From childhood on I observed and assimilated, through some process of osmosis, the thousand little tricks, shortcuts, and secrets that are part and parcel of a French cook's makeup. I also learned to take for granted that thriftiness can and ought to be an integral part of good cooking, and that the way food is served—that is, in a visually attractive way—is almost as important as the food itself.

My aim in this book, therefore, is threefold: first, to explode the myth that fine or gourmet cooking is difficult, time consuming, and a draining experience for the cook. Second, to show that even the most sophisticated dishes do not necessarily require long, arduous preparations. (How would you like to make a *mousse au cognac*, one of the most elegant of French pâtés, in only ten minutes, for very little money? Or a *jambon en croûte* in twelve? I do; and there's no reason you can't.) My third aim, which is perhaps a direct corollary of the first two, is to convince you that cooking can be not only rewarding and challenging, but great fun.

Through the years, armed with the secrets I assimilated as a child and young girl, I have evolved a series of further "secrets" and shortcuts for complicated recipes. They sacrifice nothing to taste, are quite inexpensive, and most can be done in a twinkling. If I did so it was because I had to.

As a professional musician and mother of three, and with a gourmet-oriented husband, I early had to make a decision: what to do about cooking. We could limit our gourmandise to occasional dinner parties, outings to French restaurants, or trips abroad, meanwhile resorting to plain, expedient food the rest of the time. Or I could give up my career and cook all day long. The other possibility was to try to preserve both: career and gourmet life style. But how? There were, after all, only so many hours in a day, and work and children took most of them. As I pored over the various cookbooks and encyclopedias day after day, I was put off and discouraged by the length and seeming opacity of the recipes. Too often, I abandoned the reading and, more regretfully, the cooking that might have resulted from it. But I refused to give up: I wanted to have my *tarte aux pommes* and eat it, too. Little by little I dared to try shortcuts. Sometimes they didn't work, but to my surprise they often did. And even in the cases where they didn't, I went back and tried again until I had found, for any dish I refused to let go, a new, succinct formula.

It is these "formulas"—revised, shortened recipes and tips—that I would like to share with you in these pages. What I have discovered over the years is that cooking creatively takes no more time or effort than cooking mechanically. And it's a lot more fun both for you and for your audience.

Another myth I would like to explode in this book is that having people to dinner is a production, one that must be planned six days, if not six weeks, in advance, so that by the time the event itself occurs one is in a state of nervous exhaustion. That to me defeats the purpose. Entertaining, which is part of good living—in fact of civilization—should be pleasure, not pain. And that does not apply just to the wealthy, or those with help or "staff." It applies as well to all of us who have to prepare everything, from soup to nuts to setting the table, ourselves.

In days gone by, the classic order of a French meal used to consist of no less than ten courses. These were:

>Soup
>Hors d'oeuvre
>Fish
>Meat
>Vegetables
>Salad
>Cheese
>Fruits
>Dessert
>Coffee

These courses were all accompanied by their wines, naturally. How there are still any Frenchmen left to tell the story remains a mystery, and somewhat of a miracle, to me. This "protocol" of eating has, however, been simplified to some degree (!), and the "classic" French meal now consists of:

>Soup *or* hors d'oeuvre
>Fish *or* meat
>Vegetables
>Salad
>Cheese
>Dessert *or* Fruits
>Coffee

Despite efforts to further simplify and reduce it, the classic French meal still remains stolidly entrenched to this day. Does it seem excessive? Perhaps; but I have generally found that behind most food customs or culinary traditions there lurks a dietary mission of sorts. And I remind myself that, despite what may strike some as aberrations or idiosyncrasies when it comes to food, the French are also nonetheless well known for their wisdom, their logic. While clearly motivated by a seemingly incurable pleasure complex, the French also have a strong sense of self-preservation, of measure, that acts as a kind of governor for the sensual impulses. If the French start a meal with soup, it is because soups tend to calm even as they nourish, and soothe and prepare the diner for the next dish. If they start with an hors d'oeuvre (and both soup and hors d'oeuvre will or should be served in modest quantities), it is to "tease" as well as please the appetite. The notion of equilibrium is present in any French menu, be it for health or gastronomic reasons. A vegetable accompanying a meat course is conceived to either enhance or counterbalance, never to "overload." If cheese appears so widely on French menus, it is not because it "feeds" but because it acts as a calming transition from the salty main course or courses to the sweet portion of the meal, and also enhances the last bit of wine. As desserts round off a meal sweetly, so coffee acts as a digestive . . . as do the brandy or liqueur which are so often served after coffee. "Joindre l'utile à l'agréable" is one of the basic mottos of not only French cuisine but French life: "Combine the useful and the pleasurable." It may not always be an easy motto to live by in this harried age. But it strikes me as a good one to strive for.

"A woman's place is in the kitchen!"

— *(Very) Old Saying*

It is not my intention to add further fuel to the much discussed and often abused topic of whose place is what or where in today's society. My situation is: I am female, and a working female, on the one hand. On the other, I love good food. If that seems to create an immediate conflict, for me it doesn't, in that I am not among those who consider the kitchen a place of confinement or punishment, but rather one where fun, creativity, and repose are the order of the day.

Since I consider the kitchen a pleasure site, I would like—rather than debate the matter politically—to invite one and all, male and female, adults and children, into it.

Cooking is an art, true. But unlike most of the other arts, which require long and arduous training, the art of cooking can be approached—and mastered—at any point in one's life. My four-year-old is so enamored of cooking—the smells, the doughy materials, the edible results—that I can't keep him out of the kitchen; similarly, a friend of mine in her fifties who has worked in an office all her adult life confided to me recently that she has just "discovered" cooking, and it is fast becoming a passion with her.

Cooking is also an art which does not require all kinds of complex, expensive, or fancy equipment. You should be able to cook "gourmet" in a cabin in the mountains, with only a wood stove or alcohol burner to go on. As you will see, there is some basic equipment I highly recommend, but even if you don't have it or can't afford it, there are ways to obtain fine results without it. Throughout this book I will give you these alternate methods.

Having spent many years in both Europe and the United States, I have seen and experienced the best (and the worst) of both worlds from a culinary point of view. In Europe, until recently, cooks had no refrigerators, freezers, blenders, mixers, or any other appliances which are part and parcel of virtually every American kitchen. Therefore, they had to shop almost every day of the week, and sometimes twice. Anyone who knows France will doubtless remember the image of the housewives with their *filets*—string baskets—laden with groceries from the local market or store, from which generally protrude golden brown sticks of freshly baked bread. It is all very picturesque —except perhaps to the French woman herself, who would gladly trade the habit for her American counterpart's ability to shop once a week.

The point is, and it is one that has always intrigued me, that the cook in France, for whom not only shopping itself but the entire spectrum of meal preparation is relatively more difficult than it is for the American, produces meals day in and day out that are good, savory, and generally elegantly presented. Nor is this standard exclusive to the upper strata of the so-called social or economic scale. It prevails throughout the population. If you don't believe me, stop in and see what the local people are having for lunch at some out-of-the-way French village.

There is no question but that great progress has been made in the United States over the past fifty years. Back in the 1920s, Frank Crowninshield could write, in his Foreword to Brillat-Savarin's *Physiology of Taste:*

> Consider the present debasement of a smart dinner-party in New York! No flowers on the table. Most of the guests thirty minutes late. Two cocktails for everybody. And how can one truly appraise the flavor of good food after two cocktails? . . . Then a soup, plenty of champagne, a meat that has been kept on the edge of the stove for thirty minutes, two vegetables, and a bottle of Scotch—a carafe would border more nearly on the realm of aesthetics. The host wholly unaware of what dishes are to be put before him. Cigarettes, of course, smoked with the meat. . . . Everybody bolting his food. The women eating a little too little, the men drinking a little too much. . . .

How the situation has evolved as far as your own dinner parties are concerned I leave you to judge. But obviously, the many millions of Americans who have traveled and sampled the cuisines of different lands, plus the generally increased awareness of cooking as a fine art, have broadened horizons in general. Cooking out of cans, and frozen TV dinners, still do exist, but hopefully are on their way out. I hope that this book will demonstrate that no one need resort to such barbarities, simply because anyone with 45 minutes a day at his or her disposal can prepare an elegant, several-course meal.

Elegance. To me the ceremony of eating is virtually as important as the art of fine cooking. And by ceremony I do not mean stiff collars and stuffed shirts, but simply the creation of a pleasant environment wherein to partake of your meals, be they family dinners or formal invitations for fifteen or twenty.

At times, I have the feeling that every pressure in the modern world is combining to militate against elegance, to do away with any kind of ceremony. The thrust is toward instant everything, be it instant rice or frozen baked potatoes. The theory is: since you, the cook, no longer have the time in this hectic age to slave over a hot stove, we (the packagers) will slave for you, and make your life easy. The only problem is, the resulting quality is rock bottom. But the other, more important point is: why accept poor quality when —I maintain—all you need is 45 minutes to an hour a day to become a fine cook.

But cooking is only half the battle. The other half is presentation. What is presentation? Simply "dressing up" your food, whatever it may be, in an attractive dish, bowl, or platter. It's candles, maybe, or a bouquet of flowers as a centerpiece. It's a tablecloth rather than a bare board; a pretty crock for your pâté or pickles or cheese; in a word, it's caring. For cooking—and the presentation thereof—is not only an art but an act of generosity. When you cook thoughtfully, you are really telling people that you care for them. You are giving them a gift, in the same sense that performers give of their talent and ability. And as performers need and expect applause, so do cooks need appreciation—concrete, verbalized appreciation. I therefore urge you not to be reticent in complimenting the cook.

Eating—good eating—is great fun. Not only in the consumption but also in the preparation. What is more, it is the most democratic of all the arts, in that it is accessible to all. It does not have to be expensive (although it can, and doubtless ought to, look that way); it can be indulged in and appreciated daily, and even twice daily. And you don't have to travel far, be it across town or across the ocean, to experience it. The main problem is convincing yourself of the truth of the above. There are so many old wives' tales about the drudgery of cooking that too many people equate kitchen and cooking with a kind of slavery.

I hope and trust that in some measure this book will help dispel those myths forever.

GOOD COOKING BEGINS WITH GOOD MANAGEMENT

All of us have seen graphic depictions of the "laden board," filled with untold culinary delicacies, and the bon vivants of bygone eras who made a cult of eating and drinking. What we sometimes tend to forget is that for every such baronial banquet there was, in the kitchens below, a veritable army of cooks and bakers and helpers working day and night to maintain this high level of sensual pleasure. In other words, behind the pleasure principle was an exploitation principle—and this was true in bourgeois cooking up through the end of the nineteenth century . . . and on into the twentieth.

Today, there has been a real democratization throughout the world, which has virtually destroyed that former society and most of its amenities. While few may regret its passing, the fact remains that too often this democratization has been used as an excuse for lowering standards, for eliminating the pleasure principle from life, on the basis that there is no longer any time for the amenities.

I disagree. While admittedly it is more difficult for a working mother of two or more with little or no help to maintain high culinary standards, it can be done. For one thing, as machines have replaced manual labor in the fields and factories over the past two centuries, so have labor-saving devices gone a long way toward making up for the lack of "help" which produced the *haute cuisine* in times past. The point is: one can, with a bit of planning and management, still produce "gourmet" cooking in the context of today's tempo and pressures. If one does not, it is because one does not want to. Only in that case no one should resort to the excuses of lack of time, of "help," or of strength.

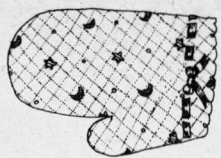

"Management," which derives from the Latin word *manus*—hand—is the art or manner of handling something successfully. In our context it means handling one's time, one's energy, and one's equipment.

Let's take each of these three separately.

Time: It is not only how you use it during that crucial hour just prior to mealtime, it is how you use it in general, long before any given meal. It is how you anticipate.

By anticipation I mean very simply the act of composing and visualizing your menu ahead of time. How far ahead will depend on the occasion, of course, on whether you are giving a large dinner party or planning a family dinner. Projecting a particular recipe, as well as an entire meal, has become a daily habit with me. It takes no more than a few minutes, but in the beginning at least requires a bit of discipline. They are minutes that can be easily fitted into your daily "dead" time: in the shower, on the subway going to work, or at any other idle moment of day or night.

The first step is to formulate a general idea of what your menu will consist of, from first course to last. It may be only a tentative menu, which you may later modify, but at least it will give you a basic structure from which to work. The menu may be dictated by what you know is in your larder or by what is in season. Or by what you know is this week's special at your local supermarket. When projecting, it is not necessary to plan from the first course to the last. Most likely, you'll think of the main course you'd like, then build around it. But you may well decide that it's a meal that must finish with chocolate mousse, and that will inspire the rest.

Once you've got your tentative menu clearly in mind, check your shelves to see what you already have on hand and what remains to be bought. At this point you're ready to break down your meal—that is, the sum of the various recipes involved—into several preparation phases. This is the area where the timesaving may be the greatest, when properly applied, but it is also a great energy saver.

Energy: Many people think of preparing a meal as a strictly chronological affair: first you make the hors d'oeuvre, then you start the entrée, then you clean the salad, after which you go out and buy your cheeses. If you have any time or energy left, you'll use it for a dessert. But cooking does not have to be chronological any more than making a movie does. Movies are not shot in chronological sequence, or in the order the story occurs; on the contrary, scenes with the same actors are combined and shot one after the other, as are scenes with the same sets. This is as logical as it is economical. For this same reason, breaking down your menu into logical preparation phases will minimize your expenditure of energy. Many of these phases can be fitted into loose ten-minute periods either fairly early in the day of your planned meal or even the night before. For example, suppose you have settled on a main course of lasagna (see page 112) for your Wednesday dinner. Today is Tuesday. On Tuesday evening, while you're cleaning up the kitchen, put your pasta in to boil. While it's boiling, you can make your meat sauce, including the tomatoes and seasoning. When done—and it should take no more than twenty minutes in all—put in separate bowls, cover, and store in the refrigerator. For those who can't stand the sight of any food after dinner, you can accomplish the same result by doing the above on one side of the stove while cooking Tuesday night's dinner on the other. Same time; double results. On Wednesday evening, when you come home from school, work, or whatever, it will take no more than ten minutes to assemble and top your lasagna, and another fifteen or twenty minutes for it to bake, while you are doing other things.

Even more important than this daily planning is the overall planning for the week. The basic concept, and the phases, are roughly the same.

Plan your menus for the week. That doesn't mean that you'll stick to them like a good soldier, but again it gives you a basic structure. In any formal plan there's also plenty of room for frivolity and caprices—and they're always welcome. On the basis of your tentative menus, make a shopping list. Check your shelves, both refrigerator and pantry, to see what you already have in plentiful supply, and what you need. Since virtually all refrigerators today are large enough to store at least a week's supply of food for a normal family—with the exception of dairy products and perhaps a few perishables which will taste better being fresh—there's no reason you shouldn't be able to do your shopping once a week. In many areas, dairy products can be delivered to your door daily at little extra cost, and for a relative pittance most supermarkets will deliver, too. It's a small luxury well worth it. Phone ordering is another time and energy saver, but you'll feel the difference in your pocketbook.

Obviously, your own particular schedule, tastes, and purse will dictate your weekly planning. But I cannot stress too strongly the notion of thinking ahead, when you are planning any main course, to the various derivatives or leftovers that you can possibly make from it. As you will discover, I am a staunch advocate of "leftovers," not only for economic reasons but also for gastronomic pleasure. For example, let's assume that you have chosen two main meat courses for the week (they were on sale this week at your local market): ham and ground beef.

For the ham, let's assume you serve baked ham as the main course for your Monday meal . . . and there's plenty left over. For Wednesday, think quiche lorraine, using scraps of ham. For Friday or Saturday, *jambon en croûte*—ham in pastry—will use up another portion of your remaining ham. If any is left after these three meals, you may want to try French pancakes with ground ham, ideal for a weekend lunch but also delicious for another dinner main course.

For the ground beef, use some of it to make a lasagna for Tuesday's dinner. On Thursday, make a *hachis parmentier* (a dish utilizing mashed potatoes and ground beef in several layers), and with the rest of your leftover ground beef, make a *chou farci* (whole cabbage stuffed with ground beef) or *piroshki* (a Russian "turnover" stuffed with meat).

Weekly planning in this sense will not only prove a boon for your budget but, even more important, will be fun, a constant challenge to your creativity. I have always enjoyed knowing that from only two basics five, six, or even seven main courses can result. What you should also bear in mind in this game of "leftovers" is the other items you will need depending on your choices: for instance, if you know that from your original ham you'll be making a quiche, a ham soufflé, or French pancakes, you'll also know you should buy an extra dozen eggs.

The whole point is, in anticipating your weekly menus, plan your leftovers rather than simply letting them happen.

Here are some other items to remember in the "anticipation" department. In the morning, whether you're leaving for the day or staying home, remember to defrost any frozen foods—especially meats—that may figure in that night's menu. Frozen casseroles, homemade soups, and frozen vegetables may of course be heated or cooked without prior thawing.

It's also worthwhile to spend the four or five minutes (maximum) it takes you in the morning to wash your salad and immerse it in a bowl of water for the rest of the day. You'll come home to find it crisp and fresh. Most people have a favorite salad dressing, which they've evolved from experience or from cookbooks, a dressing seasoned with their personal herbs no doubt. If you're among them, it's a good idea to mix up a good quantity of the dressing, which you can store in a quart jar in the refrigerator, ready for instant use. Purists may object—and even in France today most people mix their dressings fresh for each new salad. I did too for years, thinking it was the only way, until I realized it was completely unnecessary. Not only was the time saving appreciable but the quality of the dressing remained the same from day to day. I usually mix up a quart at a time.

There are times when you have to be in the kitchen, when feeding younger children or keeping them company, when waiting for a phone call or a delivery. Use these "idle" moments. In the same way that some people knit or crochet or just plain doodle, pick some item from this week's menu, or even next's, and do some preparatory work on it. For instance, make enough pie crust for two or three dishes and freeze it. Make stuffing for poultry; try your hand at *pesto* (see page 163). Also freeze. In the case of the pie crust, it takes only minutes but it can save some future "orphan" meal, when you have no time or mind to plan. It's evening, you arrive home too late to shop, and despite all my admonitions you haven't planned ahead: a quick quiche lorraine, or an apple pie, will be a welcome zesty addition. "As easy as apple pie" is more than a cliché: it's a truth, especially if you have the pie crust ready and waiting to be rolled. The same goes for quiche, which sounds as though it should be difficult but is just as easy. It takes about an hour to defrost your dough and make it "rollable." So remove it from the freezer as soon as you get home.

Most dishes can be frozen; therefore, whenever possible make double the quantity of whatever you're preparing: use one half for your current meal and freeze the other, labeling before you do. At some later date you'll be delighted you did.

Soups. I'll have much more to say in a later chapter about the virtue and charm of homemade soups. But for planning purposes, assuming I have convinced you that not only are homemade soups worth ten times any canned or dried soup you can buy, but also that they are easy to make—whenever you make a soup, divide it into several medium-size containers rather than one large one. The point is, each of the medium containers, which should be large enough to hold soup enough for four to six, can be defrosted individually. If the entire quantity is in a large container, you'll not be able to refreeze and you'll have to waste the extra, unused portion. Or eat nothing but soup for supper.

In our family we have soup fairly often, and I have evolved something the children jokingly refer to as "my eternal soup." Whenever I have some soup left over, even if it's only a cupful or so, I reconstitute it using whatever else may be left over from the same meal: a couple of potatoes, a handful of chopped parsley, fifteen green beans, some meat scraps, or whatever. Stretched with some milk, they reappear with a new personality.

EQUIPMENT

Most cookbooks will give you a basic list of "required kitchen equipment" that varies in length from one page to ten. Personally, I have always operated with a minimum of material. If I were asked what was the one absolutely necessary appliance I would have to reply: the blender. There are literally dozens of elegant dishes that can be made with a minimum of effort by using a blender.

Other Appliances: As for the rest, let's take a look at my kitchen:

Mixer: not as important as the blender, but a close second. If your budget forces you to choose between the two, choose the blender. You can always get a cheap, manual mixer at the hardware or ten-cent store which will serve your interim purpose.

Juicer: electrical is handy, but manual is fine too.

Grater: the French make is called *Moulinette* by Moulinex. It comes in both manual and electrical models. Outside of major cities it may be difficult to find, but it can usually be ordered by mail from a good kitchenware house or major department store. In any case, it's a treasure. Most helpful for cole slaw, grated carrots, *céleri rémoulade,* and so on.

Utensils: Still from my own kitchen:

Dutch Oven (in French, *cocotte*) : can be found in enamel, cast iron, as well as in some newly developed Teflon-coated material. Whatever you choose, it should be heavy, because it is called on to sit on the stove and simmer for hours. Essential for soups and stews. I recommend a five-quart size.

Deep Fryer: everyone loves good, crisp, fried potatoes—the *frites* you get at French restaurants. For that reason alone, a deep fryer is basic, in France. I've had one since the first day I set up housekeeping, and I warn you I intend to proselytize in these pages for deep frying. You can use simply a pot with a wire basket.

Pressure Cooker: as time-saving as ever.

Frying Pans: two, one large (12 inch), one small (8–9 inch). I prefer cast iron, but many people prefer Teflon.

Pots: two or three medium-sized, with lids.

Saucepans: two, large (2 quart).

Casserole Dishes: one or two, Pyrex or other (8 inch square).

Roasting Pan: one, large (12 by 18 is a good bet).

Coffee Pot.

Tea Kettle.

Colander.

Fondue Dish: optional, but great fun.

Soufflé Dish: optional (3-quart size). I term this "optional" because any Pyrex dish of the same size will do. But a soufflé dish enhances your dinner table.

Timbales (small individual soufflé dishes or molds): even more optional than the above, but lovely to have.

Pie Plate and/or Quiche Molds: two 9-inch molds. If you can buy the French variety, which lifts out of its rim, I recommend it.

Springform Mold: optional but very useful.

In addition, you will need a set of flatware, half a dozen wooden spoons of different sizes, a large stirring spoon, a butcher knife, a serrated bread knife, a set of sharp steak knives, a couple of spatulas, a whisk, a rolling pin, measuring cups and spoons.

STAPLES

An integral part of *haute cuisine* planning and anticipation is stocking in your pantry an assortment of canned goods that can provide either the basis for what amounts to an instant gourmet lunch or dinner or a key supplement that can raise an ordinary meal to epicurean heights. I am not referring here to the regular and relatively standard pantry provisions—to each cook his or her own—but to a list of items I have used time and again to good purpose, often in emergencies. Emergencies? How with all my planning can I have emergencies? Very simply: it's one o'clock Saturday afternoon and all of a sudden four people drive up to your door. They are just passing through, and wanted to say hello. You offer them a drink. By now it's one thirty and you can see *haute cuisine* written all over their faces. So what do you do? You retreat to your kitchen, take a deep breath, and check your pantry shelves, or your cupboard. Here are some of the things you are likely to find:

Anchovies: an exotic and tasty plus for several hors d'oeuvres.

Artichoke Hearts: a salad in itself, or an hors d'oeuvre. Can also be a meat garnish sautéed with garlic and parsley. Delicious with any meat.

Asparagus: excellent for salads or with vinaigrette as an hors d'oeuvre.

Baking Powder: an essential ingredient used as a leavening agent in countless recipes, from doughnuts to cakes.

Beets (sliced) : served in a vinaigrette sauce, part of the traditional hors d'oeuvre variés (in the French sense of the term, that is as a first course, *not* as canapés) .

Black Bean Soup: Despite my own strong feelings about the homemade kind, this is the exception that proves the rule. Actually, I'm not suggesting here that you serve it as is; it needs some very personal attention but nonetheless serves as an excellent basis for one of my favorite soups (see page 30) .

Carrots and Peas: a fine accompaniment for veal, as well as an hors d'oeuvre in itself when served in a mayonnaise sauce (called *mace-*

doine in French, this too is one of the staples of the hors d'oeuvre variés).

Bread Crumbs: necessary for all sorts of breaded dishes, both meat and vegetable. I make my own with stale bread, using the blender, but you can of course buy them as well. But it has always struck me as rather silly and wasteful to throw away stale bread with one hand and buy bread crumbs with the other.

Cereal: there are hundreds of kinds, literally, and aside from oatmeal I don't generally use dried cereals myself. But my children do, and your choice will doubtless be dictated by your family's preferences.

Chestnut Purée (au naturel): this imported canned vegetable won't be available in your supermarket, but can usually be found in most specialty and gourmet shops. Unsweetened, it is concentrated, mashed chestnuts, especially good with roast turkey, any poultry, roast beef, or leg of lamb. It should not be served as it comes out of the can.

Chestnut Purée (sweetened): also imported, and doubtless available only at gourmet shops. What I do is serve it with a mixture of sour cream and whipped cream (which is my method of simulating French *crème fraîche*) to make a marvelous albeit rather rich dessert. It is also a basic ingredient for some (also sinfully rich) cakes.

Chickpeas: good as salad in a vinaigrette sauce, with shallots and parsley, a staple for lunches and picnics. Can also be puréed into a Lebanese delicacy called *hummus* and served as an appetizer (see page 195).

Chocolate: for baking, and desserts in general. Sweet or semi-sweet.

Clams (au naturel): great for instant spaghetti clam sauce.

Clams (smoked): mixed with sour cream, a perfect instant dip. Also part of antipasto.

Corn Meal: for bread, and also necessary for baking French bread (see page 36).

Cornstarch: essential as a thickener, for soups, sauces, desserts, and so on.

Creamed Corn: gives a hearty touch to soups.

Deviled Ham: can be turned into an ultraquick pâté (see page 138).

Evaporated Milk: very important. Can be the basic ingredient for innumerable recipes which call for cream or milk, whenever your fresh dairy products are in short supply.

Flour: I prefer the unbleached variety.

Gelatin (unflavored): essential for a variety of desserts, including cold soufflés. Also necessary for any dishes in aspic.

Mustard: another basic, needed for salad dressings, *céleri rémoulade*, preparation of gigot (French-style roast lamb), and an infinite number of other recipes. I suggest Dijon style, of whatever brand.

Oil: you'll need oil for eating and oil for cooking. I prefer olive oil for my salads, but you may prefer another kind. For my cooking and deep frying I use peanut oil, as does all France.

Onions (canned): boiled onions are handy for garnishing a number of meat dishes. They can be used alone as a vegetable or be mixed with another vegetable.

Oysters (smoked): for instant canapés, or part of an antipasto.

Pastas: this includes everything from spaghetti to noodles to lasagna. I always keep a supply of several different kinds, since one can serve as a meal in itself at a moment's notice, or as a side dish.

Peas: preferably the small or tiny variety. A must with veal or poultry.

Pimiento: mostly decorative, in antipasto or on an hors d'oeuvre tray, but can man—or woman—live by necessities alone?

Rice: regular long grain—not Minute rice.

Salmon: keep a can or two handy for cold salads or salmon mousse. Also for casserole dishes.

Salt: I keep two kinds, the coarse for dipping fresh vegetables and for pot-au-feu; the fine for daily use.

Sardines: a traditional member of the hors d'oeuvre tray.

Tea: I keep both regular tea and tea bags handy, for although the former unquestionably tastes better there are times when only a single cup is needed and tea bags are useful.

Tomato Paste: a little goes a long way—*always* dilute.

Tomato Purée: has the virtue of often being more economical than tomato sauce—for which it can be generally substituted.

Tomato Sauce: as above, for all sorts of sauces, from spaghetti on down (or up).

Tomatoes (whole, canned): always needed, for gazpacho, bouillabaisse, and sauces galore, when fresh tomatoes are unavailable.

Truffles: a necessary nonbasic. A sinfully luxurious addition to your pantry shelf, which will give you the opportunity of turning the blandest or skimpiest leftover into something exquisite. I keep a can on hand because I know they aren't easy to find, and just when I desperately need them they'll be unobtainable. Expensive, but worth it.

Tuna: numerous uses in salads, casseroles, and so on.

Vegetable Bin: a corner of my cupboard is devoted to my vegetable bin, where I keep those basic vegetables that do not require refrigeration: potatoes, onions, shallots, garlic.

Vinegar: I, like most French people, use red wine vinegar.

White Beans (very small) : with the proper herbal marriage, delightful with gigot.

NOTE: A monetary tip which I have found has worked for me: for the most exotic staples suggested above, such as the truffles, smoked clams, or oysters, buy them when you *don't* need them. If you wait until the day you do, you will invariably find (at least I have) that that is the very day my food budget has run out. Or the store has run out of what I want. I don't know whether you have ever put on a coat or jacket you haven't worn for a while and found a crumpled dollar bill in the pocket. You'll have something of the same feeling the day you open your cupboard in an emergency and find one of your exotic staples sitting there.

Next I turn to my herb shelf and quickly glance at the herbs and spices there. Here is a list of those I consider basic to fine cooking. Some, you will see, are not specifically French, for though my cooking is basically French, I am a transplanted French cook and have absorbed other influences. The following list, therefore, is of varied origin and quite personal. In Chapter 3, I give a more complete and detailed herb and spice list, but these I use in one way or another on a daily basis:

    Basil   Mint
    Bay Leaf   Nutmeg
    Caraway Seeds Oregano
    Cinnamon   Paprika (sweet)
    Cloves   Paprika (strong)
    Dill Weed   Thyme
    Ginger   Vanilla

Next I check my refrigerator to see what else might serve or inspire. Among its multitude of treasures are:

Almonds (sliced): for sauces, soups, baking. NOTE: All nuts keep better refrigerated.

Almonds (whole): when ground, basic for cakes, cookies, macaroons, and so on.

Anchovy Paste: will put zest in a bland sauce.

Apricot Jam: I use it to glaze my *tartes aux pommes,* and as a filler for crêpes.

Bacon Slab: the basis for many a hearty dish, from pâtés to cassoulets.

Bread: I keep two or three loaves of sliced bread always handy: white, whole wheat, and pumpernickel.

Butter: I recommend having on hand both sweet and salted, for varying uses.

Carrots: I'm never without at least one bunch. Three or four carrots can be quickly transformed into a delicious first course—*carottes rapées*—or integrated into any number of soups.

Celery: hors d'oeuvre, salads, snacks. Also, like carrots, a basic for my homemade soups.

Celery Root: for *céleri rémoulade.* Also a great delicacy as a cooked vegetable.

Cheese (cheddar): preferably the sharp variety. Will add zest to sauces. One of the ingredients for my homemade cheeses. Always wrap airtight.

Cheese (cream): for pie crusts, pâtés, dips, casseroles . . . and also for my homemade cheeses.

Cheese (mozzarella): delicious cold, in salad. Or for some casserole dishes.

Cheese (Swiss): domestic or imported. Dozens of fine dishes depend on Swiss cheese, from gratins to sauces, sandwiches to cheese pie.

Cornichons (French): a small, sharp pickle, a basic accompaniment for pâté.

Cream (heavy): for pie crusts, pâtés, dips, casseroles . . . and for my homemade cheeses.

Cream (sour): will improve many stews and sauces. I also use it in many of my baking recipes.

Eggs: a basic.

Escargots (snails): may or may not be among your favorite appetizers, but if it is keep a can or two in your refrigerator (although canned, I always refrigerate). Escargots are served in *beurre d'escargot,* a judicious mixture of butter, nutmeg, garlic, parsley, pepper, and salt, which can be made well in advance and even frozen. Thus you can serve escargots literally at the drop of a guest's hat.

Ham: keep a one-pound can ready; it will be a friend indeed for a short-notice meal. (Ham, too, I keep refrigerated, even though it is canned.)

Hazelnuts: not an essential, but I've blessed their presence more than once when I've needed a glamorous dessert such as hazelnut mousse or macaroons.

Lemons: a cook's best friend. Never be without one, and preferably several. Lemon rind, juice, and pulp can all be a plus for countless recipes.

Margarine: for baking, I need and use it all the time, from puff paste to brioches. There's a myth about French cooks and butter, but more and more often margarine is used.

Mayonnaise: I've always made my own mayonnaise, and I urge you to do the same. It's better, and less expensive. See page 47 for basic recipe.

Oranges: for breakfast, naturally and for a number of desserts. Both juice and eating oranges should be among your supply. About twenty of the former and four or five of the latter should suffice for a week for a family of four. If you dislike the chilled ready-made orange juice, or even the frozen variety (as I do), and yet don't have the time or pocketbook to serve fresh orange juice for breakfast every morning, here is a compromise that I've found satisfies even the most demanding palates:

3–4 oranges (squeezed)
3 tablespoons frozen orange juice concentrate
2 cups cold water
3–4 ice cubes

Blend for 30 seconds until all ice is integrated, and serve.

Parsley: like lemon, one of my best friends. Keep in jar with water, the way you would flowers.

Peaches (canned): not a "must," but also good to have on hand, whether for a compote or a peach melba.

Pears (canned): in themselves a lovely dessert, served chilled in their own juice. They also provide the basis for one of my favorite desserts, pear sherbet (see page 178).

Raspberry Syrup (German or Swiss): another superfluous but wonderful essential, required for peach melba, recommended with strawberries, and so on.

Salad: if you feel you have to buy your salad fresh daily, try buying all your green salad for the week at once. If by midweek some of it seems wilted, you can revive it to perfect crispness by immersing it in cold water for at least an hour.

Scallions: for salads and soups as a substitute when chives or leeks are called for. Also will prove a pleasant seasoning for numerous vegetables.

Walnuts: for salads, cakes, cookies, pies. Also an essential ingredient for Greek soup.

Yeast: for doughs and breads. Active dry is most readily available, but of course fresh yeast will do, too.

Now, finally, I turn to my freezer, to see what it contains that might also be qualified as "gourmet basics." Obviously, some of the items that follow reflect my own tastes, but I have tried to limit the list to the things I recommend you consider keeping in your own freezer, if you have one. I cannot emphasize too strongly the value of the "squirrel complex" as your best method of avoiding any emergencies. Remember that whenever you bake—be it bread or brioches, croissants or pies—whenever you make a pâté terrine or quiche or quenelles, it is wise to make double or even treble what you will need immediately—and freeze the rest. I do this automatically now. Thus my freezer is filled with an array of delicacies just waiting to be thawed at a moment's notice.

Bread: baked or unbaked. It takes only minutes to heat, or bake, in your oven.

Brioches: the same as above.

Casseroles: any casserole dish, from *hachis parmentier* to moussaka to lasagna, can be frozen. Be sure to freeze it in aluminum or ceramic dishes, so that you can transfer it directly from freezer to oven without fear of the dish breaking. Pyrex can and does crack.

Coffee Cake: as you know, many store-bought coffee cakes come frozen. So can your homemade variety, an instant festive touch to an otherwise mundane breakfast—or tea.

Dough: any dough can be frozen: puff paste, pie crust, or whatever. I keep dough for one or more pie crusts handy in the freezer at all times. It takes one to two hours to thaw out.

Ice Cream: vanilla.

Orange Juice (frozen): one 16-ounce can should suffice for your weekly breakfast needs.

Pâtés: whenever I am making pâté of any kind, I always make double or more than I know I will need. Especially important for *rillettes*, which take longer to make than most pâtés. But apply the rule generally.

Pie: you can freeze any baked pie. Also make sure you freeze in a metal pie mold—for the same reasons indicated for casseroles above. Defrost and warm slightly in a 250° oven before serving.

Quenelles: will turn any improvised meal into a celebration.

Quiche: ditto above. I always have at least one frozen quiche on hand.

Soup: I generally have half a dozen or more homemade soups frozen. They can be defrosted and served very quickly, and I find retain the full, homemade flavor of the original.

Stock: always have a plastic container or two of stock in your freezer. You'll use it all the time, but you should always be replenishing your stock. Whenever you roast any poultry, or pick up some soup bones from your butcher, remember to make some stock with the untouched leftovers, by putting them in a kettle, adding enough water to cover, plus a bay leaf, one onion pricked with a couple of cloves, and a sprig of parsley. Bring to a boil, reduce flame, and let simmer for an hour. Strain, cool, and freeze (remembering to mark your container as to contents and date).

Turkey Roll: a worthy replacement for veal, and much less expensive, this can quickly become the main course of an impromptu menu on a day when you haven't had time to shop.

For my four unexpected guests, I settle on the following menu, which I quickly estimate should take no more than eight to ten minutes to prepare. Just for fun, I decide to time myself. Glancing up at the clock, I see it is just 1:40.

> Wine and Black Bean Soup
> Mozzarella Cheese Provence Style
> Sliced Beets Vinaigrette
> Sardines in Olive Oil
> Peach Melba

I begin by taking a couple of loaves of French bread from the freezer and sticking them in the oven at 425° (this of course is a far hotter oven than I would normally use, but given the time factor it will serve the purpose. Just be careful not to place bread too low in the oven, or even in my ten-minute time limit you might singe the bottom crust.)

Next, I open two cans of black bean soup, to which I add a can of red wine and a can of water. Into this heady mixture I squeeze half a lemon. I let it simmer on the stove, stirring a few times to mix the ingredients.

For my mozzarella dish I will need the following ingredients:

½-pound piece mozzarella cheese
1 can anchovy fillets
1 shallot, chopped
1 clove garlic, finely chopped
½ cup chopped fresh basil (or
   1 tablespoon dry basil)

½ cup chopped parsley
3 tablespoons olive oil
1 tablespoon wine vinegar
Pepper and salt

Slice the mozzarella thinly and place lengthwise on an attractive platter. On top of and around the cheese place your anchovies in crisscross fashion. Sprinkle the shallot, garlic, basil, and parsley on top. Add the olive oil, vinegar, and pepper and salt to taste (and, for added zest, pour over the cheese the oil remaining in the anchovy can).

As another dish, for this impromptu buffet, open a can or two of beets, reserve the juice for a later use, and pour the beets onto a separate serving platter. Add some vinaigrette sauce and top with a sprig or two of finely chopped parsley.

Now open a can (or two) of sardines, put in a glass bowl, and surround with quartered lemons.

I glance again up at my kitchen clock: it is just 1:52. The only course I have not prepared is the peach melba, which obviously cannot be prepared in advance. But that will take me no more than four to five minutes to prepare after the table has been cleared: simply the time required to open the refrigerator door, take out some vanilla ice cream and chilled peaches, and spoon them into dessert plates (champagne glasses if you have them!), then top with raspberry syrup and sprinkle with blanched almonds.

Bon appétit!—as we always say to one another in my family at the beginning of a meal and as you will hear it said throughout France.

I have discussed planning in general and certain specific aspects of good management, which basically depend on thinking ahead to anticipate problems and situations, and solve them before they arise. This anticipation program applies not only to the kitchen, but to the dining room as well.

In later chapters I'll discuss in detail how to set up your dining room for dinner parties as far in advance as practical, in order to minimize last-minute panic. Here I'd like to stress the importance of creating a daily routine for yourself which will cut down on your work and correspondingly increase both your own pleasure and that of your family. For no meal can be fully enjoyed and savored—no matter how fine the cooking—if you or a member of your family has constantly to get up and leave the table, to fetch some missing condiment, utensil, dish, or whatever, which with a little planning would have been on the table. It's not just a matter of efficiency; it's also a matter of thoughtfulness—which is an integral part of the culinary art.

On an everyday level: run quickly through your menu and see what it calls for in the way of serving utensils. Do you need a mat under your casserole dish? Put it on the table ahead of time, so that you don't end up rushing another person to fetch it while you stand holding the hot dish. If bread and butter are part of your meal, rather than have one big butter dish on the table, use small, individual butter dishes—or in the case of larger families, one for every two members. It's amazing how much that simple item will cut down on traffic jams. The same principle applies to salt and pepper shakers. On the sideboard, or somewhere at your elbow, close to but not actually on the table, keep ready your salad bowl (the dressing already in the bottom of the bowl but the salad not yet tossed), your cheese tray, and plates you may need for a subsequent course or courses, extra serving utensils, an extra pitcher of water or milk: anything for which you might have to get up and leave the table were it not right next to you.

Most of us lead fairly hectic lives, and mealtime should be a time of enjoyment—both of the palate and of the mind—a "truce" from the trials of the world outside. Good management, which is nothing more nor less than thinking and planning a little ahead, can go a long way toward making mealtime that much needed and much appreciated respite.

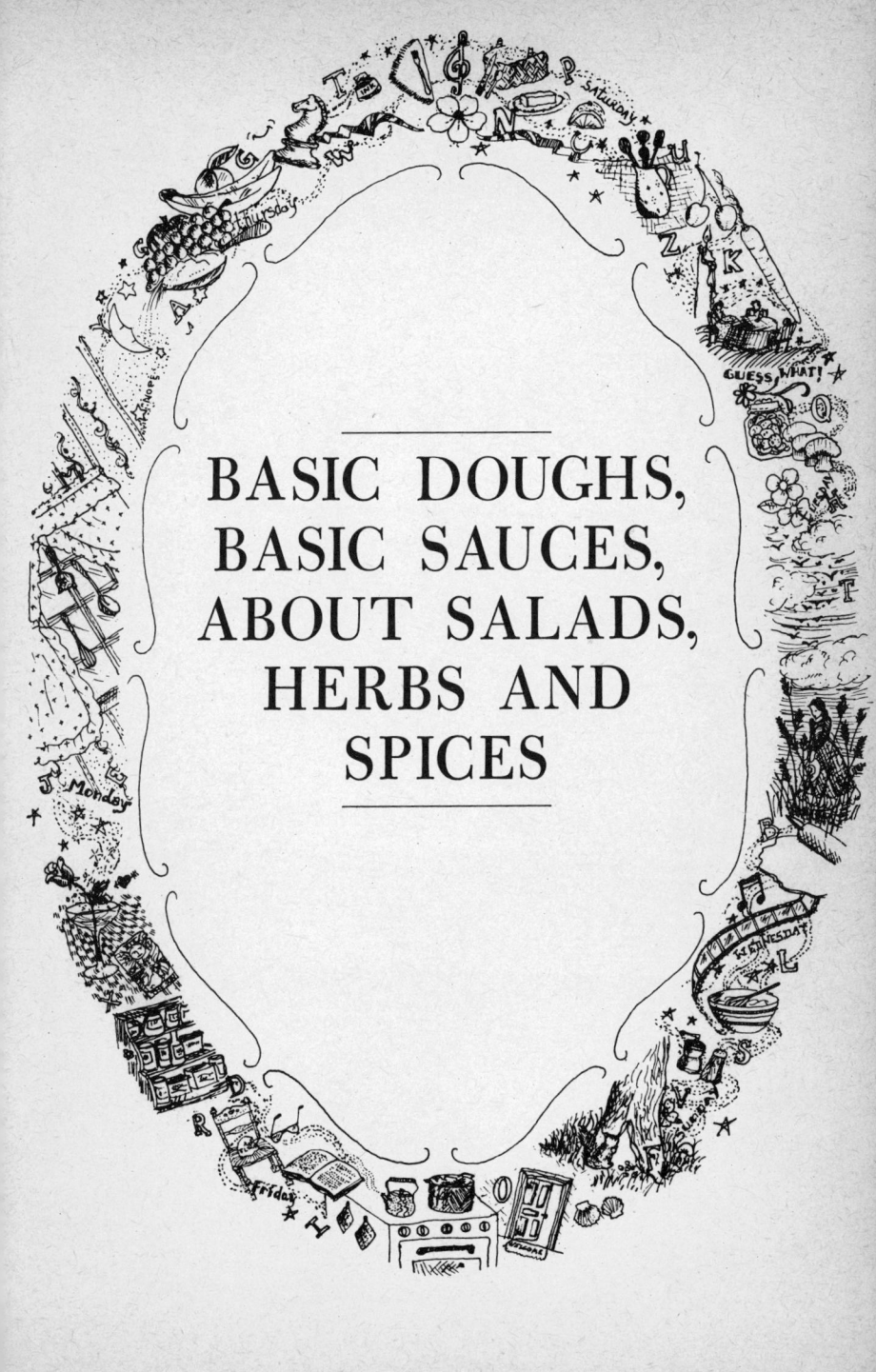

BASIC DOUGHS, BASIC SAUCES, ABOUT SALADS, HERBS AND SPICES

MY BASIC DOUGHS

I have found that part of good culinary management—and so-called quick gourmet cooking—is keeping readily available a variety of basic doughs in my refrigerator or freezer. The simplest way to assure such a supply is to make double or treble the amount of any dough you need for your immediate use. If you're making the dough for a quiche today, remember that that same dough can be used for any pie crust, or any *en croûte* dish, so think ahead to the apple pie you can make in ten minutes if your dough is ready and waiting, or that piece of ham you can dress up as *jambon en croûte* next Wednesday—again in only minutes.

The basic recipes I offer below are not so much new—people have been baking bread and pastry for several thousand years, after all—as recipes adapted and simplified from a number of classic baking formulas. I use them in one way or another almost every day. And, like most of my recipes, they can easily be fitted into even the most busy schedules.

The first recipe is for my homemade French bread, which I make once or twice a week (and, when I make it, there's plenty for several days). Next is a pizza dough that's so simple (and fun) to make you'll wonder why you went out and bought pizza all those years. Then there is my basic pie crust. Also included is my puff paste, considered the queen of the pastry doughs, which can be used for the fanciest desserts as well as for virtually any *en croûte* dish. Another *en croûte* pastry I hope you'll want to try is the brioche variety, which is lighter and different in texture from the other two, especially suited to fish and other delicate fillings. Speaking of brioche, I have evolved a relatively simple method of making breakfast brioches, those marvelously light yet sinfully rich French "rolls" which, together with croissants, feature in most Gallic morning menus. Last, a dough which serves me a dual purpose: first for my homemade coffee cakes, but also, without fillings, and shaped as crescents, a reasonable facsimile of the French croissants.

I am well aware that entire books have been devoted to baking, to offering literally hundreds of recipes for breads, pastries, doughs, and cakes. I have no desire to duplicate these comprehensive and very often excellent works. All I am suggesting with the following recipes is that, with these few, you will be able to accomplish in a few minutes what many have long considered arduous tasks. If you find that I seem to be skipping steps or breaking rules . . . well, I do. For instance, most books seem to call for sifting flour; mine doesn't. Why? Simply because one day when I was in a special hurry I made my dough without sifting, and found the results just as good. I tried it again . . . and again, until I became convinced that nothing was lost by eliminating it. You'll find, too, that my doughs call for very little kneading, compared to most recipes. Again, necessity was the mother of invention: when a certain classic recipe called for kneading for twenty minutes, sometimes twice, or (for brioches, to take a flagrant example) when recipes asked you literally to throw the dough onto a floured board for fifteen minutes, I began, like a bad schoolchild, to try to find the easier way, cutting down on time and kneading (or "throwing") until I felt I could cut no more.

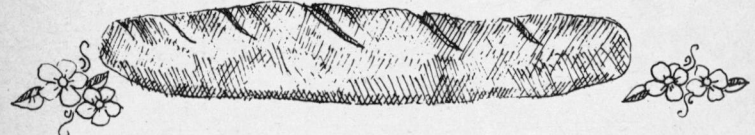

Homemade French Bread

There has been in the past a serious misconception regarding homemade bread—the myth that baking bread is difficult, particularly French bread. But I'm glad to see that more and more people are discovering that baking your own bread is not only fun, it's easy. And quick. Moreover, it is the *only* way you will get a good French loaf in most parts of America.

All you need to do to make your own French bread is the following, which will give you the equivalent of six short *baguettes*—real

French *baguettes* are three to four feet in length, but home ovens make loaves of fifteen or so inches your best bet.

½ cup warm water
2 packages active dry yeast
7 cups flour

2 tablespoons salt
2¼ cups warm water
½ cup corn meal

In a small bowl, mix ½ cup of warm water with the yeast. It will take a few minutes for the water and yeast mixture to interact and start to foam (also: yeast can be defective, and this initial step will give you a chance to make sure the yeast is "alive"), during which time, in a larger bowl, you mix the flour, salt, and the 2½ cups of water. Combine the contents of both bowls into one, kneading for two to three minutes. Divide dough into two mounds. Place each mound in a separate large bowl. Cover with plastic paper and put into an unlit oven, where it will be safely out of drafts. Forget about it, and go about your business, from a minimum of three hours to all day—or overnight.

The point is, all the above—step one of only three brief steps—can be accomplished literally in 5 minutes. So it's all a question of fitting those 5 minutes into your schedule during any given day.

Meanwhile, the dough in the oven will have been busy doing its own thing, namely rising. Remove. Uncover. Flour your hands, and gently punch both mounds to deflate them. Remove from the bowls and place on a floured board or countertop. With a knife, cut the dough into six roughly equal parts. On two or three cookie sheets, sprinkle corn meal, to cover the surface. Roll out each of the six pieces of dough into a rectangle, then roll or fold to form a flute as long as your cookie sheet and three to four inches wide. With the tip of a knife, make a number of light incisions every inch or so along the top surface. Leave the loaves for an hour or so to rise a second time; no need to cover them. (Again, the unlit oven is fine; or in a cupboard—just so they're away from drafts.) All of this—step two—will take you at most 10 minutes.

Now move to step three: preheat your oven to 450°, insert your loaves, or as many as your oven has room for at a time, and bake for 30 to 35 minutes. Repeat process until all loaves are baked.

The above quantity should more than suffice for from 10 to 12 people (if that seems like a lot—about half a loaf per person—you'll be amazed at how fast your bread goes), but bear in mind that you can always freeze what you don't need. To serve the frozen homemade bread, remove from the freezer and heat in your oven for 15 minutes at 400°.

Instead of running to your specialty shop, or dreaming of French bread, remember that all it entails is 20 minutes of your time. I urge you simply to give it a try. Chances are you'll be hooked for life.

Pizza Dough

Pizzas are popular in our family. We discovered they're so easy to make, and such fun, that we almost always make our own. For your dough, you will need:

½ package active dry yeast
½ cup warm water
2 cups flour
½ teaspoon salt
1 tablespoon olive oil

In a bowl, dissolve the yeast in the warm water, then mix with the remaining ingredients to form a smooth, elastic dough. Knead for 10 to 12 minutes (if you prefer, remove the dough from the bowl and knead on a counter or tabletop). Return to the bowl (if removed), and cover with a damp towel, at room temperature but out of a draft, and let rise for 1 to 2 hours.

Punch to deflate. Roll the dough on a floured board until it is about a quarter-inch thick. Line an oiled 10 by 12 roasting pan, cookie sheet, or any other ovenproof dish with the dough.

For the "standard" filling you will need:

15-ounce can tomato sauce
8 ounces mozzarella cheese, diced
½ teaspoon oregano

Over the rolled-out dough, spread the tomato sauce, top with the cheese, sprinkle oregano. Bake in a preheated 400° oven for about 20 minutes. (The edges should still be pale; otherwise the dough will be too hard.) Vary the above filling by adding: precooked Italian sausage, sliced; mushrooms; anchovy fillets; green pepper and onions, fresh sliced tomatoes, and so on.

Remember, when making pizzas you can make several for about the same amount of time and energy it takes to make only one. Whatever you don't eat, you can freeze and save for later use.

My Basic Pie Crust

My basic pie crust, which I use for countless dishes from quiche to *tarte aux pommes,* has the virtue of being extremely easy, quick, and reliable.

For an 8–9-inch pie mold you will need:

4-ounce package cream cheese
1½ sticks butter
2 cups flour

In a bowl, mix all the ingredients with your fingers to form a smooth dough. It should take you no more than 3 to 5 minutes. Refrigerate for 30 minutes (or more) before rolling out and baking. If you are not going to use it immediately, you can of course freeze it for later use. If you want to double or triple this recipe and set some aside for later use, I suggest you divide the dough into balls each enough for one pie, and store in the freezer in plastic bags. Label accordingly. It can keep two to three months in the freezer. It will take little or no more time, and will assure you of a ready supply for any emergency or unplanned meal. If you freeze the dough, move to the refrigerator what you expect to use any given day in the morning before you leave the house, or leave out at room temperature one hour before using.

Pâte Feuilletée (Puff Paste)

Pâte feuilletée, or puff paste, is rarely made by home chefs, even in France, being generally considered too difficult and too time-consuming to be made by anyone but professionals in cooking schools, restaurants, and pastry shops. I, like everyone else, was awed by the myth, but finally grew impatient of it and spitefully decided to try my hand at it. The problem—and the origin of the myth—stems from the fact that to make this pastry puff into many fine, flaky layers, it has to be rolled out, folded, and refrigerated at least six to eight times (to form the "layers"). Unfortunately, there is no shortcut here. However, since the pastry is unique, I refused to give up so easily and devised the following way to make it. I realized that it was not the rolling or folding that took the time, but rather the chilling in between, which varies according to the recipe from a half hour to an hour. Being excellent in math I soon came to the conclusion that the actual work time consisted of only 30 to 40 minutes. What I do is make enough for several pies, and not worry that the whole operation may go on for perhaps two or three days. Every time I have 5 free minutes in the kitchen I roll and fold, then put the pastry back in the fridge for an hour or a day, that is until I have another 5 minutes free.

Here is the recipe for four 8-inch pie crusts:

4 cups flour
½ tablespoon salt
¾ cup ice water
5 sticks butter (or margarine)

Mix the flour and salt and make a well. Pour ice water gradually into well, kneading with your fingers. It will become rubbery; if it is too sticky, add a touch of flour until a workable consistency is attained. If it is too dry, add a bit of water. Form dough into a ball. With a rolling pin, flatten ball into a rectangular shape, until it is about the size of a kitchen towel. Cut each stick of butter into 12 slices and, allowing for an inch or two margin all around, place butter patties side by side covering the middle area. Fold along all four sides to meet (as though you were wrapping a package). Roll out again carefully, making sure butter doesn't spurt (if it does, sprinkle with flour and continue; it will soon integrate properly into one smooth dough). When you have re-created a new rectangle, approximately the same size as the first, fold into thirds, wrap in wax paper, and refrigerate. You can begin your aforementioned 5-minute rolling stints an hour after this first operation. Roll out the dough again to a rectangle, fold into thirds, wrap, and refrigerate. Repeat this procedure at available intervals. The more rolling and folding, the flakier the pastry will be. I recommend a minimum of six rolling-folding stints.

Brioches: There are two kinds of brioches. The first are the golden-brown, shiny little cupola-shaped "rolls" that together with croissants form one of the two bakery pillars of French breakfasts.

It wouldn't occur to a French person to make breakfast brioches, because they are available in every French bakery throughout the land. The small, individual size is more common, the big you generally have to order. But for someone who has acquired a taste for brioches and who does not live in France, they are (a) difficult to find and (b) very expensive. But you can make them yourself—for only pennies apiece.

The second "brioche" is the name of a pastry dough used to wrap meat, fish, or a wide variety of fine fillings. Both brioches are made with a yeast dough. While the breakfast brioches are quite rich, the other dough is not, since it is rightly assumed by the French that the filling itself will be rich and that, therefore, the *croûte* should not be.

There is a myth that making brioches *must* be difficult, complicated, and time consuming. It's not. As is the case with puff paste, there is a time element, but it is one where you do not need to be present. Your involvement will require no more than 20 to 30 minutes. The rest of the time the dough will be doing its own thing—resting or rising—without any help from you. Again, it's a matter of planning rather than presence. Therefore, whenever you are in the mood for brioches, think one day ahead. Between the desire and the realization a minimum of eight hours is needed. You can, for example, begin your preparation in the evening before you go out, let the initial rising take place while you are out, take step two when you come home, and finish in the morning.

Individual Brioches

Here is what you will need to make 24 individual brioches which, if you bought them in a store would as of this writing cost you about ten dollars. The cost here will be under two dollars.

3 sticks butter	1 package active dry yeast
6 eggs	¼ cup warm water
3½ cups flour	⅔ cup flour
3 tablespoons milk	1 egg mixed with 2 tablespoons water
2 tablespoons sugar	
½ teaspoon salt	

In a bowl, mix one stick of the butter with four eggs, and add the 3½ cups of flour, milk, sugar, and salt. I recommend using the mixer, but if you don't have one a bowl and a wooden spoon will do nicely.

In a smaller bowl (roughly pint-sized, or a little larger) dissolve the yeast in the warm water, then add the ⅔ cup of flour. Form a ball. Now cover this ball with warm water from the tap, and watch (and if they are in the vicinity invite your children to watch the "magic" yeast ball) : it will rise to the surface (this "ball" is called *levain* in French, from the verb *lever*, "to rise") .

In a third, large bowl (big enough to contain the contents of the other two) mix the remaining 2 sticks of butter with the 2 remaining eggs to creamy consistency. Now mix the contents of the three bowls together until a smooth dough is obtained. Cover with a damp towel (or wax paper) and set dough aside to rise—give it at least an hour and a half, but longer is fine if your schedule demands —in a place away from drafts.

Remove the risen dough from its *cache,* punch down gently in the bowl to deflate, and put it in the refrigerator for a second rising, this time from 6 to 8 hours.

If this double rising, and the time required, deters you from this recipe, let me remind you that *your* time—the time you will actually have to be in the kitchen working—adds up to no more than 10 or 12 minutes, most of which will be taken up by the original mixing. Step two, the deflating and transfer from *cache* to refrigerator, is a matter of only a minute. The final step requires perhaps another 10 minutes. Thus your total preparation time will be no more than 25 minutes.

Remove your dough from the refrigerator, deflate, and with floured hands form small balls about the size of Ping-Pong balls. Place each ball into a cupcake tin. Make an indentation in the center of each, on which place a second, marble-size ball (which will become the top, or cupola). When you have made all your "brioche balls," allow them to sit on the tabletop for 45 to 60 minutes, where they will rise again, for the third and final time, to about triple their original size. Brush them with the egg and water solution, and bake in a preheated 425° oven for 15 to 20 minutes, until golden brown.

The above quantities will give you about two dozen small brioches, or two large ones made in an 8- or 9-inch cake mold. Or make one large and a dozen small.

Brioche Dough *(for "en croûte")*

The quantities below should be enough to cover two average-size sea bass, or two five-pound hams.

- 1 package active dry yeast
- ¼ cup warm water
- 3½ cups flour
- 2 eggs
- ¾ teaspoon salt
- 2 tablespoons sugar
- 1 stick butter, melted

In a small bowl, dissolve the yeast in the warm water. In a second bowl, mix the remaining ingredients, then add the yeast mixture. Knead to form a smooth, rubbery dough. Cover with a damp towel (or wax paper) and set aside away from drafts to rise. Allow 3 hours' rising time. Deflate by punching dough down gently in the bowl. Roll out the dough onto a floured board into any desired shape required for the filling you are using. It should be no more than a quarter to three-eighths of an inch thick. Wrap the dough around your meat or fish and proceed with whatever recipe you are preparing *en croûte;* glaze with an egg and water solution and bake in a preheated 350° oven for about 20 minutes. Serve.

Homemade Coffee Cake, Simplified

This dough belongs to the puff paste family. The following proportions will give you at least three large coffee cakes, or roughly 3 dozen smaller ones. Your total preparation time should come to no more than 20 minutes—about four 5-minute sessions. But as for any puff paste, there is a resting time required between these four "stages." Thus it is all a question of working these 5-minute sessions into your daily schedule.

Here is what you will need:

2 envelopes active dry yeast	1/3 cup milk
1/2 cup warm water	2 eggs
1/3 cup sugar	1 teaspoon salt
4 1/2 cups flour	4 sticks butter (or margarine)

In a small bowl, dissolve the yeast in warm water and 1/2 teaspoon of the sugar. With a mixer, mix the flour, remaining sugar, milk, eggs, and salt. All this should take you no more than 3 minutes. If you don't have a mixer, you can do it with a wooden spoon, and it may take you 3 to 4 minutes more. Add the contents of the yeast bowl, and mix again. Refrigerate for 30 minutes (or more: if you're going out for a couple of hours, that's fine too).

On some wax paper, place the sticks of butter side by side, then flatten with your hands or a rolling pin, until you have a rectangle roughly 8 inches by 6 inches. Sprinkle with flour to make it more workable. Wrap in the wax paper and refrigerate.

After your initial half hour (or more) is up, remove the dough and the chilled butter from the refrigerator. On a floured board, roll out the dough into a rectangle roughly 12 by 18 inches. Place the chilled butter in the center, and fold all four sides as you would a package. Sprinkle a little flour over the top, and roll out, adding flour as needed, into a new rectangle. If the butter "spurts out," don't worry: just keep adding flour, which will integrate it into the dough. Now fold this new rectangle into thirds, as you would a letter. Refrigerate, again for at least half an hour.

Remove the dough and roll again, in the opposite direction, that is lengthwise, and fold into thirds again. This is the principle of puff paste—rolling several times in different directions, which gives it its "layers" of flakiness. In any case, each of these operations will take no more than a couple of minutes. What I do for my puff paste is take one step at a time, not worrying about the length of time between rollings. It's perfectly all right, for example, to let a whole day go by between rolling sessions. Just make sure that, between rollings, it is covered and refrigerated. You will need a minimum of three rollings; but sometimes I do as many as five or six, simply to give the dough added flakiness.

Whatever your number of rollings—which you can work out according to your own taste and the time you have available—you are now ready to make your coffee cakes.

Cut your dough into three roughly equal pieces. Put the two pieces you're not working with immediately back into the refrigerator, and store for later use; it will keep in the refrigerator one week. For longer storage, freeze. Roll out your dough on a floured board into two 20-by-15-inch rectangles, then cut into about 12 squares, from which you will shape crescents or rectangles or triangular envelopes.

What you decide to use as a filling is entirely up to you. Here are several fillings I use; the quantities are for *one* coffee cake (or 12 small ones). If you're making several at the same time, increase accordingly. What I do, generally, is use different fillings for each.

Almond Paste and Butter Filling

4 ounces almond paste
½ stick sweet butter
¼ cup sugar

1 egg mixed with 2 tablespoons water

In a bowl mix the almond paste, butter, and sugar well. Spread into the center of your rolled-out dough. (If you are making individual "Danishes," a teaspoonful in each center will do.) Fold over and set on a cookie sheet, and allow to rise at room temperature for 30 minutes. Brush with the egg and water solution. In a preheated 400° oven bake for 5 minutes, then reduce to 350° and bake for another 20 to 25 minutes, until puffy and golden brown.

Sugar and Cinnamon Filling

If you like cinnamon, try this filling:

½ stick sweet butter, melted
⅔ cup sugar
1 teaspoon cinnamon

¼ teaspoon ground cardamom
1 egg mixed with 2 tablespoons water

Pour the melted butter over the center of the rolled-out dough, concentrating on the center. Combine the sugar, cinnamon, and cardamom, and pour the mixture into the center of the dough. Fold over the dough to enclose the filling, either lengthwise like a letter or into a crescent, or whatever. Allow to rise. Brush with egg and water mixture. Bake as in preceding filling.

You can also vary the sugar and cinnamon filling by adding chopped walnuts.

Some people like jam fillings. About a cup of your favorite jam should suffice.

Whichever you choose, your homemade coffee cakes will cost you about a third of what you would have to pay at your bakery shop or grocer's, and be twice as delicious.

Croissants: If you would like to obtain a reasonable facsimile of those marvelous French croissants, omit all fillings. Simply roll out the dough, cut into squares (3 to 5 inches is about right), bring any two opposite corners together, then shape into crescents. Bake as in preceding recipes.

Doughs, like bread, are the staff of life, and once you find how easy and economical they are, I'm sure you will want to make ever-increasing use of their almost endless bounties. Baking bread, working with doughs, seeing the magic of the yeast dough rising, is to me both stimulating and rewarding. And for those who share the results, the rewards will be equally satisfying.

The point to remember is that all these basic doughs can be made and put to endless uses with very little effort, and no more than a few minutes of your time, carved out, as you find them, from even the busiest schedule.

BASIC SAUCES

This book refers time and again to cream sauce, vinaigrette, and mayonnaise. They are all basic to French cooking, and essential to literally hundreds of recipes, either in the form given here or in some variation. They are the ABC's of good cooking. Further, I urge you to make all three—plus the many variations you will soon find yourself making as you experiment with new dishes—for they are first of all very simple and easy to whip up and, second, far better than any ready-made equivalent you can buy.

White Cream Sauce

Makes 1½ cups
1½ tablespoons butter
1½ tablespoons flour
1½ cups milk

In a saucepan melt butter over a low flame, then stir in the flour, cook a few seconds. Turn off the flame. (The reason for turning off the flame at this stage is that flour hardens when heated, and if you don't you'll have an immediately lumpy sauce.) Gradually stir in the milk, using a wooden spoon. Once your milk is all stirred in, return to low flame and continue stirring until the sauce thickens (which should take no more than 2 minutes or so). Season to taste, according to what the recipe calls for.

Vinaigrette (or Lemon Dressing)

Makes about 1½ cups
⅓ cup red wine vinegar (or lemon juice)
1 cup olive oil
1 tablespoon prepared mustard (preferably Dijon)
Pepper and salt to taste

Mix all ingredients thoroughly. You may prefer a lemon dressing, in which case substitute the juice of 2 or 3 lemons (depending on taste) for the wine vinegar. To this basic dressing you may also add a tablespoon or so of basil, tarragon, shallots, or chives, as you prefer.

As I indicated, I usually make up a quart jar of my vinaigrette at a time, since it lasts for quite a while under refrigeration. If you follow my example, remember to remove your vinaigrette from the refrigerator as you begin preparing dinner, since well-chilled oil separates and thickens; it needs half an hour or so to "thaw out."

Mayonnaise

Mayonnaise can be made in one of three ways: in the blender, in which case it will take you about 40 seconds; in the mixer, where it will take perhaps 6 or 7 minutes; by hand, with a whisk or fork, which may take you 10 to 15 minutes' mixing in a bowl.

I will start with the blender because it is so much faster.

Makes 1 cup
1 whole egg
Juice of 1 lemon
1 tablespoon prepared mustard
1 teaspoon dried tarragon
   (or 1 tablespoon fresh)
Pepper and salt
1 cup olive oil

Put the egg, lemon juice, mustard, tarragon, pepper, and salt into a blender. Turn it on, blend a few seconds, then trickle in the oil with the blender running full speed. Your mixture will thicken almost immediately. Transfer to a bowl and refrigerate. You can make as much as you want, that is more than enough for your immediate needs, since it stores easily in the refrigerator.

After you've made this mayonnaise to formula, you may want to vary it somewhat, according to your own taste or preferences. Some people prefer only half the amount of lemon, some a trifle more; I've known cooks to double the amount of mustard, while others use only a teaspoon. You may also want to substitute (I do for fish dishes) a tablespoon of white wine (dry preferably) for half the quantity of lemon juice.

A reassuring tip: one time out of ten, because of climate, altitude, or gremlins, your mayonnaise will not thicken. If this happens, transfer the still-liquid contents of the blender into a bowl; now put an egg into the blender, and blend; slowly pour in about a third of a cup of oil, then trickle in the contents of the bowl. That should do it.

If you use a mixer or make the mayonnaise by hand, use 2 yolks rather than the whole egg, and incorporate the oil more slowly—drop by drop—in the beginning until it thickens. Some people feel that it is important to have the egg at room temperature (about 30 minutes) or to warm it up more quickly by putting it in a bowl of hot water for a minute, but I often forget that step, and the mayonnaise ends up as good.

ABOUT SALADS

I divide salads into two categories, both of which are important although they serve quite different culinary purposes.

The first kind of salad is an integral part of daily meals. It is served after the main course and consists of greens in any combination, seasoned with one of several kinds of dressing, and offered either just before the cheese course or, sometimes, together with it. This salad course serves as a transition from the rich or copious main dish to the sweets that will conclude the meal, the lemon or vinegar of the dressing acting as an astringent agent to modify the mood and prepare the palate for what is to follow.

The second category is called salad because it makes use of greens in one form or another, but is essentially a main dish, an entity unto itself, consisting of either a single ingredient—chicken, shrimp, mussels, salmon, and the like—or a mixture of several, such as the chef's salad found on virtually every restaurant menu. This variety, in small portions, makes a fine first course for most menus. Or, served with warm French bread, it suffices for a lunch, cold supper, or picnic.

Throughout this book I offer a number of recipes for this latter type of salad, but here I would like to focus briefly on the former "green" variety.

There are literally dozens of kinds of salad greens, some of which are: Boston, Bibb, salad bowl, and iceberg lettuce; escarole, chicory, and watercress. And, of course, one that is less green: endive. Each green is good by itself, or can be mixed in any proportion according to taste and availability. Whatever your choice, the following four steps regarding preparation apply:

1. Wash each leaf thoroughly under running water (no matter how clean a head of leaves looks, it's amazing how bits of sand or earth can lodge in the nooks and crannies and will, if not removed, ruin your enjoyment).

2. In addition to washing the salad, immerse it in a bowl of fresh water, from a half hour to a whole day. This will serve a dual purpose: it will keep the leaves crisp, and it will rid them of any last lingering grains of sand that might have escaped your washing.

3. As important as washing is the drying. The trick is to dry carefully without crushing the leaves. There are several ways to do this: first, you can take a few leaves in your hands, then, forming a ball and leaving your fingers slightly ajar, shake vigorously over the sink (being careful not to crush the leaves!) ; second, put your leaves in a salad basket and shake it vigorously up and down over the sink or, if you have a backyard, balcony, or the like, swing it with a broad pendulum motion (if you have a colander, you can substitute it for a salad basket for the sink-shaking method). All these methods have been used since time immemorial, but none is entirely satisfactory in that, in all cases, the additional step of pat-drying is required for desired results. There has recently come on the market a simple

but rather ingenious salad-drying device which, while doubtless to be classified in the luxury appliance category, does do the job quickly and perfectly. It has an inner basket in which you put your salad. The basket sits on a cog which is activated by a string which self-winds after the first pull. But enough of mechanics: the point is it's a nice toy which has the virtue of being functional.

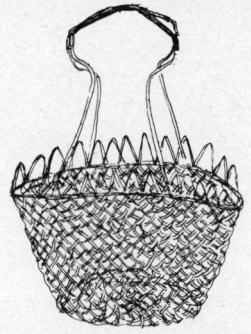

4. Do not "drown" your salad with too much dressing. Too much dressing will kill it; therefore, I've always found it better to use perhaps too little at first, adding slightly more if insufficient.

It is difficult, if not impossible, to advise as to proper proportions or precise amounts of dressing for your salad, both because tastes in dressings vary considerably and because heads of lettuce vary in size. However, be that as it may, I use roughly a third of a cup of salad dressing for an average-size head of Boston lettuce (for four people).

Because they are (almost) all green and physically similar, salads may seem the most unvaried of courses, the one where your creativity has the least possibility of exercising itself. Actually, there is considerable variety in texture and taste, and near-infinite possibilities of "marrying" your salads with what preceded or is to follow. Endives, for example, work wonderfully well after veal, because they are both delicate and rather subtle to the palate. Boston lettuce is pretty safe with everything; it is crisp (though not aggressively so), tender, and flavorful. Watercress and arugula lend themselves well to rather spicy meals (about watercress: when you see it in the store, one bunch may look puny and inadequate, but it seems to expand once you put it in fresh water; therefore, one bunch ought to suffice to serve four. Also: go extra easy with your dressing, since watercress is fragile and tends to wilt when subjected to an excess of oil and vinegar).

Don't hesitate to experiment with your salads, mixing one, two, or more greens to taste. If you have a few fresh basil leaves available, add them to any salad (except watercress): it's marvelous. So is arugula (also known as rocket, rucola, or roquette). Also guaranteed to add zest to any salad are a number of herbs—tarragon, dill, parsley —but how much or how little of each will of course be a matter of taste.

HERBS AND SPICES

Why herbs? What is their function? Do they really add something to a dish, to a meal? How does one know which herb or spice to use with what dish?

These are but a few of the questions I have been asked—and have asked myself—on the subject. The point is: herbs and spices, properly utilized, offer the possibility of turning a bland or ordinary dish into something seductive and irresistible. There's a theory that a pretty girl suffices unto herself; she needs no perfume or makeup to enhance her natural beauty. That may be true for some rare beauties, as it may be true for some rare dishes. But most dishes can profit from the proper utilization of herbs and spices. Eating is a sensual experience, and like all sensuality can be heightened by piquant refinements.

All this said, when we're dealing with herbs and spices we're involved with matters of taste—and taste is individual. Nonetheless, making due allowances for individual tastes, there are certain culinary principles and practices that derive from long experience and have proved themselves over the centuries.

For one thing, fresh herbs are preferable to dried; their fragrance is stronger and more distinctive when fresh. But most people, for geographical or seasonal reasons, have to resort to using dried herbs and spices. Remember that the dried variety is sharper, more pungent (though less aromatic) than the fresh. For example, when making lasagna, you would need half a cup of fresh oregano for the recipe, whereas one and a half tablespoons of the dried herb would suffice.

An advantage of the dried variety, however, is that they can be kept on your shelf for months, and are "instant helpers" in that you don't have to wash, peel, or chop. But beware: all these miracle herbs do have a limited life and cannot remain on your shelf forever. I suggest you check your jars every once in a while. If any of them have a scent reminiscent of straw (it's strange, but that is how they all seem to end up), you know time is up: discard and renew your supply.

Fresh herbs, such as parsley, basil, oregano, chervil, and chives can and should be stored in the refrigerator with their stems in a jar of water. Or they may be washed and frozen (labeled, since they look so much alike when frozen) in plastic bags.

If your supply of any herb is plentiful (that is, if you have a garden), pick the leaves (mint, basil, or whatever), wash them, and spread them on a roasting pan. Light the oven and "roast" them at 150° for from an hour and a half to two hours—until they are "crumbly." Store in jars, seal, and label.

The French have entire bouquets of various herbs, but most notably thyme and bay leaf, tied and attractively hung on their kitchen walls for winter use.

If you have one sunny window, try growing any one (or several) of the following: basil, parsley, tarragon, or oregano. Basil is a very docile plant, and will adapt especially well to apartment living, assuming there is a modicum of light.

The earliest use of herbs goes back to the mists of recorded history. Frankincense and myrrh were of course part and parcel of Biblical literature, the former burned as incense, the latter used for the same purpose and also as a basic ingredient for making perfumes. Most of the herbs we think of today in culinary terms, in fact, were used originally for perfume and medicinal purposes. Cinnamon, one of the oldest spices known to man, worked its way westward from China to the Middle East as long ago as two thousand years before Christ. It was also known in India at least a millennium before Christ, as was black pepper, one of the oldest spices known to man.

In any event, there is plenty of documentary evidence to indicate that very early on in his civilized existence, man was preoccupied with improving the quality of his cooking through the use of a multitude of spices and herbs.

Bear in mind as you read what follows—which is a distillation of ancient culinary experience and my own personal tastes—that although hard and fast rules regarding herbs and spices do exist, they can be bent and modified to suit your own palate.

Anise: seeds from a small plant of the carrot family, with a strong licorice flavor. Grows freely in Italy, the south of France, Greece, and North Africa. The Italians utilize it extensively in making their sausages. It is also used in numerous Italian desserts and candies. In the south of France, from the looks of every café counter and terrace, the principal adaptation seems to be Pernod, a very potent and treacherous apéritif distilled from the anise seed. Interestingly, many of the Mediterranean countries have a similar drink: in Greece it's known as ouzo; in North Africa, raki.

Basil: another Mediterranean herb, from the mint family. In Italy, basil is considered a symbol of love: in our house, it is definitely a symbol of pleasure. Its fragrance is exceptional, and picked fresh from the garden it serves in countless salads and stuffings, it flavors fish or chicken, and last but far from least it constitutes the basis of that divine sauce, French or Italian depending on who claims it first, called *pesto* in Italian, *pistou* in French.

If you use basil to flavor fish or chicken, I urge you not to mix it with other herbs, which might threaten to neutralize it.

Bay Leaf: the bay tree is also a native of the Mediterranean basin. In Italy bay leaves are still considered good luck charms. In France, they are a virtual must for all sorts of dishes: from broth to fish, from stews to pâtés. Use 2 leaves for approximately 10 cups of liquid, 2 or 3 for a 3-pound meat stew.

Capers: green, unopened flower buds from a bush that grows extensively throughout the Mediterranean basin. Excellent for sauces. Often served with fish and tartar steak. Capers have a distinctive taste; use them in moderation, a teaspoonful at a time.

Caraway Seeds: our English term derives from the Arab *karauya*. Also known in various parts of the world, including France, as *cumin*. Interestingly enough, whatever its geographical origins, it seems to have settled in Middle Europe. A great deal of the food originating in Germany, Czechoslovakia, Hungary, and Austria is flavored with caraway seeds: breads, cheeses, cabbage preparations, meat dishes such as goulash and spareribs, and potatoes. Usually the seeds are used intact, in quantities ranging from a teaspoon to one or two tablespoons. With the blender, I make my Hungarian cheese by mixing in the blended caraway seeds with all the other ingredients.

The Germans also have a sharp brandy distilled from caraway seeds and called *kümmel*.

Cardamom: a subterranean root stock from the ginger family. Sold generally in powdered form. *Not* from the Mediterranean area, cardamom stems from India and Ceylon and is one of the basic spices used in Indian cuisine. Such dishes as curried chicken, curried shrimp—in short, any curried dish—will contain a teaspoon or so of cardamom. Also very popular in Arab countries, where it is used both as a spice and as the source of "cardamom coffee." The aroma is reminiscent of lemon rind. Good in many desserts and meat sauces.

Chervil: a small plant with flat green leaves. It's not readily available in the United States, but is quite widely used in Europe. More delicate and sweeter than parsley, it can be substituted almost anywhere parsley is called for. I recommend growing it in pots near a window during the winter.

Chives: a milder cousin of the onion, chives (like onions and garlic) belong to the lily family. They can be used virtually anytime onions are called for. But in salads, for example, where onion might be overwhelming, chives will give just the right added touch. Can be successfully frozen.

Cinnamon: one of the oldest spices known to man, cinnamon is made from the inner bark of a shrub or tree of the laurel family. Dates from Old Testament times, for Moses refers to it. Actually it was the Lord no less who, in speaking to Moses, told him to use it to anoint the tabernacle. Reference in Exodus was made to both "cinnamon" and "cassia," the former the tree and the latter the shrub, both of whose barks supply the spice. In the United States virtually all, if not all, the cinnamon you buy comes from the shrub—cassia.

Cinnamon is one of the most widely used spices in the world, and appears in many, many cuisines. The sticks may be used to flavor drinks. In compotes, the fresh fruit may be cooked with one to two sticks of cinnamon. Powdered cinnamon is used in countless recipes, mostly in sweets and desserts but also in some places in meat and vegetable dishes.

Cloves: cloves are the dried flower buds of a tropical evergreen tree that originated in East India, and more specifically in the archipelago known as the Spice Islands. Its name comes from the French *clou* or "nail" (short for *clou de girofle,* the name of the tree itself being *giroflier*), because the clove resembles a nail. Exceedingly pungent, cloves must be used sparingly. Pricked in an onion, cloves are part of the basic flavoring of broth (poultry, or beef). Also good pricked directly into Virginia ham. Cloves are also widely used in any number of baked desserts, from cookies to fruitcakes, and they add taste to stewed fruits.

Coriander: an herb originating in southern Europe and the Mediterranean basin, also known and used by the ancients. Mostly used in Indian cooking.

Cumin: first cousin to the caraway seed. Widely used in Indian and Mexican cooking. A basic ingredient of both curry and chutney.

Curry: the word comes from the Hindustani *turcarri,* which in daily usage was shortened to *turri*. The English mispronounced the term and brought it home as curry. Actually it is not a single spice in itself but a blend of several spices: cumin, coriander, turmeric, pepper, cardamom, mustard, saffron, ginger and allspice. All Indians mix their own proportions and vary the flavors according to the dish. When asked once whether it had any use outside of curried dishes I had to reply: "No; as soon as you use it in a dish, the dish is curried."

Dill (seed) : dill is a plant of the carrot family. The seeds are mostly used for pickling preparations. In France, they are used to flavor a number of pastries.

Dill (weed) : the weed (leaves) is distinctive for its fragrance. Dill is widely grown throughout the Mediterranean region but originated in southern Russia and thence made its way to Scandinavia, which explains its longtime popularity in Russian and Scandinavian cuisines. For reasons unknown, it is seldom used in French cooking. Because of its delicate flavor, it should not be mixed with other herbs. Use it to flavor fish, salads (cucumber salad is especially good with dill), and certain meat dishes such as piroshkis. Sour cream with dill makes a good dip, served with fresh vegetables. Dill may be frozen successfully.

Fennel: a very ancient herb, from the celery family. Fennel is one of the herb plants with the highest productivity: virtually every part of the plant can be utilized. The bulb is edible and can be used, like the celery stalk, in salads, or plain. It has an anise flavor. Delicious, too, braised with butter. The leaves are often used for fish, as an aromatic addition to various sausages, and poultry. The seeds are also used in making sausages and breads, and are distilled to make a liqueur.

Garlic: the bulb of a plant of the lily family, each section of which is called a clove. It is hardly news that its fragrance is very pungent indeed, and most people connect it with the cooking of the Mediterranean basin. In southern France, I have often seen truckloads of the garlic tresses being transported to market, enough to pep up many thousands of meals. Personally, I love it. I use it in many recipes, from *beurre d'escargot,* croutons in salad, in my *pesto,* my gigot, and in my bouillabaisses—both fish and chicken. But garlic is potent indeed, and tends to overwhelm what follows; therefore, use it in moderation.

In addition to its myriad culinary uses, garlic is purported to have numerous medicinal properties, not the least of which is aiding circulation.

Also comes in powdered form: I find that powdered garlic has an artificial and sour taste; avoid it at all costs.

Ginger: a tropical plant, from East India and China, the rootstalk of which is used widely in both Chinese and Indian cuisines. You can buy the rootstalks fresh and grate or powder them yourself; or you can buy the powder in a can. A basic for curry. Also for desserts and cookies—the best-known of which is ginger snaps. It is very strong, and should be used with discretion.

Juniper Berries: dark, bluish purple berries from an evergreen shrub. They give an added flavor to sauerkraut.

Laurel: see Bay Leaf.

Mace: the ground outer coating of the nutmeg. It is used in desserts.

Marjoram: like its first-cousin oregano—with which it is often confused—marjoram was well known in both ancient Greece and Rome. Actually, marjoram is a much milder herb than oregano. Both are members of the mint family. Its dried leaves are used to flavor poultry, stuffings, vegetables, and meat pies. Also salads.

Mint: there are many forms of mint—spearmint, peppermint, horsemint—some of which were well known in ancient times, when mint's fresh, cooling quality made it a medicinal cure-all. Understandably, it is used extensively in hot countries, where it appears not only in main courses and desserts but in numerous beverages. Greek, Armenian, Lebanese, and North African cuisines frequently flavor their food with mint. I use its dried leaves to sprinkle over Greek-style lamb. Also in my yogurt soups.

Mustard: in France, hardly a steak is consumed without mustard near to hand. I personally never indulged in the practice, but I admit being the exception. So imbued with the spice are the French that Anatole France once noted, "A story without love is like beef without mustard." What is called commercially French mustard is made from ground brown mustard seeds, salt, vinegar, and other spices, each brand including its own "spice secrets." Used basically as a flavoring for various meat dishes, and sauces. Also salad dressings. I recommend Dijon-style mustard.

Nutmeg: the seed of the nutmeg tree, a tree indigenous to East India that soars as high as 60 feet. An exceedingly fragrant spice, to be used with economy and discretion. Has a basic place in many, many recipes, from creamed spinach to turnip purées, from quenelles to *escargots*. Also in numerous desserts. I couldn't cook without nutmeg.

Onions: bulb of a plant of the lily family. Among the oldest cultivated plants known to man. The Romans purportedly brought it to England, and the story also goes that Columbus brought onions to the New World. To my mind, it is one of the pillars of good cooking—or even less than good cooking. It seems to create a consistency in stews, a sweetness (yes, interestingly so, despite its pungency when raw), and generates a sauce with the natural juices of whatever meat it is cooking with. I would say that it ranks now almost with pepper and salt as a staple of flavoring: open any cookbook and count the number of recipes that begin with "sautée the onions." Avoid the powdered variety.

Oregano: leaves of a bush of the mint family. Sometimes confused with marjoram, but much stronger. Popular in Italian cooking, as well as Greek—and in American adaptations of southern European cooking such as pizza.

Paprika: the ground powder of dried red pepper capsicum. The best paprika is made from Hungarian red peppers. Comes hot and sweet. The hot is fiery, the sweet aromatic. Quite naturally, features widely in Hungarian cooking.

Parsley: the key to my cooking. If it would be difficult to live without nutmeg, it would be impossible without parsley. I even go so far as to make parsley soup. Like a bouquet of flowers, I keep parsley in a jar of fresh water in my refrigerator.

Pepper: the world's most important spice, and one of the oldest known to man. There are references to pepper in Sanskrit literature, where it was referred to as a medicine, and our term for it comes from the Sanskrit *pippali*. Pepper originated in the Orient, and what we use as spices are the berries—*piper nigrum*—of pepper plants; these should not be confused with the various pepper plants of the genus—capsicum—to which hot peppers, like cayenne and chili as well as sweet green peppers belong. In the Middle Ages pepper was so sought after, and so expensive, that the economies of many major ports depended on the "pepper trade." Most commonly used, of course, is black pepper, which is obtained by picking the berries when green and allowing them to dry in the sun. White pepper, on the other hand, comes from fully ripened berries divested of their hulls, and most often ground. White pepper is more common in European cooking; black is preferred in the United States. But in either case, pepper is truly the essential spice in cooking. Only salt ranks as its peer.

Poppy Seeds: from the poppy flower, they have a flavor similar to that of walnut. In Middle European cooking, they are used extensively in baking breads, cookies, and cakes. Poppy seeds also feature in many Hungarian main dishes. An exquisite dessert which my mother often made consists of noodles, poppy seeds, sugar, and butter.

Rosemary: grows extensively in the Mediterranean region, especially in Provence. Aromatic, it flavors beautifully poultry, salads, roasts, and meats in general. Another delight from the mint family.

Saffron: very expensive, so you will use it seldom. Many Spanish recipes call for it, as do a number of Mexican and South American, and it is used in some French dishes such as bouillabaisse.

Sage: again from the mint family. The long, furry leaves of this herb, with its delicate fragrance, are ideal for leg of lamb, pâtés, stuffings, and fish.

Savory: also of the mint family, was used in ancient Rome to fulfill many of the culinary functions that pepper assumed later on. I use it but seldom.

Sesame Seeds: records indicate that they were one of the earliest spices known to the Eastern Mediterranean. Used in baking many varieties of bread and pastries, mostly from the Middle East. A paste from the sesame seed, *tahini,* which resembles peanut butter in texture, is used as a spread, an appetizer, and a component of many fine Middle Eastern dishes and sauces. Both Chinese and Jewish cuisines utilize sesame seeds in making candies.

Shallots: another pillar of the French cuisine. Somewhat milder than garlic, they are more aromatic than onions, and when you don't want to go garlic in any recipe, shallots are your best bet. You can substitute shallots in virtually any recipe that calls for onions. Where one onion is called for, substitute two to three shallots.

Soy Sauce: of Far Eastern origin, made from the soybean, and fermented in brine. Featured in Chinese and Japanese cuisines, where it is an almost automatic accompaniment to countless dishes, from soups through main courses to salads. Also used in cooking. I use it as a component for one of my dressings for gigot, as well as in certain of my salad dressings.

Tabasco: a sauce made from hot peppers, vinegar, and salt. Ultra-hot, to be used with extreme care. A drop or two, literally, will suffice to sharpen gazpacho, all manner of Mexican dishes, not to mention the drink "Bloody Mary."

Tarragon: leaf of a plant from the mint family. Extremely aromatic, it is used extensively in French cuisine. There is a perfumed vinegar in France which contains the stalks in the bottle. Part of the bouquet the French refer to as *fines herbes,* which can also include chervil, chives, and parsley. Although, as I have suggested, various herbs cannot be mixed indiscriminately, tarragon can be and often is used in combination with other herbs. Often used in salad dressings and with poultry, fish, stuffings, and pâtés.

Thyme: one of the basics of French seasoning. Also of the mint family, and like tarragon extremely fragrant—but even more potent. To be used with moderation. Among its many uses are in marinades, stuffings, pâtés, poultry, meat, fish, stews, soups. One of those herbs I couldn't cook without.

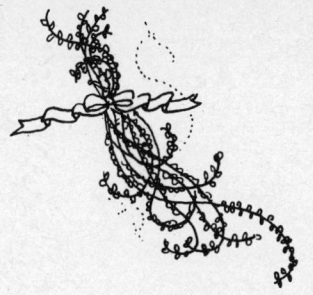

Turmeric: a plant of the ginger family, originating in Southern Asia. Of a bright yellow color, its pungent flavor and color add a distinctive touch to most curries.

Vanilla: one of the few spices the western hemisphere has contributed to the world spice trade. The flavoring is made from the "bean," or "pod" (actually, the name derives from the Spanish *vaina,* meaning "pod"), which is the dried and cured fruit of a towering vine of the orchid family. It was discovered in Mexico by Cortés and his men in the sixteenth century and brought back to Europe. But Mexico remained the primary source of vanilla until about a hundred years ago, when methods for artificially pollinating the flowers were finally discovered, thus permitting widespread cultivation in various tropical countries around the world. Used as a basic flavoring ingredient in practically all desserts. Also a component in many chocolate-flavored candies, sweets, and beverages. Most common in the United States in liquid form, but is also available as a bean. In France, powdered vanilla is the most common form used, though beans are used widely in the mixture called "vanilla sugar," which is simply a premixed package of sugar and vanilla.

Vinegar: from France, its name derives from the two words *vin* (wine) and *aigre* (sour). Contains acetic acid and is made through a special process of fermentation. In France, wine vinegar is *de rigueur,* but in other countries, including the United States, one finds cider vinegar made from apples, and a white vinegar made from an all-grain recipe. I always use red wine vinegar.

Worcestershire Sauce: a prepared sauce, originating in Worcester, England, made up of vinegar, soy sauce, various spices, and molasses. Used to flavor meats, fish, poultry, sauces. An absolute must for tartar steak.

FAMILY DINNERS

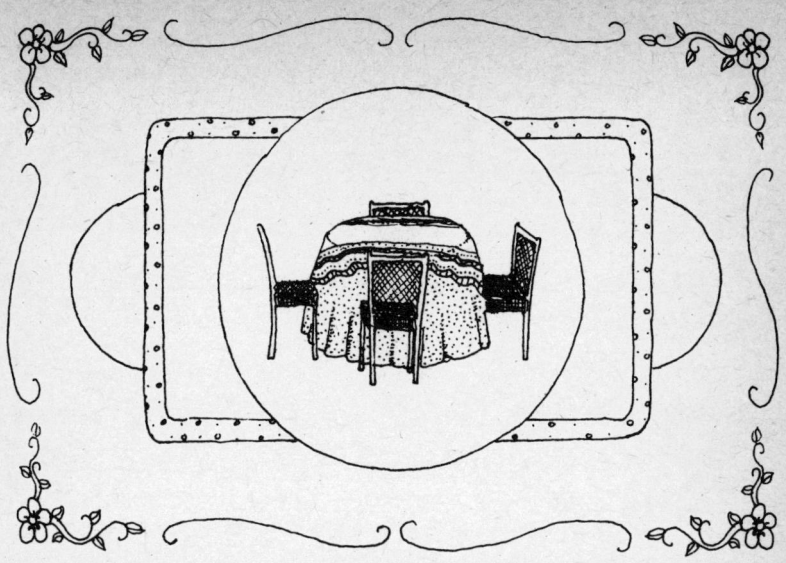

Virtually everyone can manage to carve time out of a busy life to prepare a dinner party successfully. The very fact of inviting guests compels a certain formality, both in the setting and in the quality of the menu. But how often do we carry over this effort, this presentation of our social selves, into the intimacy of our family? Why is it that daily meals are so often "sacrificed" under the pretense that, after all, "it's only family"?

We have a strong sense of family in France, and it is precisely for the family that good meals, presented with a certain formality, are created. At least once a day, and often twice—though things are changing, and less emphasis is put on the noon meal—there is a rendezvous around the table. French families are spoiled, in that they treat themselves as guests. But is that such a bad idea?

I have no scientific basis on which to judge, but I have partaken of and witnessed the cult of eating sufficiently to state unequivocally that this *sens de famille* derives at least in good measure from the solemn act of sharing the pleasures of food around the table, day in and day out throughout the years. I do not mean to imply that culinary pleasures are the sole key to this unity, but there can be no question but that they contribute to it. The mere fact of sitting down together at table, of relating to one another and sharing a general sense of well-being as well as sharing the fruit of your day's experiences, keeps the family closer together. I have noted, as doubtless you have too, how at dinner parties guests are often reluctant to forsake the table for the living room; it is as though they feared to break the magic. (The word is not too strong.) If one doesn't make the effort to bring the family together over dinner, if on the contrary one slips into the "method" of allowing various members to splinter and eat when they like, the very possibility of creating this moment, this unity, is lost.

For me, the family dinner is and always has been an important element in my life, a ritual both my husband and I believe in. From the time my children were old enough to stay up until dinner time without dropping with fatigue, I have included them in our dinners. We've always had candles, and a pretty tablecloth (even if we ate in the kitchen). The darkness, the flickering candles, the fact of sharing the evening meal with their parents, make children feel, very early on, that they belong and are full-fledged members of the family unit. Very early on, too, I introduced them to good cooking, first because my husband and I liked it, but also because we liked them and wanted to expose them to it. What resulted, as an added and unexpected side effect, was that our children very early learned to appreciate good—and often rather exotic—cooking, and voiced their appreciation. And I cannot emphasize too strongly that aspect of cooking: as performers need applause, so cooks need recognition.

Here are a few practical suggestions I have found helpful in creating, without any big effort, that feeling of formality:

Even though it's "only" a family dinner, don't ignore aesthetics when setting the table. Use a tablecloth or pretty mats. Try candles, even in the kitchen. Don't serve milk directly out of its container, or leave the carton on the table; use a pitcher. If the wine you are serving is jug wine, I likewise recommend using small individual pitchers or carafes, which are both prettier and easier to handle. Try not to bring any cooking pots to your table, unless they happen to be ceramic, earthenware, or other attractive pots, and arrange your food on serving platters. It will take only a couple of minutes more, and will make all the difference.

Unless your meat dish is to be carved directly at the table, slice it before bringing it to table, arrange on a meat platter, and crown with vegetables. If the vegetables are served separately, it is pleasant to decorate your meat slices with a few sprigs of parsley.

If you are serving custards, ice cream, or any other soft or liquid dessert, use stemmed glasses, which create a festive culmination to the meal.

In your mind, run through the needs or tastes of your family members and try to provide for them prior to sitting down. Perhaps one likes his or her food more seasoned than others; have the various seasonings handy. Ice water may be a must for another. Someone may need an ashtray. These are tiny details, true, but to remember them initially avoids the irritating necessity for someone to hop up from the table. I feel, too, that children learn by seeing thoughtfulness practiced in the home.

The meals I propose in this chapter are among those that I make daily for my own family. Without exception, they are easy and quick to put together. And, most important, they are fun.

Before turning to the menus themselves, however, a few words about two other quite unrelated matters; first, cooking aromas; and second, the question of variety.

Most of the menus in this chapter will give the cook an opportunity to seduce the family even before people sit down to the meal. The smell of bread cooking in the oven, or a pie, or soup simmering on the stove not only whets the appetite but creates a feeling of intimacy and "home" to those members of the family who arrive at the end of the day, be it from school or work, tired and, perhaps, cross. It is amazing what the odor of vanilla or yeast dough can do for the morale.

It is important to remember, too, that it takes but little extra effort to create this culinary fragrance: five minutes more or less for biscuit dough; no more than fifteen for homemade soup or a pie. The difference between coming home to a place permeated by tempting culinary odors and one without is to me like the difference between walking into a house or apartment tastefully and personally furnished or into one impersonally furnished by the management: a hotel or motel room.

As for variety, I mention this in the context of family dinners because I know how tempting it is for a cook to solve the question of what's for dinner by reheating yesterday's roast. Don't. There is nothing duller than the constant repetition of anything, no matter how good it was the first time around. This is true of art, music, behavior, you name it. It is certainly true of food. The point is, you don't have to repeat: you can vary. And that does not mean you're going to become wasteful. Rather, yesterday's meat dish or main course can be so disguised that even your own family won't recognize it. A second-day leg of lamb, for instance, can quickly be turned into a Middle Eastern delight. Or, if there is insufficient lamb left over for a casserole dish, think moussaka. Or, if the leg of lamb was indeed large enough to serve your family two meals, simply skip a day or two and offer a repeat performance, preferably with new side dishes.

Hopefully, my chapter on leftovers will provide a number of ideas on how to vary your menus from day to day or week to week.

One final point about family meals: it's not just the eating that's important, but the preparing as well. I love to cook. But I enjoy it even more when one or more members of my family participate. On weekends and holidays, I sometimes have the whole clan working or pottering around in the kitchen. I won't say that this collective enterprise necessarily speeds up the cooking process, but it does democratize the workload and introduce children—and spouse—to both the pleasures and the secrets of the culinary art. It may be a contribution only as mechanical as a teenager grating the cheese; a child making a vinaigrette sauce, carefully following instructions as he or she measures out the ingredients; making meatballs; cutting cookies; the possible tasks are endless. I even have a four-year-old who insists on getting into the act, whether rolling out pie crusts or breaking eggs for an omelet. For every child who participates, you might want to add five minutes to the time prescribed in each recipe—but it's worth every minute of it!

MENU 1

This is a simple, fairly classic French menu, which begins with something fresh and crisp and ends in like fashion. Only the potatoes need any length of time to cook—about an hour in all—which will give you more than enough time to prepare the rest of the meal: the grated carrots, 10 minutes; the cucumber salad, a mere 5; and about the same for your Greek-style cheese. Therefore, you'll have 15 to 20 minutes of "free" time—to set the table, read the paper, or whatever —before starting the pork chops.

Carottes rapées
(Grated carrots with vinaigrette)

Côtes de porc, sauce moutarde
(Pork chops in wine, mustard, and cream sauce)

Pommes de terre au four
(Baked potatoes)

Salade de concombres
(Cucumber salad with dill)

Fromage grec
(*Greek-style cheese*)

Fruits frais de saison
(*Fresh fruit basket*)

Grated Carrots with Vinaigrette

This hors d'oeuvre may seem plain, but it offers several virtues for family dinners: (1) it's very healthy, fresh carrots containing a lot of vitamin C; (2) it's a crisp and tasteful dish: even children who balk at most cooked vegetables will love it; (3) it's extremely economical; and (4) it takes no time at all to make, providing you have a Moulinette or any other automatic grater. Speaking of collective cooking, kids enjoy helping to grate the carrots, even if all you have is a manual grater.

Serves 4–5

1 package carrots, or 6–8 carrots
1 onion, finely chopped
2/3 cup vinaigrette (see page 46)

Wash, peel, and grate the carrots. Add onion and dressing and mix.
If you like, you can make this hors d'oeuvre well in advance—in the morning for your evening's meal, for example—cover, and refrigerate.

Pork Chops in Wine, Mustard, and Cream Sauce

Pork is a rich meat, so it is frequently, if not always, accompanied by a condiment or garnish—mustard, pickles, apples or apple sauce, relish—in order to counterbalance this richness.

Serves 4–5

4–5 pork chops, preferably lean
1/2 teaspoon thyme
Pepper and salt
1 onion, finely chopped
1/3 cup heavy (or light) cream
2 tablespoons prepared mustard, Dijon style or American
1/2 cup white wine (optional)
Fresh parsley, finely chopped

Brown the pork chops in a skillet. (NOTE: It is not necessary to use any shortening unless your chops are very lean, in which case you may have to lubricate the skillet with a dab of butter or oil, or even a teaspoon of bacon fat. Normally, pork chops will render their own fat and cook in it.) The browning should take no more than 5 to 7 minutes on each side, over a medium flame. Season with thyme and pepper and salt to taste. Add onion and continue browning for another 5 minutes, stirring until onion is golden brown. Reduce flame, cover, and cook for 20 minutes. Mix cream and mustard in a cup, then stir into skillet. If your children are of age and consenting, you may want to add wine to the sauce. (Wine loses its alcoholic potency when cooked.) Sprinkle with parsley and serve.

Baked Potatoes

Wash the potatoes and put them in the oven to bake at 350°. Since the rest of this meal will take only 30 to 40 minutes to prepare, start your baked potatoes roughly half an hour before you begin the pork chops. If you're too pressed for time for that, substitute boiled potatoes, which take only 15 to 20 minutes, starting them roughly at the same time you begin your meat.

Cucumber Salad with Dill

Cucumber salad, like the condiments already mentioned, tends to offset the richness and texture of pork. Dill, I find, marries especially well with cucumbers.

Serves 4–5
- 3 cucumbers
- 1/3 cup vinaigrette (see page 46)
- 2 sprigs fresh dill, finely chopped (or 1 teaspoon dry dill)

Peel and slice the cucumbers, add dill and dressing, and serve.

Greek-style Cheese

Cheese is expensive, and French cheeses are more expensive than most. Thus, increasingly, I have resorted to making and improvising my own. This Greek-inspired cheese is not only delicious but very inexpensive.

Serves 4–5
- 8-ounce package cream cheese
- 1 small onion, finely chopped
- 1 clove garlic, finely chopped
- 1 teaspoon thyme
- 1 teaspoon salt
- 1/2 teaspoon pepper
- 1 teaspoon sesame seeds
- Thyme and sesame seeds for garnish

In a bowl, mix all the ingredients except garnish with a fork. When thoroughly mixed, place on a serving platter and reshape into a mound or rectangle. Top with more thyme and sesame seeds, and serve with warm bread or crackers.

Fresh Fruit Basket

One of the best finales of any meal is a basket of fresh fruit. Its contents will vary according to the season, of course. If you're serving pears, apples, or oranges, don't forget to set the table with fruit knives. If you have cherries or grapes, it's nice to put a small bowl of water on the table.

MENU 2

At least three items can be prepared in advance: the beef could (and should) be put in to marinate in the morning, and the salad immersed in cold water to soak. If you expect to be home late, I suggest making your clafouti *the night before. The rest of the dinner will take you only about 20 minutes; the soup will need just that time to cook in one kettle while the celery hearts are cooking simultaneously in another.*

Potage Saint-Germain
(*Vegetable soup with peas, leeks, and salad leaves*)

Hot Biscuits

Marinade de boeuf
(*Marinated beef*)

Coeurs de céleri gratinés
(*Celery hearts au gratin*)

Salade de laitue
(*Boston lettuce salad: pages 47–50*)

Clafouti de prunes
(*Plums in custard cake*)

Vegetable Soup with Peas, Leeks, and Salad Leaves

This may sound like a very exotic soup, but actually it is part of the basic repertory of good, homemade French soups, and full of nourishment.

Serves 4–5
- 1 stick butter
- 2 leeks, washed and cut in small pieces
- 1 head escarole, washed and cut in small pieces
- 4 cups water
- Salt and pepper
- 1 package frozen peas
- 1 egg yolk
- ½ cup heavy cream

Melt half a stick of butter in a soup pot, and add leeks and escarole. Cook for 5 minutes over medium flame, until greens wilt. Add water, salt, and pepper, cover, and let cook for 10 minutes. Pour contents into blender and blend until smooth. Return to pot, add frozen peas, and cook another 5 minutes. In a bowl, mix the remaining half stick of butter, egg yolk, and heavy cream, and pour into soup pot. Stir and serve.

I generally serve, with this and most other soups, hot biscuits, if I have not had time to bake any bread that day. I don't pretend these biscuits are my invention. Actually, I learned to make and appreciate them in America, and I can say that my family likes them fully as much as French bread. But I would like to stress again that they add immensely to a meal and are very quick and easy to make from scratch: no more than 15 minutes in all—at most 3 to 5 minutes to mix and 10 to 12 minutes to bake. These are 15 minutes that can usually be found while the other dishes are cooking. Like homemade bread or pie being baked, the smell of hot biscuits adds that certain something to the home.

TIP: If the phone rings bring the bowl and mix while you chat. By the time you hang up, your biscuits will have been made.

Hot Biscuits

Makes about 16
- 2 cups flour
- 2 teaspoons baking soda
- 1 teaspoon salt
- ½ stick butter
- ¾ cup milk
- 1 tablespoon sour cream

Preheat oven to 450°. In a bowl, mix all the ingredients together, using your fingers, until the dough is smooth. Shape dough into little balls the size of Ping-Pong balls and place them on an ungreased cookie sheet, or any roasting pan. There should be about 16 biscuits. Bake for 12 minutes, and serve wrapped in a napkin in a breadbasket.

This recipe has been my standard for years, but more recently I have made biscuits from the following recipe. I find the results somewhat lighter and more delicate.

2 cups flour	2 teaspoons baking powder
1 cup whipped cream	1 teaspoon salt

Prepare as in preceding recipe. As opposed to a kneading finger movement, however, this one requires a very light touch, by which I mean simply that in mixing you should apply less pressure.

Marinated Beef

A 2½–3-pound London broil or flank steak should adequately feed a family of five; if yours is larger or smaller, adjust your purchase accordingly. Also: this is something that can easily be prepared a day in advance (if you do, don't worry if you haven't enough room for it in your refrigerator; the bowl, which should be kept covered, can safely stay on your counter while the meat is marinating). Advance preparation should also enable you, in days of soaring meat prices, to substitute a cheaper cut for London broil—flank or cheap chuck for instance—with little noticeable difference in quality. The marinating process has a tenderizing effect, and if you marinate a full day or even more, the chuck should be very tender. For the marinade, put the following ingredients into a large bowl:

Serves 4–5

1 bottle red or white wine (inexpensive jug wine is fine; even leftover wine will do)	½ teaspoon basil
	½ teaspoon oregano
	1 peppercorn, mashed
	3 shallots, chopped
1 cup vinegar	2 carrots, thinly sliced
½ cup olive oil	½ teaspoon sage
1 large onion, sliced	2 cloves garlic, finely chopped
1 teaspoon thyme	4 sprigs parsley

Immerse meat in the marinade. The minimum length of time you should marinate is 4 to 6 hours.

At time of cooking, remove meat from bowl and wipe it with a paper towel. Pan-broil, which means preheating skillet with only salt (the salt will keep the meat from sticking to your frying pan). The amount of cooking time depends both on the thickness of the meat and personal preferences. To check, insert the point of a sharp knife after meat has cooked about 5 minutes on each side. If still too rare for your taste, cook a few more minutes on each side. Carve at an angle into thin slices. If you have some left over, don't fret: it is delicious cold.

What about the marinade? By now you know how much I hate to throw anything away, and this is no exception. Pour the marinade into a saucepan and boil for 1 or 2 minutes. Then pour into a plastic container and freeze. You can use it at least twice more, if you boil it before refreezing.

Celery Hearts au Gratin

Serves 4–5

1½ bunches celery (or 6–8 stalks celery)
1 quart salted water
1 cup beef or chicken broth
½ cup grated Swiss cheese
1 stick butter
Pepper and salt

Wash the celery well, discarding damaged parts. Cut each stalk into four pieces. In a saucepan, bring the salted water to a boil and cook the celery for 20 minutes. Drain. Preheat the oven to 400°. Arrange the celery neatly in a casserole dish. Add broth. Cover with cheese and dot with butter. Add pepper and salt to taste. Bake for 12 to 15 minutes, or until the cheese has turned blond and crisp. The broth should be entirely absorbed. Serve.

Plums in Custard Cake

Clafouti—sometimes spelled *clafoutis* but pronounced without the *s*—comes from the Old French verb *clafir*, meaning to fill or stuff. It is hearty, true, but delicious, an integral part of French bourgeois cuisine, especially after a relatively light main course. Cherry clafouti is the most common kind, with apple a close second. But plum is my favorite.

Serves 4–5
1½ pounds plums
½ stick sweet butter
3 eggs
1 cup milk
½ cup flour
⅔ cup sugar
2 teaspoons vanilla extract

Preheat oven to 400°. While oven is heating, wash, halve, and pit the plums. In your mixer or blender, combine the butter, eggs, milk, flour, sugar, and vanilla extract, and beat or blend until you have a smooth batter. Put plums in a buttered casserole dish, and pour batter over them. Bake for 45 minutes, or until batter has become firm on the surface, although the center will have a custardlike consistency. Remove from oven and sprinkle with granulated sugar. Serve warm preferably, but cold is good too.

NOTE: If your kids aren't looking, sneak ¼ cup of Kirsch or rum into the batter; it's delicious.

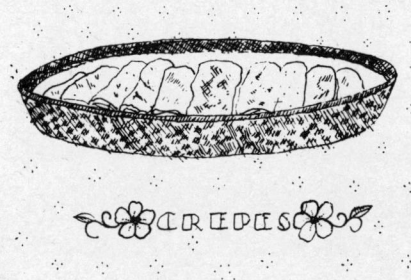

MENU 3

This almost meatless meal is as much fun to prepare as it is to eat. There are three things you can do ahead of time to make the evening's work simple: make the crêpe batter, which will take only a couple of minutes, and refrigerate it for the day; and wash the spinach and radishes in the morning and immerse them in water to soak for the rest of the day. In the evening, make your crêpes while the tomatoes are baking and the rice is cooking, then cover and put them in the oven at 250°, just to keep them nicely warm, while you are having dinner.

Radis beurre
(*Radishes served with sweet butter*)

Tomates farcies
(*Stuffed baked tomatoes*)

Riz
(*Rice*)

Salade d'épinards aux croûtons
(*Spinach salad with croutons*)

Crêpes à la confiture d'abricots
(*French pancakes, filled with apricot jam*)

Radishes Served with Sweet Butter

In France, radishes will inevitably appear on the hors d'oeuvres variés tray and, on most menus they are offered as a separate appetizer—always, you will note, with butter. The reason for the butter is that it complements the natural sharpness of the radishes. The French actually put a dab of butter on each radish, treating it as if it were a tiny roll. Dip in salt if desired. Like the grated carrot appetizer in menu 1, this is light, economical, and healthful. The butter is served in a separate bowl, and each person takes what he or she needs. Or you can put your butter on a serving platter and crown with the radishes.

Stuffed Baked Tomatoes

Serves 4–5

- 6 tomatoes
- 1 stick butter (or margarine)
- 1 onion, finely chopped
- 3 slices stale bread, softened in water
- ½ cup walnuts, coarsely chopped
- Chopped parsley
- ¼ pound ground beef
- Salt and pepper
- 1 clove garlic, finely chopped (optional)
- ½ cup bread crumbs

Wash the tomatoes and scoop out their insides, reserving the pulp for a future sauce or soup. Place tomatoes side by side in a buttered casserole dish. In a skillet, melt half the butter and sauté onion until golden brown. Squeeze out the bread; in a bowl, mix it with walnuts, parsley to taste, onion, and meat. Salt and pepper to taste. If you wish, add the garlic. Neatly fill the hollowed-out tomatoes with the stuffing, top with bread crumbs and parsley, and dot with remaining butter. Place in a casserole dish, add half a cup of water, bake at 350° for 35 minutes, and serve.

NOTE: Instructions for cooking the boiled rice which I recommend as a side dish will be found on the package of whatever brand you buy.

Spinach Salad with Croutons

Serves 4–5
3 slices bread, cubed
2 tablespoons cooking oil
¼ stick butter
Pepper and salt

1 pound fresh spinach
1 clove garlic
Vinaigrette (see page 46)

Sauté bread cubes in oil and butter. Season with salt and pepper. Using a spatula, agitate your croutons until they're evenly toasted. Remove the stems of the spinach, wash several times (when one of our children was little, he asked, as he saw a truck filled with sand going by, "Mommy, are they taking that to put it into the spinach?"), and drain thoroughly. Rub a clove of garlic several times around the inside of the salad bowl. Mix spinach, croutons, and vinaigrette in salad bowl. Start with 4 tablespoons vinaigrette, taste, add more if necessary. Toss just prior to serving.

French Pancakes, Filled with Apricot Jam

Crêpes, as French pancakes are called, are a traditional dish in France, still served not only for breakfast but for both lunch and dinner. They can be stuffed with literally hundreds of fillings, and served either as a main dish or as a dessert. During the past decade or so, the "crêpe" concept has been imported into the States, and many restaurants have sprung up, generally called "crêperies," which serve only these delicious, thin pancakes. In France, there is one particular feast day, February 2, called La Chandeleur— which stems from the Latin *festa candelarum,* or "candle festival"—celebrating the presentation of Jesus at the Temple and the purification of the Virgin Mary. It is a festive occasion on which a family, or group of families, gathers around an enormous pile of crêpes. Various jams, preserves, and sugar complete the picture. Everyone rolls his or her own crêpe with the preferred fillings. Children drink cider. The adults drink either cider or wine.

Here is the batter for about ten crêpes. Most recipes give milk as one of the basic ingredients, but I have found, after experimenting over the years, that water is better. What you want in a crêpe batter is delicacy and lightness, and water provides this. Another important tip: crêpe batter seems to cook better when prepared several hours ahead of time, so take a few minutes to mix it in the morning and let it sit during the day. However, it's not absolutely essential to making good crêpes; if you haven't had a chance to do your batter well in advance, you can still make it just prior to cooking. It tends not to bind quite as well, but many a time I have made crêpes from start to finish in a total of 5 minutes.

Serves 4–5

2 eggs
2 cups flour
⅓ cup sugar
2 cups water
1 tablespoon vanilla extract
  or Kirsch or rum
1 teaspoon salt
1 tablespoon cooking oil
Apricot jam

Put all the ingredients except jam into a blender and blend at high speed until smooth and liquid (if you have no blender, a whisk will do nicely), which should take no more than a minute. If this is your first try at making crêpes, I suggest you confine yourself to using a single skillet. Later on, when you get more comfortable, you can use two skillets simultaneously, one on either side of the stove.

Over a medium flame, lubricate the skillet by rubbing lightly with butter or margarine. Wait until the frying pan is good and hot, then pour into the middle slightly less than a ladleful of batter, or just enough to coat the bottom. Remove the skillet from the flame and tilt it in various directions so that the batter spreads thinly over the entire surface of the skillet. For you who are used to pancake batter, remember that all you want for crêpes is a very thin layer, almost a film. Return skillet to heat. When you see that batter looks fairly solid and dry (don't look for bubbles, as in American pancakes) take your spatula and flip it over. The color you are looking for is blond; never brown. I find that about 20 seconds on either side is all you need.

Repeat the above process until you have the desired number of crêpes or have run out of batter (a minimum of two crêpes per person should be allowed, if my family is any criterion).

Another tip: whether you make your crêpes before the meal or just prior to serving, keep them warm and covered in the oven (at 250°) until time to bring them to the table. My mother used to make marvelous crêpes, but she stood by the stove and doled them out to us one by one, right out of the skillet. We enjoyed them, but I can't believe she did. I like to think that the cook will enjoy eating them along with the rest of the family.

Each member of the family takes a crêpe, which just about fits a dessert plate, spreads it flat, fills the center with jam, rolls the crêpe into a flute shape, and sprinkles with sugar. Crêpes are also eaten with only sugar sprinkled over them.

While this recipe proposes apricot jam, virtually any preserve is in order. Often, I put two or three different jams on the table, together with a bowl of granulated sugar.

MENU 4

Here, the stewed peaches gain from being cooked in the morning (10 minutes), then chilled for the day. You can also, if you like, make your Greek soup ahead and refrigerate it in its tureen, thus saving 5 to 10 minutes in the evening. Make the dough for your friands chauds *ahead, or if you have some in the freezer, remember to move it to the refrigerator in the morning or take it out at least one hour before rolling out.*

Soupe grecque
(Greek soup)

Petits friands chauds
(Sausages in pie crust)

Salade d'haricots verts à la flamande
(Green bean salad, Flemish style)

Mon fromage aux herbes
(My cheese with herbs)

Compote de pêches au vin
(Stewed peaches with wine)

Greek Soup

The minute I first tasted this soup on the island of Corfu ten years ago, I knew I had to incorporate it into my culinary repertory. Since that time this soup has emigrated to America. I often serve it, especially in the summer, because it is so refreshing, but I find it just as appetizing during the winter.

Most recipes call for yogurt as a basis, but I prefer buttermilk, which from the taste point of view is just as good and has the advantage of already being liquid. My recipe calls for mint and chopped walnuts, which give an added zest.

Serves 4–5

1 quart buttermilk
10 radishes, washed and sliced
1 cucumber, washed and diced
1–2 cloves garlic, squeezed
2 tablespoons mint, fresh or dry
½ cup coarsely chopped walnuts
Pepper and salt to taste

Mix all the ingredients in a soup tureen, and refrigerate.

NOTE: If you've had no time to prepare at least an hour before serving, therefore have not had a chance to refrigerate the soup, add two or three ice cubes directly into the tureen, and stir.

Sausages in Pie Crust

This is an extremely economical main course, yet with its pastry crust enclosure is both attractive and festive. Either plain old-fashioned hot dogs or Polish sausage will do: they both should be readily available at your regular market. If you live in urban areas or where delicatessens abound, you can obviously vary your meat filling considerably.

Serves 4–5

Double recipe for Basic Pie Crust (see page 39)
1 package hot dogs (or 1 large Polish sausage)
8 slices domestic Swiss cheese
1 egg yolk mixed with 2 tablespoons of water
Chopped parsley

In the morning remove two bags of previously prepared dough to thaw, or make dough according to directions, doubling the recipe. It should be at room temperature for rolling. In the evening, cook the hot dogs for 5 minutes in boiling water. (If you use Polish sausage, cook for 15 minutes, then slice into 4-inch pieces. If you use another sausage, follow the instructions for cooking.) Drain the meat. Roll out the dough onto a floured board to form two thin rectangles. With a knife, cut small rectangles about 5 inches long and 3 inches wide. Wrap a hot dog or piece of sausage in a slice of cheese, and place one on each small rectangle. Draw up sides and close by pressing with your fingers along the open edges of the dough. It will seal tight. Brush each "package" with the mixture of water and egg yolk. Bake in a preheated 400° oven for 35 minutes. Sprinkle with chopped parsley and serve.

You can if you like—and have a little more time to spare—make your own sausage meat. I do, and I prefer the end result. There are many variations I could suggest, but here is one that is not overly complex:

1 pound ground pork, with fat
1 clove garlic, minced
½ cup finely chopped parsley
1 teaspoon thyme
1 teaspoon tarragon
½ teaspoon oregano
Pepper and salt

In a bowl, combine all the ingredients until well mixed. Shape into one sausage, place into an ovenproof dish and cook in a 350° oven for 20 minutes. Remove, and divide the meat into sausage-length portions.

Green Bean Salad, Flemish Style

This is an ideal side dish for the preceding main course, because it completes it while not adding any starch. It also becomes the "condiment" that will cut the richness of the *friands*.

Serves 4–5
5 slices bacon
2 packages frozen whole green beans (or 2 pounds fresh beans)
½ cup vinaigrette (see page 46)
1 onion, finely chopped
½ cup finely chopped parsley
1 tablespoon bacon fat

Cook the bacon and drain on a paper towel. Reserve the fat. Cook beans in salty, boiling water for 5 minutes. (If fresh, cook for 15 minutes, but remember in both cases that the salad gains if the beans are slightly undercooked.) Drain. In a salad bowl, mix the beans with the dressing, onion, and parsley. Crumple bacon over it, and add the bacon fat. Toss and serve. May be served warm or cold. Warm is more authentically Flemish, but I find cold just as good.

My Cheese with Herbs

Here is another personal variation which, in an era of steeply rising prices for French and other cheeses, I have worked out. It ranks as a cousin of the better-known *Boursin aux herbes*.

Serves 4–5

- 8-ounce package cream cheese
- ⅓ cup sour cream
- ½ cup whipped cream
- 4 shallots, finely chopped
- 1 clove garlic, minced
- ½ cup finely chopped chives (or ½ cup finely chopped greens of scallions)
- 2 teaspoons thyme
- ½ cup finely chopped parsley
- Salt and pepper

In a bowl, thoroughly mix with a fork all the ingredients, seasoning to taste. Refrigerate until ready to serve, either in a pretty crock or reshaped on a platter. It can be eaten as soon as you have made it, but refrigeration will give it an added firmness.

Serve with warm bread, or crackers. In contrast to other cheeses, you may keep this cheese refrigerated until serving time—it does not require "breathing" time.

Stewed Peaches with Wine

- 2 pounds peaches, whole and unpeeled
- 2 cups water
- 1 cup wine (red or white)
- ½ cup sugar
- 1 cinnamon stick

Wash fruit. Cover with water, wine, sugar, and cinnamon in a pot. Bring to a boil, reduce flame, and let simmer for 10 minutes. Transfer to a deep dessert serving bowl. Refrigerate. This dessert gains by being served chilled: therefore, make it in the morning or well ahead of time.

MENU 5

For this rather exotic Mediterranean menu there are only a couple of things you can do to advance your dinner preparations: one is to soak, and preferably scrub, your mussels, and the other is to make your brik dough and refrigerate. But remember, too, that your brik dough will take you only about 5 to 7 minutes if you haven't had a chance to do it in the morning.

Brik de Tunisie
(*Fried turnovers stuffed with herbs, egg, and capers*)

Moules marinière
(*Steamed mussels in white wine and herbs*)

Salade de laitue
(*Boston lettuce salad: see pages 47–50*)

Fromage américain
(*Sharp cheddar cheese*)

Oranges

Fried Turnovers Stuffed with Herbs, Egg, and Capers

When I first saw "brik" on the menu in Tunis several years ago I envisioned a heavy dish fraught with danger for the unwary tourist. The maître d' described it to me, however, and recommended it as hors d'oeuvre. I have never regretted heeding his advice. Contrary to so many recipes in this book, in which I proselytize for advance preparation, this delicacy unfortunately requires last-minute cooking, which explains why I tend to limit it to my family or an intimate dinner with a few close friends: not only does it take you away from your guests for perhaps 15 to 20 minutes in all, but the odor of deep frying can be offensive to some. (It is to me.)

You can make only 2 briks at a time, since they take up half the surface of the deep fryer. It will take a minute or two to cook the turnover on one side. Therefore, it will take 8 to 12 minutes maximum to cook 4 to 6 briks. Normally, people eat only one, since it's rather filling, but I have had gourmets—both guests and family—so smitten by briks that they've come back for seconds. Thus, if you have 4 for dinner, I would advise you to make at least 6.

For the dough:

Serves 4–5
2 cups flour
1 teaspoon salt
½ cup cold water

Mix the flour, salt, and water together with your fingers until you obtain a light, rubbery consistency. This should take no more than 6 or 7 minutes. Roll dough out onto floured board and cut into six to eight 5-inch squares.

For the filling and frying:

1 quart peanut oil
1 cup finely chopped parsley
8 teaspoons capers
½ cup finely chopped chives (or 6 teaspoons dried chives)
8 eggs
Salt

Start heating the oil in the deep fryer. Mix parsley, capers, and chives in a bowl. Place one tablespoon of this mixture in the center of one dough square. Break an egg over it, quickly fold the square into a triangle, and seal tightly with your fingers. (I say "quickly" simply because if you linger the liquid of the egg will seep away.) Repeat the process for all your dough squares. When the oil in the fryer is very hot (when it begins to fume, you know it's very hot), reduce flame. Immerse two briks at a time; when gold on one side, turn over with a fork or spatula. When cooked golden on both sides, remove and drain on a paper towel. When all are cooked, sprinkle with salt and serve.

Steamed Mussels in White Wine and Herbs

Moules marinière are delicious, and coveted the world over, with good reason. But they're a bore to prepare. One considerable advantage to serving steamed mussels after briks is that the latter are so substantial you'll have to clean and prepare fewer of the former. I consider 2 quarts of mussels sufficient for 4 to 5 people. They *must* be scrubbed mercilessly, then scrubbed again. I use a hard-bristle nailbrush purchased specifically for that purpose, and clean them under cold, running water. You also must remove the "threads" that cling. You'll know when they're clean: the shell will be smooth and free of sand and other grit. (Note: discard any mussels whose shells are opened before cooking.)

Serves 4–5

2 quarts mussels, cleaned
1 cup dry white wine
4 shallots, finely chopped
1 cup finely chopped parsley
1 bay leaf, crumbled
1 teaspoon thyme
Pepper and salt

Put all the ingredients in a large kettle. Cover with a lid, and cook over a medium flame for approximately 4 minutes. Once or twice during this 4-minute period, give your kettle a good shake to distribute both mussels and steam. Uncover and stir with a wooden spoon until all the mussels are open. If you see that some have still not opened, give it another minute or two. After that, throw away any unopened mussels. Transfer to a deep platter and serve immediately, with hot French bread. The server will ladle out to each person a goodly pile of mussels, plus a ladleful of juice. The mussels are eaten directly from their shells, by hand. The juice can be eaten with a spoon, but the French use a mussel shell. It's easier, and closer to nature.

NOTE: Be sure to serve the mussels in individual soup plates (because of the juice), and provide at least one and preferably two extra empty soup plates for the discarded shells.

The richness of this menu—and by rich I don't mean heavy—obviates the necessity of any prepared dessert. However, one does need to finish on a sweet note, and eating oranges is refreshing, appropriate, and in keeping with the Tunisian brik. Serve them in a basket. If you should have some green leaves handy, line the basket with a few.

MENU 6

Do two things ahead—and the rest of the meal will take only 30 minutes. Wash your salad (I hope this will become as automatic as rolling your dough; if you don't have time to wash your salad in the morning, at least immerse it in cold water so that when you come home in the evening it's crisp and fresh); second, take 5 minutes to mix the batter for Lily's cake, then let it bake for 45 minutes during breakfast, or make it in a spare moment during the day.

Your soup and your cauliflower will be cooking at the same time half an hour before dinner, and your meat course requires—say, 3 minutes just prior to serving.

Potage purée Crécy
(Cream of carrot, turnip, and potato soup)

Foie de veau aux fines herbes
(Calf's liver with shallots and herbs)

Choux-fleurs au gratin
(Cauliflower au gratin)

Salade de scarolle
(Escarole salad: see pages 47–50)

Gâteau de Lily
(Lily's cake)

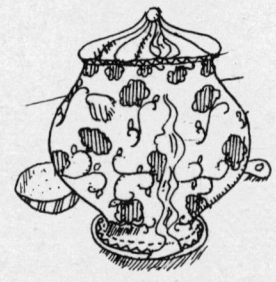

Cream of Carrot, Turnip, and Potato Soup

Serves 4–5

- 8 carrots, peeled and cubed
- 2 turnips, peeled and cubed
- 3 potatoes, peeled and cubed
- 3 onions, peeled and cubed
- 4 cups water
- ½ teaspoon nutmeg
- Pepper and salt
- ½ stick butter
- ½ cup finely chopped parsley

In a large soup kettle, place all vegetables (except for one onion), water, nutmeg, salt, and pepper. Bring to a boil, reduce flame, cover, and let simmer for 20 minutes. Pour into the jar of your blender, filling it halfway. Blend at high speed, until creamy consistency is reached, and return to soup kettle. Sauté the remaining onion in butter until golden, then add to soup with parsley, and serve.

Calf's Liver with Shallots and Herbs

In the United States, English-style calf's liver is more common than the following French recipe. The English method is to broil the liver and serve it garnished with a slice or two of broiled bacon. We sinful French bathe our liver in butter, herbs, and sometimes wine. I have found that even those—like my husband—who are not liver lovers nonetheless love this recipe.

5 shallots, finely chopped
1 stick butter (or margarine)
4–5 slices calf's liver
Flour
2 tablespoons tarragon
1 cup finely chopped parsley
Pepper and salt

In a skillet, sauté the shallots in butter over a medium flame. Wash liver under cold water and dry with paper towel. Dip in flour and, when shallots are slightly golden, put into skillet and cook no more than 2 minutes on each side. While the liver is still in the skillet, add tarragon, parsley, and pepper and salt to taste. Serve.

Cauliflower au Gratin

Serves 4–5
1 head cauliflower
1½ cups cream sauce (see page 46)
½ teaspoon nutmeg
1 cup grated Swiss cheese (or cheddar)
Pepper and salt
Butter

Remove the green leaves of the cauliflower, slice off the root end, and cut the cauliflower into flowerets an inch or 2 in diameter. Cover in a pot with 2 inches of salty water and cook for 12 to 15 minutes. Meanwhile, make your cream sauce, and add the nutmeg, half of the grated cheese, and pepper and salt to taste.

Drain cooked cauliflower and place in a casserole dish. Pour cream sauce over it, and cover with the remaining grated cheese, plus a few dots of butter. Bake in a preheated 350° oven for 15 minutes, or until top is light and crusty. Serve.

Lily's Cake

This recipe, given me by a Haitian friend, is a personalized version of a standard island dessert. It is reminiscent of the French *quatre-quarts,* a rather rich pound cake which requires no frosting. It will take less than 10 minutes to prepare, even if you have no mixer and have to mix the ingredients with a wooden spoon in a bowl.

Serves 4–5

1 stick sweet butter, softened (or margarine)
1 cup sugar
3 eggs
2 cups flour
1 cup milk
2 teaspoons baking powder
1 teaspoon almond extract
1 tablespoon vanilla extract

In a bowl, mash butter and sugar until smooth. Use a mixer if you have one; otherwise, your wooden spoon. Add the eggs one at a time, stirring. Add 1 cup of flour, then half the milk, still stirring. Now add the rest of the flour, then the rest of the milk. Add baking powder, almond, and vanilla. Butter and flour an 8- to 9-inch cake pan, then pour your batter in. Bake at 350° for 40 minutes. Cool and unmold before serving.

An ideal accompaniment for Lily's cake is any stewed fuit.

NOTE: To vary the flavor, you can substitute a cup of orange juice in place of the milk, and two tablespoons of orange extract in place of the almond.

MENU 7

Gazpacho gains triply by being made ahead (preparation time: 10 to 12 minutes): you'll be one step ahead for the evening meal, the soup will chill to proper temperature, and it will season by the sitting. You can also move things forward another step by taking 10 minutes to blend your ham and herbs for the quenelles: refrigerate them in a bowl for the day, together with the other ingredients. Again, remember to defrost your pie crust if you're using frozen dough for your wine tart.

Gazpacho de Seville
(Gazpacho from Sevilla)

Quenelles de jambon à la chapelure frite
(Ham dumplings with fried bread crumbs)

Salade de cresson
(Watercress salad: see pages 47–50)

Roquefort beurre
(Roquefort cheese mixed with butter)

Tarte au vin
(Wine tart)

Gazpacho from Sevilla

Virtually unknown in America a few years ago, gazpacho, like Greek soup, is fast becoming a part of the American culinary repertory. Actually, there are almost as many varieties of gazpacho as there are towns and cities in Spain. I've eaten at least a dozen different gazpachos in Spain. The present recipe derives from a soup I had in Sevilla. It contains almonds, which adds that little special "something," and is somewhat more creamy than most gazpachos, because of the bread. It has been approved and acclaimed by even my most demanding Spanish friends.

Refreshing and delicious, gazpacho is the answer to many a mother's dream: faced with the problem of how to make children love vegetables, which so often they instinctively hate, this is a festival of vitamins. If my children are any indication, you'll have requests for a repeat performance after you've served them gazpacho for the first time.

Serves 4–5

- 8 tomatoes, peeled, or 15-ounce can whole tomatoes
- 1 quart water
- ½ loaf French bread or 5–6 slices American bread, soaked in water
- 1 onion
- 3 cloves garlic
- Juice of 1 lemon
- ½ cup wine vinegar
- ½ teaspoon Tabasco
- Pepper and salt to taste
- ½ cup olive oil
- 1½ cucumbers, peeled and cubed
- 3 green peppers, chopped
- 1 cup almonds

Blend all ingredients—*except* half a cucumber, one green pepper, and ½ cup almonds—filling the blender only three-quarters full each time to ensure proper blending. It makes no difference in what order you blend your vegetables: in other words, you can blend all your tomatoes at one go or combine them with whatever else might fit to make your blender three-quarters full. In any case, empty the successive blender loads into your soup tureen, and stir to make sure all ingredients are evenly mixed.

Add the remaining half cucumber, the green pepper, and the almonds, coarsely chopped. Refrigerate. If you've had no time to refrigerate, you can add 3 or 4 ice cubes directly to the soup tureen.

NOTE: If you feel that your gazpacho is too thick, don't be afraid to add half a cup, or even a cup, of cold water or cold broth. If it's too liquid, you can obtain proper consistency by blending two or three more slices of stale bread and adding.

Some chefs may take umbrage at my advocating water rather than chicken bouillon. I have used broth, but frankly I find water just as good: it is the raw vegetables that count.

Ham Dumplings with Fried Bread Crumbs

This is a *very* inexpensive dish, though it comes on with style. You need only half a pound of ham, or you can use leftover meat or scraps from a baked ham.

Serves 4–5

- 7 slices bread, cubed
- 1 stick butter
- ½ cup milk
- ½ pound ham, ground in blender or meat grinder
- 3 eggs
- ½ cup finely chopped chervil (or ½ cup finely chopped parsley)
- ½ cup cottage cheese
- Pepper and salt
- ½ cup flour

Sauté the bread cubes in butter over a medium flame. Transfer to a mixing bowl and pour milk over them. Add ham, eggs, herbs, and cottage cheese. Season to taste. Knead with fingers until well mixed. Shape into little balls, roll in flour, immerse the dumplings in boiling, salty water, and reduce flame. Cook for 10 minutes, or until dumplings rise to the surface. Drain and arrange on a serving platter.

While the dumplings are cooking, make your fried bread crumbs as follows:

- 1 onion, finely chopped
- 6 tablespoons butter
- 1 cup bread crumbs
- ½ cup finely chopped parsley

In a skillet over medium flame, sauté the onion in butter until it becomes light brown. Add bread crumbs and stir, over low flame, until crumbs are toasted. Add parsley. Pour over the dumplings and serve.

NOTE: These dumplings need no side dish; a green salad will suffice.

Roquefort Cheese Mixed with Butter

Roquefort tends to be a trifle sharp. Therefore, at home we always used to mash it with an equal amount of sweet butter. This can be done with a fork in 2 to 3 minutes.

Wine Tart

You may well wonder what a wine tart is doing in a family dinner. Actually, the wine evaporates in the course of baking, but as it goes it imparts a lovely flavor.

Serves 4–5
Dough for 8-inch crust (see page 37)
5 tablespoons flour
5 tablespoons sugar
1 teaspoon cinnamon
½ bottle white wine, dry or sweet (about 1⅔ cups)
2 eggs, beaten
1 stick sweet butter or margarine

Preheat your oven to 400°. Roll out the dough and line a pie mold. Evenly spread a layer of flour over the pie crust (use all 5 tablespoons). Make a second even layer using the mixed sugar and cinnamon. Mix the wine and the eggs and pour evenly over the pie. Distribute dots of butter until the surface is covered. Bake for 45 minutes until crust is golden and the filling has a custardlike consistency. Serve warm.

MENU 8

There are two or three advance steps you can take, all admittedly minor but all of which will make the evening's work a cinch; prepare the crêpe batter in a matter of 2 or 3 minutes and refrigerate, or if you have another 10 or 15 minutes, make all the crêpes in the morning and store them, covered, for the day—which means you'll only have to do the filling in the evening. Again, don't forget to soak your lettuce in cold water.

Potage velouté
(Velvet soup)

Crêpes farcies aux épinards
(French pancakes stuffed with creamed spinach)

Salade de laitue
(Boston lettuce salad: see pages 47–50)

Fromage de Camembert
(Camembert cheese)

Pêche melba
(Peach melba)

Velvet Soup

You will note that many of my family dinners start with soup. This is because I have found that soup adds a hearty touch and helps create a cozy mood for the evening meal.

Serves 4–5

4 cups chicken or beef consommé	1 egg yolk
½ cup tapioca	½ stick butter
Pepper and salt	½ cup finely chopped parsley

In case you have not defrosted your chicken or beef stock several hours in advance, remove from freezer and place, still in its plastic container, in hot water or under a stream of hot water. When it has loosened enough from the sides, invert and place contents in a kettle. (If you have no previously made stock, you can also use water and bouillon cubes, but only in a real pinch! You'll be able to taste the difference.) Heat to boiling point, then add tapioca and pepper and salt to taste. Lower flame and let simmer 8 to 10 minutes.

In a small bowl, mix egg yolk, butter, and parsley, and mash until well mixed. Add to your soup just prior to serving.

French Pancakes Stuffed with Creamed Spinach

Make your crêpe batter according to the directions on page 76, omitting both the sugar and the vanilla extract, since this batter will serve as the basis for a main course rather than a dessert. In a skillet, make 8 to 10 crêpes, set aside, and prepare the following filling:

Serves 4–5

- 1 package frozen spinach
- 1 pint cottage cheese
- ½ stick butter
- ½ teaspoon nutmeg
- Pepper and salt
- 8-ounce can tomato sauce
- 3 tablespoons grated Swiss cheese
- Butter for "dotting"

Cook spinach according to instructions on the box. Drain well, pressing the water out through a sieve, using a fork. In a blender put the spinach, cottage cheese, butter, nutmeg, pepper, and salt, and blend at high speed for one minute. It should be creamy, not liquid. If it is too liquid, add a slice of stale bread and blend for another 15 seconds or so. Fill each pancake with its fair share of the creamed spinach and roll it. Place the crêpes side by side in a casserole dish, cover with tomato sauce, and sprinkle grated cheese over the top. Add dots of butter, bake for 10 to 15 minutes in 375° oven, and serve.

A delicacy, this main course is both inexpensive and fairly quick to prepare. Like meat covered with pastry crust, crêpes tend to add an element of elegance to what might otherwise be considered an ordinary meal.

Peach Melba

Serves 4–5

- 5 fresh peaches, peeled and halved, or 15-ounce can peaches in syrup
- 1 pint vanilla ice cream
- Raspberry syrup
- Whipped cream, blanched almonds (optional)

This dish, named for the famous singer Nellie Melba, for whom it was first prepared at the turn of the century, is as simple as it is delectable. It deserves to be finely presented, so take out your long-stemmed glasses, if you have any. Champagne glasses will do. Place a scoop of ice cream in each glass, cover each scoop with both halves of a peach (if in season, fresh peaches are infinitely to be preferred, but canned will do nicely off-season). Top with raspberry syrup. Some of my friends have come back to me asking how to make the raspberry syrup. You don't: you buy it, ready-made, at virtually every supermarket. There are both German and Swiss varieties, of equal quality. You need only a little syrup for each serving, so each bottle will last you for some time. It keeps well, though, refrigerated.

If you happen to have some whipped cream handy, or blanched almonds, you can add them as a trimming.

MENU 9

Céleri rémoulade, *which takes but 10 to 15 minutes to prepare, can be done well ahead, since it keeps under refrigeration for several days. Your* hachis parmentier *can be made in a matter of 20 to 25 minutes either in the morning or even the day before. For the apple tart, make your dough in the morning, unless you have some frozen, in which case transfer it to the refrigerator for the day or take it out of the freezer 2 hours before rolling out. You can peel and slice your apples and let them macerate in sugar; or, if it's more convenient, bake the tart ahead and refrigerate.*

Céleri rémoulade
(Celeriac with rémoulade sauce)

Hachis parmentier
(Beef and mashed potatoes au gratin)

Salade melangée
(Mixed green salad: see pages 47–50)

Tarte aux pommes
(Apple tart)

Celeriac with Rémoulade Sauce

One of the classic hors d'oeuvres in France is *céleri rémoulade*. While you'll probably find it on the menus of most French restaurants in America, that does not necessarily mean that your local greengrocer or supermarket will have celeriac. Also known as celery root, it is a large turniplike root which, peeled and grated, forms the basis of this delicious appetizer.

Serves 4–5
- 2–3 celery roots
- 1 cup mayonnaise (you'll prefer your own homemade, see page 46, but prepared will do)
- ¼ cup dry white wine
- ¼ cup Dijon mustard (or American)
- ¼ cup milk
- Pepper and salt to taste

Peel the celery roots (I suggest using a potato peeler; it does a better job than a knife). Wash. Grate, using an automatic grater if available. In a bowl, mix remaining ingredients. Add to grated celery root and stir.

A good point to remember: since celery roots are not as common as some vegetables, whenever you come across them locally buy a few pounds. They're roots, and will keep. Wrap them in paper and store with your potatoes in a cool, dark place. That way, when the fancy strikes, or when your family clamors for another round of *céleri rémoulade*, you'll be able to meet the request.

Beef and Mashed Potatoes au Gratin

Hachis parmentier was named after Antoine Augustin Parmentier, who brought back the potato to France from the New World and was instrumental in cultivating it in the Old. According to legend at least, Parmentier described the vegetable as an "earth apple"—hence the French term for potatoes: *pommes de terre*.

Hachis parmentier is traditionally served the day after pot-au-feu. The leftover meats of the pot-au-feu are ground up—*hachis* means "ground up"—and combined with mashed potatoes to make a main course.

In the following menu I am giving a recipe using freshly ground beef, but the way you make it will depend on what you have on hand.

Serves 4–5

4–6 medium-sized potatoes
½ cup hot milk
¾ stick butter
½ teaspoon nutmeg
Pepper and salt
1 onion, finely chopped

1–1½ pounds ground beef
  (round or chuck)
½ cup grated Swiss cheese
  (or cheddar)
½ cup finely chopped parsley

Prepare the mashed potatoes as follows: peel, wash, and quarter the potatoes, and cover with salty water in a saucepan. Bring to a boil and cook for 15 to 20 minutes. Drain. Add milk, ½ stick of butter, nutmeg, pepper, and salt. Mix vigorously in an electric mixer or with a whisk.

Now on to the meat mixture: In a skillet melt the remaining butter and sauté the onion until golden brown. Add meat, pepper, and salt. Stir. If you are using fresh meat, cook 5 minutes; with leftover boiled meat, cook 1 minute.

In a buttered casserole dish, arrange a layer using part of the mashed potatoes. Spread over it a layer of the meat mixture, then add another layer of potatoes. Cover with the grated cheese, parsley, and dots of butter. Bake for 15 minutes at 350° until top is crisp and golden. Serve piping hot.

Apple Tart

"As American as apple pie," goes the saying. I say there ought to be an equivalent, "As French as *tarte aux pommes*," if only because in the smallest, remotest patisseries throughout France you will always find a *tarte aux pommes*. How does it differ from apple pie? For one thing, it has no covering. For this reason—because the apples are visible to the naked eye—the French arrange the slices meticulously, with all the rigor of the *jardins à la française* (see Fontainebleau, Versailles, 1,000 French châteaux, etc.). Finally, we glaze our apples. I do not claim one is better than the other: they are simply different.

As for pie crust, any kind is welcome: *pâte feuilletée, pâte brisée, pâte sablée,* or my quick, safe cream cheese and butter dough (see page 39).

Serves 4–5

Dough for 8–9-inch pie pan
  (see page 39)
6–7 apples (tart if possible)
⅔ cup sugar

Almond extract
Vanilla extract
⅔ stick sweet butter
4 tablespoons apricot jam

Roll out dough and arrange neatly in buttered pie mold. Peel apples, slice into a bowl, and cover with ½ cup sugar. Do this a little ahead of time, so that the apples have a chance to release some of their juices, which will prevent excessive moistness later on the pie crust. Arrange the apple slices over the uncooked dough in neat circular rows, starting on the outer rim and working inward over the crust. Cover with the remaining sugar, add almond and vanilla extracts to taste, and dot generously with butter.

Preheat your oven to 350° and bake for 45 minutes. In a small saucepan, melt the apricot jam. After you have removed the pie from the oven, pour jam over the apples to form a glaze.

MENU 10

For this hearty menu, which does not need a first course, I recommend taking 5 minutes to wash and shred the cabbage early in the day—it's one step less later. If you have an additional 15 minutes available, boil it. If you have another 15, complete the recipe and refrigerate it, then reheat for 10 minutes before serving. One of the virtues of cabbage is that it gains from being reheated. For the pear turnovers, make your dough ahead, unless you have some frozen (in which case remove from the freezer 2 hours before rolling out). In another 10 minutes you can peel the pears and wrap them in the dough circles, then either refrigerate unbaked or bake to completion.

Jambon aux olives et au vin blanc
(Ham slices with green olives and white wine sauce)

Choux à la campagnarde
(Cabbage peasant style)

Salade de cresson
(Watercress salad: see pages 47–50)

Fromage de chèvre
(Goat cheese)

Chausson aux poires
(Pear turnovers)

Family Dinners / **95**

Ham Slices with Green Olives and White Wine Sauce

This is a good recipe to serve two or three days after you have had a large baked ham. Or, starting afresh, buy two ham steaks and divide into four or five slices. The olives act as an excellent counterbalance to the ham's richness.

Serves 4–5

- ½ stick butter or margarine
- 1½ tablespoons flour
- 1½ cups white wine
- 1 cup green olives
- 4–5 slices of ham
- Pepper and salt

Melt the butter in a skillet, add flour, lower flame, and stir, gradually adding the wine to form a smooth sauce. Add the olives, continue stirring, then add ham slices and let simmer in the sauce for 5 to 8 minutes. Season to taste. Serve.

Cabbage Peasant Style

Cabbage is a hearty vegetable, much in vogue in the French countryside, and it seems to marry well with ham and pork.

Serves 4–5

- 1 white cabbage
- ½ cup vinegar
- 2 onions, coarsely chopped
- 2 tablespoons lard
- ¼ pound bacon, cut in 1-inch pieces
- ½ cup finely chopped parsley
- 1–2 cloves garlic, finely chopped (or squeezed)

Under running cold water, wash cabbage thoroughly. Add vinegar to a pot of cold water, and rinse cabbage in it. Quarter the cabbage, then cook in boiling water for 10 minutes. Drain. Shred cabbage with a knife (this will be easy, since the cabbage is soft from cooking).

Sauté onions in lard until golden. Add bacon. Cook for 5 minutes. Add the cabbage and stir. Cook, covered, over a medium flame for 15 minutes. Mix in parsley and garlic and serve.

NOTE: If there is any left over, don't worry: this is just as good, if not better, the next time around.

Pear Turnovers

A festive yet reasonably inexpensive dessert. In my family, I invariably get requests to "serve it again soon" every time I make it.

Serves 4–5
1 pound pears
¾ cup sugar
Juice of ½ lemon
Dough for 1–2 pie crusts
   (see page 39)
8-ounce can almond paste
   (optional)
1 egg yolk mixed with water

Peel and quarter the pears, and toss in a bowl with sugar and lemon juice. Roll dough out on a floured board and, using a wide cup or metal mixing bowl about 6 inches in diameter, cut out six or seven circles. If you have opted to use the almond paste, dab a slice on each circle (the almond paste tends to be so hard that you cannot actually spread it; but don't worry, it will melt in the cooking) in the area where you'll place your quarters of pear. Into each circle, put two pear pieces. Fold dough and seal tightly with your fingers. When finished you will have a collection of half moons. Brush them with the yolk and water mixture. Preheat oven to 350° and bake for 35 minutes.

MENU 11

Here there's not much you can do ahead of time. But if you have 15 minutes available earlier in the day, you can prepare the soup (which will require another 20 minutes to cook). You can also peel your potatoes at the same time and immerse them in water until cooking time.

Soupe portugaise
(Portuguese soup)

Filets de sole amandine
(Fillets of sole amandine)

Pommes vapeur, persillées
(Steamed potatoes with parsley)

Salade d'endives et de bettraves
(Beet and endive salad)

Petits soufflés de bananes
(Little banana soufflés)

Portuguese Soup

Whether this is Portugal's national soup or not, or whether it's even popular there, I have no idea, since I've never visited sunny Portugal. But in the French cuisine it's called *soupe portugaise*. It is an excellent opener to a meal in which the main dish will be relatively light, such as broiled meat or fish, and it is relatively quickly made.

Serves 4–5

2 onions, chopped	1 teaspoon thyme
3 tablespoons olive oil	1 cup finely chopped parsley
1 pound tomatoes	Pepper and salt
3–4 potatoes, peeled and cubed	4–5 slices bread fried in olive oil
4 cups broth or water	

In a skillet, sauté the onions in olive oil until golden. (If you have a metal or heatproof soup tureen, do your cooking directly in it. It will save you extra dishwashing.) Immerse tomatoes in boiling water for a few seconds to "pop" the skin, then peel. To the sautéed onions, add the potatoes, broth or water, tomatoes, thyme, half the parsley, and pepper and salt to taste. Cover and cook for 20 minutes over a medium flame. Blend to a creamy consistency. (If you have no blender, mash through vegetable mill or a colander.)

To serve, place toast, either full slice or halved, at the bottom of each soup plate. Pour soup over and decorate with remaining parsley.

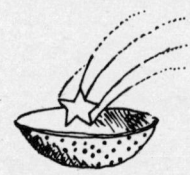

Fillets of Sole Amandine

This is an increasingly common and popular fish course in America, not only in French restaurants but also in American. Sole, however, is a very delicate fish, and requires tender loving care in preparation. There's nothing better than a good fillet of sole. But there is little worse than a sole overcooked, or too dry. Also, since it's a rather expensive fish, you might want to sacrifice an iota of delicacy and substitute flounder, which is much less costly. Before preparing the fish, start steaming potatoes in steamer basket over boiling water in tightly covered pot for about 25–30 minutes depending on their size (check by inserting tip of knife).

Serves 4–5
- 5–6 fillets of sole (or flounder)
- 1 stick butter
- Pepper and salt
- 1 lemon
- 1 cup blanched almonds, sliced
- 3 sprigs parsley, chopped
- 10–12 new potatoes, washed and scrubbed only

Wash the fish under cold, running water, and pat dry with a paper towel. Arrange fillets in a buttered casserole dish, dot with half a stick of butter, and pepper and salt, then squeeze juice of a half lemon over them. Scatter the almonds generously on the fish and bake for 10 minutes at 350°. Place casserole dish under your broiler for 2 or 3 minutes until almonds are slightly toasted. Quarter the remaining lemon half, and decorate the platter with it. Fish is ready to serve.

Remove potatoes, cover with parsley and the remaining butter, and serve.

Beet and Endive Salad

Serves 4–5
- 4-ounce can sliced beets
- 3 Belgian endives
- Vinaigrette (see page 46)

Open the can of beets and drain, reserving juice for a later use. Wash and cut the endives into one-inch pieces. Dry. Mix with the beets in a salad bowl, and add dressing.

Little Banana Soufflés

Serves 4–5
- 2 mashed bananas
- 1/2 cup sugar
- Juice of 1/2 lemon
- 3 egg yolks
- 3 egg whites, beaten until stiff

Mix the mashed bananas with sugar, lemon juice, and egg yolks. Fold in the egg whites. Pour into four or five small-size ovenproof buttered dishes. (The individual-serving aspect will make the dessert special to everyone.) Bake for 35 minutes in an oven preheated to 350°. Use your own timing, but I recommend putting them into the oven when you go out to fetch your main dish. As you take out the fillets of sole, put in your banana soufflés, which should then be ready to serve as you finish your salad.

NOTE: If your children are old enough to appreciate the flavor, you can add 3 teaspoons of rum to the banana mixture.

MENU 12

The crème caramel must be served cold, therefore has to be done in advance (preparation: 5 minutes; cooking time, 45 minutes). Put your salad to soak at the same time. The rest of the meal is a last-minute production—but a quick one.

Guacamole
(Avocado mashed with lemon juice, olive oil, and garlic)

Steak–pommes frites
(Steak with French fries)

Salade de laitue
(Boston lettuce salad: see pages 47–50)

Fromage de Brie
(Brie cheese)

Crème caramel
(Caramel custard)

Guacamole

A Mexican specialty, guacamole is frequently served as a dip with tortilla chips at parties. I prefer for ceremony's sake to serve it as an hors d'oeuvre at the table.

Serves 4–5
- 1 very ripe avocado
- Juice of 1 lemon
- ½ cup olive oil
- 1 clove garlic (or more, to taste)
- ½ red onion, chopped
- 1 tomato, cubed
- 1 large green pepper, diced
- Tortilla chips

Scoop out the meat of the avocado and put it in the blender, add lemon juice, oil, and garlic, and blend at high speed for about 2 minutes. Pour onto as many individual salad or other small plates as there are diners. Sprinkle with onion, tomato, and green pepper. Surround with a crown of tortilla chips. Serve.

Steak with French Fries

It's no mistake that *pommes frites* are called "French fries" in English, for they are virtually a national dish. Not only are they served in every restaurant in France, but one finds them being sold by vendors on street corners, the way hot dogs are in America. Every French kitchen has a deep frying pan specifically for *frites*. The importance of "steak–pommes frites" for the average Frenchman—or Frenchwoman—cannot be exaggerated. I would be willing to wager that if one took a public-opinion poll among French citizens residing outside France, asking what dish they dreamed of most at night, the answer would be overwhelmingly: "Steak–pommes frites, Camembert, et vin rouge."

"What's so great about French fries?" you may ask as an American. In answer, I must say the question is valid only because what so often parades under the title "French fries" here has little to do with *pommes frites*. So soft and large, in fact, are the American French fries that ketchup is apparently needed to make them more palatable.

If I were limited in this book to proselytizing for one basic culinary change, I think I'd choose the following method for making French fries.

Serves 4–5

1–2 quarts peanut oil   4–6 medium-sized potatoes
(corn oil will do)

Heat up the oil in the deep fryer (see page 22). While it's heating, peel and wash your potatoes. Pat dry. Slice finely and cut into thin strips. How thin? There is a variety of *pommes frites* called *pommes allumettes* which translates literally as "matchstick potatoes," and they are, indeed, about matchstick thin. "Normal" French fries should be anywhere between matchstick and pencil thickness. No more, or you'll get into the "puffy department." When the oil is hot—and you can tell if it is by dropping in one *frite:* if it sizzles, you're fine—drop your potatoes into the deep-fry basket. Lower the basket into the hot oil. Cook for 10 minutes. *Do not reduce the flame*. I have found that there are some electric, thermostatically controlled deep fryers on the market which automatically reduce the temperature when it reaches a certain point. They will not make good *frites*. Better to remove French fries all at once from hot oil, rather than decreasing temperature, which tends to soften the potatoes. Lift the basket and let it rest on the handles of the deep fryer to drain. Don't be concerned if your potatoes are not yet crisp: that is how they are supposed to be; you are only in phase one. Lower flame, awaiting phase two. Phase one may be done hours ahead.

While your *pommes frites* drain, cook your steak. I usually pan-broil mine, first covering the skillet with a "film" of salt and letting it get good and hot. Our family tastes run from rare to medium: for the former, 5 minutes on either side is about right for a 1-inch steak. For the latter, about 7. But if in doubt you can cut the steak in the center to check its status. Two or 3 minutes before it's done and ready to serve, immerse the basket a second time in the hot oil. If you see the oil beginning to smoke prior to reimmersing, it means it is too hot and will char your potatoes. Turn off flame. You may not have to turn it back on; it's doubtless hot enough to accomplish the purpose of the second immersion, namely to seize the potatoes and make them crisp.

Remember then, the key to successful "French fries" is: (1) slicing the potatoes thinly enough; (2) two immersions in the deep fryer, the first for 10 minutes, the second for 2 to 3.

NOTE: We use peanut oil for the frying oil, but any other oil will do, *except* olive oil. Olive oil has too pungent a flavor, which it would impart to the *frites*. It's also far too expensive, but the flavor's the basic drawback. When the oil has cooled, strain and refrigerate it.

Caramel Custard

This dessert is a standard part of French *cuisine bourgeoise* as well and appears on the menus of most French restaurants. It is also a common Spanish dessert, called flan. My family loves it, and I therefore serve it to them often, but I hasten to add that it is equally good for a large or small dinner party. Although it requires an hour's baking time, it is quick and easy to prepare—no more than 5 minutes in my experience. Unmold just before serving.

Serves 4–5
1½ cups sugar
5 eggs, beaten
1 tablespoon vanilla extract
Pinch salt
4 cups milk

In a pan over a low flame, melt ⅓ cup of sugar. Stir with a wooden spoon until the sugar turns light brown, at which point turn off the flame and pour into a buttered deep dish or oven-proof mold of your choice. Tip your mold so the caramel spreads evenly over the bottom (otherwise the caramel, which tends to harden, will remain in the area where you have poured it). Preheat oven to 350°. Mix eggs, vanilla, salt, remaining sugar, and milk with a whisk or in an electric mixer. Pour into the caramelized mold. Set the mold in a roasting pan containing 2 inches of water and bake in the oven for a little over an hour, or until the custard is firm. Cool. Chill in the refrigerator. At time of serving, loosen edges and unmold onto a serving platter.

MENU 13

Pumpkin soup is as good warm as it is cold. Therefore, if you make it ahead of time, you have the option. If you're using fresh pumpkin, count on about 15 minutes of preparation time; for canned pumpkin, it will take only a third as long. The hazelnut macaroons can also be done ahead of time, so if you have a free half hour (10 minutes for preparation, 20 for baking), I urge you to spend it making your dessert.

Crème d'or
(Pumpkin soup)

Baked bluefish

Pommes de terres à l'anglaise
(Boiled potatoes with parsley)

Salade d'endives
(Belgian endive salad: see pages 47–50)

Fromage de Camembert
(Camembert cheese)

Fours aux noisettes
(Hazelnut macaroons)

Pumpkin Soup

This is a marvelous soup for fall, when pumpkins abound, but even out of season it can be made using canned pumpkin. In the late summer and autumn, I often make pumpkin pies, pumpkin casserole vegetable, and so on. The seeds too can be put to good use: washed, roasted with butter in the oven, and salted, they disappear as if by magic when the children find them. I make several kinds of pumpkin soup, and this is one of them.

Serves 4–5

- 3 cups diced (or canned) pumpkin meat
- 4 cups milk
- ½ teaspoon nutmeg
- Pepper and salt
- ½ stick butter
- 1 cup chopped onion
- 3 tablespoons finely chopped parsley

If you are using fresh pumpkin, scoop seeds out with a knife (wash and reserve them for roasting) and discard stringy matter. Peel and cut up.

In a soup kettle, cover your pumpkin with milk, nutmeg, pepper, and salt, bring to a boil, reduce flame, and cook for 10 minutes. Blend. Sauté the onion in half the butter until golden. Add to the soup. Mash the remaining butter and parsley and top the hot soup just prior to serving.

NOTE: You may substitute curry for nutmeg.

Baked Bluefish

This is a fish that does not exist in France. I learned to eat it here, and it rightly ranks high on the list of most tasteful and delicate of fish. Of the many ways to cook it, the simplest, but also one of the best, is baking it in foil, with a stuffing of herbs and butter. Because of its natural delicacy and richness bluefish needs very little in the way of outside help.

Serves 4–5

4–5-pound bluefish	1 stick butter or margarine
2 lemons	Pepper and salt
1 cup finely chopped parsley	5–8 medium-sized potatoes, washed and peeled
1 tablespoon thyme	

My family is very "picky" when it comes to fish bones, so I always have my fish filleted at the market, which simply means removing the bone and the tail. (I also like the head removed, for personal and aesthetic reasons. Many people keep fish heads for soup.)

Just before putting the fish in the oven, start cooking potatoes in boiling salty water (they'll need about 18 minutes).

Wash the fish under cold, running water, and pat dry with paper towels. Place both halves of the clean bluefish skin side down on a piece of foil a few inches longer than the fish itself, so that you can wrap and seal it. Squeeze the juice of half a lemon over the entire fish. Slice the second half of the lemon over one half of the fillet, add half the parsley, the thyme, half the butter, and pepper and salt to taste. Lay the second half of the fish sandwich-fashion over the filled half, cover with a second piece of foil, wrap, and seal tightly. Preheat your oven to 450° and bake for 20 to 25 minutes. Drain potatoes, when ready, and toss with butter and parsley.

I recommend this simple sauce over the fish: In a small saucepan, melt remaining butter and parsley, and squeeze in half the remaining lemon. At time of serving, crown the fish with slices from remaining lemon half. Serve, pouring the butter-lemon sauce over each diner's portion.

NOTE: Bluefish should always be bought fresh at your local fish market. While some fish of course can be frozen, bluefish unfortunately cannot. If you're a fisherman and come home with several, I suggest you play Santa Claus and distribute them to your friends and neighbors rather than yielding to the temptation to put some aside.

Hazelnut Macaroons

Serves 4–5

2 cups hazelnuts, ground in blender	2 egg whites
⅔ cup sugar	1 teaspoon almond extract

Mix all the ingredients together to make a sticky paste. With your fingers shape into little mounds and fill a cookie sheet with them, leaving an inch or so of space between them. Bake in a preheated 350° oven for 20 minutes.

This is such a simple recipe it's a shame not to make macaroons often for your family. If you buy them in a pastry shop, they'll be among the more expensive cookies, whereas you can make them at home for a pittance. A recommended fancy presentation for the macaroons is different-colored tissue paper for each.

MENU 14

It is imperative to make the dessert well ahead of serving time, either in the morning or preferably the night before, because it has to sit. In the evening, cook your eggplant dish at the same time as the rice, since they both take the same amount of cooking time.

Salade de tomates
(*Tomato salad*)

Aubergines à la grecque
(*Fried eggplant with yogurt sauce*)

Riz
(*Rice*)

Salade de laitue
(*Boston lettuce salad: see pages 47–50*)

Gâteau soufflé aux framboises
(*Raspberry soufflé cake*)

Tomato Salad

In both restaurants and homes in France, raw tomatoes are served sliced as a first course, with, of course, a vinaigrette sauce. If you happen to grow basil in your garden or windowbox, or have access to a farmers' market where it is sold, chop a few leaves and sprinkle liberally over the tomatoes. You'll be glad you did.

If you can't find any fresh basil, use dried. If you can't find either, substitute chives and fresh parsley.

Be aware of the possibilities that this simple dish offers visually: the red of the tomatoes, the green of the basil and parsley. You can add to the effect—and the taste—by sprinkling on chopped shallots or Spanish onions as well.

Fried Eggplant with Yogurt Sauce

This is a Greek specialty, which Greeks doubtless consider an in-between or side dish rather than a main course. But I have found that it serves admirably as a main course, substituting very nicely for a meat course. Put your rice on to cook while you are preparing the eggplant.

Serves 4–5

- 1 large eggplant, washed and sliced ½ inch thick
- ½ cup flour
- 1 cup olive oil

Dip the eggplant slices in flour, coating well on both sides. Heat the olive oil in a skillet and fry eggplant slices to golden brown on each side. Drain on paper towels. When all slices are fried, arrange on serving platter. Serve with a dish of boiled rice and the yogurt sauce, which is made as follows:

- 2 cups plain yogurt
- 2 cloves garlic, squeezed
- 1 teaspoon mint leaves
- Pepper and salt

Mix together until smooth. Serve chilled.

À propos yogurt: You may be interested to know that making it is easy and fun and that it costs about one-fourth what you have to pay at the store. My family also says homemade is better. Since we consume gargantuan quantities of the dish, I had long been tempted to make it myself, but was always deterred by the seeming complexities—and rather steep price—of the electrically operated apparatus advertised. But then one day I discovered in Claudia Roden's *A Book of Middle Eastern Food* (published by Alfred A. Knopf, 1972) the following yogurt recipe, which sounded so good and so simple I tried it at once. With one basic modification suggested by my daughter for creamier results, this recipe has served me in good stead ever since. My output averages about half a gallon every other day.

2 quarts milk
½ cup yogurt
½ cup dry skimmed milk

In a kettle, bring the whole milk to a boil. Turn off the flame, allow the milk to cool to lukewarm (to judge if the temperature is correct, drop a little on your wrist; if it's "comfortable," you're okay.) Transfer lukewarm milk to a bowl (glass, ceramic, or earthenware, but not metal), stir in the yogurt and skimmed milk. Cover tightly with Saran Wrap or equivalent, then drape and cover the bowl with a sweater, wool jacket, or shawl, and let sit overnight, thus bundled. Next morning when you unveil your bowl you'll discover what seems to be, for one used to dealing in eight-ounce containers, an enormous quantity of perfect yogurt.

Refrigerate, then serve as desired—either plain or with whatever fruit, jam, etc., you prefer. When you're down to your last half cup, repeat process.

Preparation time is virtually nil, with the exception of the time it takes the milk to cool.

Raspberry Soufflé Cake

This is a dessert truly fit for kings. Therefore, worthy of your family. You will doubtless want to make it for your formal dinner parties as well.

Serves 4–5

1½ cups whipped cream
2 egg whites, beaten stiff with
    ½ cup confectioner's sugar
2 packages ladyfingers
4 egg yolks
⅓ cup granulated sugar

½ cup raspberry jam
2 tablespoons water
2 teaspoons vanilla extract
2 tablespoons Kirsch
Raspberries or red candies

Fold gently the whipped cream into the beaten egg whites. ("Folding gently" generally means mix carefully, with a light hand, so as not to break the "foam" of both the cream and egg whites.) Set aside in the refrigerator.

Crumble or cut the ladyfingers into small pieces in a bowl. If you have an electric mixer, mix the egg yolks with the granulated sugar until you have a creamy consistency. If you have no mixer, you can do it by hand in a bowl with a whisk or wooden spoon.

In a saucepan over a low flame, melt the raspberry jam with the water, vanilla, and Kirsch. Pour over the crumbled ladyfingers.

Using a wooden spoon—or your fingers if you've a mind to—stir for 2 to 3 minutes until well mixed. Add to it the yolk-sugar mixture and stir.

In a springform mold, place a band of paper (wax paper, or typewriter paper moistened with margarine or oil) slightly higher than the edge of the mold. Secure with string or freezer tape.

Into the mold, pour the raspberry–ladyfinger–yolk mixture. Top with the cream–egg white mixture. Refrigerate at least 3 hours before serving; a day ahead is recommended. At time of serving, unmold and decorate with a few raspberries or red candies.

MENU 15

If you are using salt codfish, remember to soak it for several hours, preferably overnight, to desalt it. Whenever you're dealing with fresh spinach, you can never rinse it too often, so start that early in the day and leave immersed. Make your dough ahead and chill; if you have some frozen, transfer it to the refrigerator in the morning, or take it out of the freezer 2 hours before rolling out.

Soupe aux fannes de radis
(Radish-leaf soup)

Brandade de morue
(Whipped codfish with olive oil and garlic)

Salade d'épinards aux champignons
(Spinach salad with mushrooms)

Tarte aux abricots
(Apricot tart)

Radish-Leaf Soup

See recipe on page 135.

Whipped Codfish with Olive Oil and Garlic

Brandade de morue is a native of Provence, and, like so much from that region, is aromatic and rich. Thus a light first course is called for.

Contrary to culinary myth, this is *not* a complicated recipe to make. You can really make it in no more than 10 minutes.

Serves 4–5
1 pound codfish, salted or fresh
½ cup olive oil
1 cup heavy cream
2 cloves garlic
½ teaspoon thyme
Pepper and salt
Juice of ½ lemon

If you have bought a salted codfish, soak it overnight in fresh water. Then poach codfish for 8 to 10 minutes over a low flame. If fresh, poach directly. Drain. In a saucepan, heat up oil and cream for a minute. Pour into blender with garlic, thyme, pepper, and salt. Add fish and blend until fluffy. Add lemon juice, and serve, accompanied by toast.

NOTE: Once you have prepared this dish to the serving stage, you can keep it warm in the oven for as long as half an hour while you relax.

Spinach Salad with Mushrooms

Serves 4–5
1 pound fresh spinach
¼ pound fresh mushrooms
Vinaigrette (see page 46)

Remove spinach stems and wash spinach thoroughly several times under cold running water. Wash the mushrooms. (Some cooks will tell you not to, for fear they will lose their delicate fragrance; wipe with a damp towel, they suggest. I've tried it both ways and fail to notice any real difference. I suggest you try both and let your own experience be your guide.)

Slice mushrooms, mix with spinach, add dressing, and serve. For this salad, I urge you to use lemon juice rather than vinegar.

Apricot Tart

Serves 4–5
Dough for 1 pie crust (see page 39)
1½ pounds fresh apricots
1 cup milk
2 tablespoons flour
3 tablespoons sugar
2 eggs
1 teaspoon vanilla extract

Preheat your oven to 350°. Roll out the dough on a floured board and line an 8-inch pie mold. (To keep the pie crust from buckling, place on it five or six kidney beans, or small washed stones, to give the crust a weight.) Put the pie crust in to prebake for 15 minutes. Since the filling for this tart is very moist, the prebaking will ensure crispness of the crust at serving time. If you bake it all in one step, you're liable to end up with a soggy tart.

Halve apricots, and remove pits. On top of partly baked dough, place apricots face down. Mix milk, flour, sugar, eggs, and vanilla, and pour over the apricots. Bake for 30 to 35 minutes at 350°. Serve.

MENU 16

This entire menu can be made ahead of time. If you don't have time to prepare it in its entirety the morning of or the day before your dinner, at least cook your cherries, since they need refrigeration.

Artichauts vinaigrette
(*Artichokes with oil and lemon dressing*)

Lasagna

Salade frisée et scarole
(*Chicory and escarole salad: see pages 47–50*)

Fromage maison aux noix
(*Homemade cheese with walnuts*)

Compote de cerises
(*Stewed cherries*)

Artichokes with Oil and Lemon Dressing

No matter how young or old, people seem to respond to eating artichokes: not only are they delicious, but the very act of "artichoking" is fun. I prefer lemon to vinegar for the dressing, but you decide for yourself. One hint: we've always found that red wine does something peculiar to your palate when combined with artichokes. Therefore, I suggest you not start your wine until the main course. Another hint: you'll note that in good restaurants artichokes come with the tips of the leaves clipped. This is because the leaves are sharp and you could prick yourself while removing them. Simply take a pair of scissors and clip the leaves about half an inch from the top. Cook artichokes 35 to 40 minutes in salty water. Drain. Serve. Remember to place an individual cup of dressing (see recipe for lemon dressing on page 46) on each artichoke plate.

Lasagna

I was always impressed when any friends served me homemade lasagna, for in the strict Italian tradition preparation of the sauce is an all-day affair: the tomatoes, seasoning, and pork bone simmering for several hours imparted a flavor that no shortcut could presumably duplicate. I make my lasagna sauce in 15 minutes. And I think it is fully as good as the all-day sauces. Here is how I make my lasagna.

Serves 4–5

- 16-ounce box of lasagna
- 1 onion, finely chopped
- 1 tablespoon bacon fat
- 1 tablespoon olive oil
- 1½ pounds ground beef
- 4 tablespoons oregano
- 2 tablespoons basil
- 1 large clove garlic, minced
- 1 cup freshly grated Parmesan cheese
- 16-ounce can tomato purée
- Salt and pepper
- 8 ounces cottage cheese
- 8 ounces mozzarella cheese, sliced

Since the cooking time of the lasagna is roughly the same as that of the sauce preparation, on one side of your stove cook the lasagna. Empty the contents of the package into a kettle containing several quarts of boiling, salty water (see package for precise amount recommended). On the other side of the stove, prepare your sauce as follows:

In a skillet over medium flame, sauté the onion in the bacon fat and olive oil until transparent. Add meat, oregano, basil, garlic, half the Parmesan cheese, the tomato purée, and salt and pepper to taste. Stir with a wooden spoon as the sauce "brews" for 10 minutes over medium flame.

Now go back to the other side of your stove, where the lasagna should be cooked. Drain. In a large casserole dish spread a thin layer of your sauce. Over it place a layer of cooked lasagna. Now a generous layer of sauce. Next comes the cottage cheese. Repeat the same process: lasagna, sauce, cottage cheese. Close with a final layer of lasagna, and top with the remaining sauce and the mozzarella. Sprinkle with oregano.

In an oven preheated to 350° bake for 10 minutes, until the mozzarella cheese has melted and the lasagna is bubbling. Serve with remaining Parmesan cheese in a bowl at the table, so diners can serve themselves to taste.

NOTE: Don't be worried if you have some lasagna left over. It freezes well.

Homemade Cheese with Walnuts

Serves 4–5

1 cup walnuts
1 small onion or 4 scallions, chopped
1 tablespoon brandy
Pepper and salt
8-ounce package cream cheese
1 pint heavy cream, whipped

In your blender, pulverize ½ cup of the walnuts, the onion or scallions, brandy, pepper, and salt. Place mixture in a bowl, add the cream cheese and whipped cream, and mash with a fork until evenly mixed.

Transfer to a serving plate and shape into a rectangular or circular shape, smoothing the surface with a table knife. Dot the top and sides of the cheese with the remaining walnuts, and serve.

Stewed Cherries

A "compote" of any kind is always a good way to end a rather rich meal. Cool and light, the stewed cherries nicely counterbalance the hearty aspect of the lasagna.

Serves 4–5

1–2 pounds cherries
½ cup red wine
1 cup water
1 cup sugar
Grated rind of ½ lemon
1 teaspoon vanilla extract

Stem and wash the cherries. In a saucepan, mix all the ingredients. Bring to a boil, reduce to a low flame, and boil for 10 to 12 minutes. Transfer to a ceramic bowl and chill.

NOTE: Some people prefer to make their syrup first, before adding the cherries. If you do, let the syrup simmer for 5 to 7 minutes before adding the cherries.

MENU 17

Except for the watercress, which will be immersed some time prior to dinner, and the melon, which will take only a minute or two to prepare, the rest of the menu can be done in advance. In fact, the celery will profit from marinating in its seasoning for several hours or even a day (actual cooking time will be 20 minutes). If the rice and chicken have been cooked ahead of time, as they can be, they will require from 15 to 20 minutes' reheating in an oven at 350°; make sure both are covered to preserve moisture.

Céleri à la méridionale
(Marinated celery)

Poulet sauté aux fines herbes et à la crème
(Sautéed chicken with herbs and cream)

Riz
(Rice)

Salade de cresson
(Watercress salad)

Vermont Cheddar

Melon des îles
(Melon filled with mandarin oranges, bananas, and walnuts)

Marinated Celery

This hors d'oeuvre is best prepared the morning of the day you plan to serve it for dinner, since it should marinate for several hours. However, it is not imperative: if you have not had time to prepare it in advance, you can simply pour your vinaigrette over it prior to serving. It will obviously not have imbibed the vinaigrette, but it will still be fine.

Serves 4–5

- 1 bunch pascal celery
- 1 quart water
- 1 small onion
- 1 teaspoon thyme
- 3 sprigs parsley, chopped
- Pepper and salt
- 1 cup vinaigrette (see page 46)
- Juice of ½ lemon
- 1 can anchovy fillets

Cut off the base of the celery and discard. If the outer stalks appear dark green and tough, remove and save for later soup. Cut off the leafy part of the celery and reserve, for later decoration. Cut each stalk into roughly 2-inch pieces. Put water in a kettle: cook the celery pieces, together with the onion, thyme, parsley, pepper, and salt, for about 20 minutes. Drain. Pour the vinaigrette and lemon juice, as well as the oil of the anchovies, over celery. Make decorative designs with the anchovies, as your fancy dictates, on top of the celery. Chop the celery leaves finely and add them also for decoration.

Sautéed Chicken with Herbs and Cream

Chicken lends itself to a seemingly infinite number of preparations. Here is one I find very good and simple to make. It should take you no more than 35 to 40 minutes, including cooking time.

Serves 4–5

- 1 chicken cut up in pieces, washed and dried
- 1 stick butter or margarine
- ½ cup white wine
- 1 cup finely chopped parsley
- 3 tablespoons dried tarragon
- 1 teaspoon rosemary
- Salt and pepper
- ½ cup heavy cream (or evaporated milk)

Sauté the chicken in butter for about 15 minutes. Add wine, parsley, tarragon, rosemary, and salt and pepper to taste. Reduce flame, and continue cooking, covered, for another 20 minutes. Add cream and serve.

Rice is recommended as a side dish.

Watercress Salad

Wash the watercress thoroughly. It tends to be sandy. If the stems are not too thick you may keep them. Otherwise cut and reserve for a soup. Dry, add vinaigrette (see page 46), and toss.

This rather "sharp" salad is a good complement to the richness and softness of the chicken.

Melon Filled with Mandarin Oranges, Bananas, and Walnuts

Serves 4

- 2 small cantaloupes
- 16-ounce can mandarin oranges, drained
- 1–2 bananas, sliced
- ½ cup coarsely chopped walnuts
- ½ cup sugar

Halve the cantaloupes and scoop out insides. In a bowl, mix the remaining ingredients. Fill each cantaloupe half, chill, and serve.

NOTE: For the adults' portions, add to each melon half a tablespoon of port wine or sherry.

MENU 18

The entire preparation and cooking time for this menu should not exceed 45 to 50 minutes. You can, if you want to cut down slightly on the evening preparation, make the soup earlier, and peel the potatoes and immerse in cold water.

Soupe aux oignons verts
(Scallion soup)

Couronne de saumon, sauce aux olives et aux amandes
(Salmon ring, with olive and almond sauce)

Pommes vapeur, persillées
(Steamed potatoes with parsley, page 99)

Salade de scarole et roquefort
(Escarole salad with Roquefort chunks)

Gâteau au chocolat rapide
(Thirty-minute chocolate cake)

Scallion Soup

One of the most common and relatively inexpensive vegetables available throughout France is *le poireau*. It belongs to the onion family.

Part of the scenery at marketplaces is the *poireaux,* whose foliage is abundant, spilling over the edge of the vendors' vegetable stands. Go into virtually any French apartment building at lunch time and, emanating from kitchens, from the concierge's loge on up to the top floor, will be the odor of warm French bread and . . . *poireaux* cooking.

For some reason, leeks are considered exotic in the United States, and are therefore expensive. Since I was not ready to renounce my beloved leek and potato soup, and balked at paying the exorbitant price, I began to use scallions as a substitute. And it worked. You can hardly tell the difference. For years I've been taking compliments on my "leek and potato" soup from French and American friends alike, to whom I refused to admit the truth. Now you know: profit from it. You can make this classic French soup for pennies.

Serves 4–5

- 2 bunches scallions
- 3 potatoes
- Pepper and salt
- ¼ stick butter
- ½ cup finely chopped parsley

Cut off the scallion roots and discard. Wash thoroughly. Cut into one-inch pieces. Peel, wash, and cube the potatoes. Into a 4-quart kettle, put the scallions and potatoes, pepper, and salt, cover with about 2 inches of water, bring to a boil, reduce flame, and cook for 10 to 12 minutes. Remove from the fire and whirl in blender. Heat again and serve piping hot, topped with butter and parsley. (This soup is also good chilled. If you decide to serve it cold, you may add ½ cup of heavy cream, thus turning it into vichyssoise. In which case, omit the butter.)

Salmon Ring, with Olive and Almond Sauce

It takes only about half an hour to make this relatively "chic" main course.

Serves 4–5

- 2 cups canned or fresh salmon, drained
- ½ cup bread crumbs
- 1 medium-sized onion, minced
- Juice of ½ lemon
- 1 cup evaporated milk
- 1 egg
- Pepper and salt
- ½ cup chopped celery
- ½ cup chopped green pepper

Put all the ingredients, except the celery and green pepper, into your blender. Blend. Scatter the celery and green pepper in a buttered ring mold. Pour contents of blender into the ring mold. Bake in a preheated 350° oven for 30 minutes. Unmold onto a serving platter and serve with the following sauce, which you can make while the salmon ring is baking.

1 tablespoon flour
3 tablespoons mayonnaise
2/3 cup evaporated milk (or heavy cream)
1 1/4 cups water
1/4 cup sliced green olives
1/4 cup salted almonds

In a saucepan, mix flour, mayonnaise, milk, and water. Stir. Cook over a low flame for 5 minutes until mixture thickens. Add olives and almonds. Serve with the salmon ring.

Escarole Salad with Roquefort Chunks

With this menu I serve escarole or chicory (because of their crispness) to balance the "softness" of the fish. Adding the Roquefort makes the salad even heartier, and also eliminates a separate cheese course. The amount of cheese you want to crumble into your vinaigrette (see page 46) will depend on your palate.

Thirty-Minute Chocolate Cake

How often have you thought about serving your family—or dinner guests—a cake for dessert but have become discouraged at how much time and effort it would take? Here's a recipe that will take you no more than half an hour from start to finish, including baking time.

Serves 4–5

8-ounce package sweet baking chocolate
1 tablespoon water
4 eggs, separated
1 1/2 sticks sweet butter
1 tablespoon flour
1 tablespoon sugar
1 cup heavy cream, whipped and sweetened
2-ounce square bitter chocolate

Preheat your oven to 350°. In an ovenproof bowl, put the chocolate and the water, and place in oven for a few minutes to soften. While chocolate is melting beat the egg whites until they form peaks. Remove chocolate from oven and add the butter, flour, sugar, and egg yolks. Into the stiffened whites, fold the contents of the bowl. Line a springform pan with wax paper and pour cake mixture into it. Bake for 15 minutes. Turn off the oven, leaving the cake inside, with the oven door open slightly, for another 10 to 15 minutes.

Your cake is ready to be served. It is especially good a trifle warm, topped with sweetened whipped cream (if it's *too* warm it will tend to melt the whipped cream). Good chilled, too. Either way, I top the sweetened whipped cream with shavings of bitter chocolate. (Shaving, in case you've never tried it, is simply scraping the chocolate with a sharp knife. It will give your cake that pastry-shop look.)

Don't expect a fluffy cake from this recipe: it uses virtually no flour, you will note. It will be slightly "chewy," reminiscent of a brownie consistency.

MENU 19

Two elements—the opener and the dessert—can be made ahead. The main course must, by its very nature, be prepared just before serving (count on from 30–35 minutes total time, including cooking). You can get a bit of a head start however by grinding the ham and grating the cheese in a free moment.

Champignons vinaigrette
(Mushrooms with vinaigrette sauce)

L'Omelette du lundi
(Souffléed omelet with ham and cheese)

Salade de laitue
(Boston lettuce salad: see pages 47–50)

Croissants à l'abricot
(Apricot crescents)

Mushrooms with Vinaigrette Sauce

1 pound fresh mushrooms
1 shallot, finely chopped
½ cup finely chopped parsley
½ cup vinaigrette (see page 46)
Juice of ½ lemon

Wash, dry, and slice your mushrooms. Mix with the remaining ingredients and serve. You may, if you wish, mix ahead of time, since the vinaigrette will act as a marinade.

Souffléed Omelet with Ham and Cheese

My mother baptized this course *l'omelette du lundi* because she generally served it on Mondays, when most of the butchers and greengrocers are closed in France. But the charcuteries are open, which provide the ham.

When I was a girl growing up in France, refrigerators were still a rarity, and therefore one could not stock up in advance for several days. Thus the Monday improvisations. I might add, however, that even today, when refrigeration is fairly common, most French prefer to market daily, for they are fresh-food fetishists—and with good reason. Anyway, even though this recipe may no longer apply specifically to Monday, here it is: a delicacy.

Serves 4–5
4 eggs
1 cup milk
1½ tablespoons flour
Pepper and salt
4 teaspoons butter or margarine
1 cup grated Swiss cheese
1 cup ground ham

Separate the eggs and in a bowl, mix the yolks, the milk, the flour, pepper, and salt, using a wooden spoon. Beat the egg whites stiff and gently fold them in with the yolk mixture. The resulting batter will be quite liquid—which is the way it's supposed to be.

In a 9-inch skillet, melt a teaspoon of butter. Ladle out enough of the batter to cover the surface of the skillet. Reduce to low flame. Cook the batter on one side only: it will resemble a half-cooked pancake with a fluffy top, slightly moist. Using a spatula, slide it out of the skillet and transfer to an ovenproof dish. Sprinkle with grated cheese. Repeat process, but this time when done, sprinkle grated ham over it. Repeat twice more, alternating cheese and ham over the third and fourth layers respectively. Top with the fifth "pancake," which you will turn over to place moist side down. The souffléed omelet will now look like a layer cake. Place in preheated 200° oven for 15 minutes. It will rise slightly. Serve immediately. It cuts like a cake.

Apricot Crescents

It's a good idea to serve something crunchy after the softness of an omelet. People generally associate croissants—crescents—with that marvelous "pastry" eaten by the French for breakfast, which of course is made from *pâte feuilletée*. Here the shape is the same as the breakfast croissants, but the pastry differs. For this recipe you will need:

Serves 4–5
1 stick sweet butter
1 cup flour
½ cup heavy cream
1 jar apricot preserves
1 cup confectioner's sugar

In a bowl, mix butter, flour, and cream until the ingredients form a smooth dough and adhere into a ball. Chill for half an hour. Roll the dough out *very* thinly onto a floured board. With a 3-inch cup or glass, cut out circles. Roll trimmings and repeat until all the dough is used. In the center of each circle, put a teaspoonful of apricot preserves, fold over, and seal. Prick each three times with a fork (so that the steam from the preserves can escape without breaking the pastry crust).

Bake for 10 minutes in an oven preheated to 425°. Sprinkle your crescents with confectioner's sugar, and serve.

MENU 20

The only thing you can really prepare ahead here is the soup. Hopefully you'll have a store of green sauce in your freezer or refrigerator; if not, do that ahead—it will take only a few minutes from scratch.

Borscht du pauvre
(Poor-man's borscht)

Spaghetti au pistou
(Spaghetti with green sauce)

Salade de laitue
(Boston lettuce salad: see pages 47–50)

Melon glacé à la menthe et au citron vert
(Chilled melon, with mint leaves and lime juice)

Poor-Man's Borscht

I call this poor-man's borscht or minute borscht because it can be made in a hurry, looks like borscht, and approximates the taste. But make no mistake: borscht, which requires hours of simmering, is a whole other dish. Nonetheless, this is a rapid and effective way of turning an ordinary broth into a savory soup.

Serves 4–5

4 cups beef or chicken bouillon	1 tablespoon vinegar
8-ounce can diced beets	½ cup sour cream
8-ounce can sauerkraut	2 tablespoons dill

Into a kettle, put all the ingredients except the sour cream and the dill. (Make sure to include the beet and sauerkraut juices.) Heat until piping hot. Just before serving, add the sour cream and dill, and stir. Serve.

Spaghetti with Green Sauce

As I've indicated, I'm a *pistou* freak. That may not be classic French, but I suspect that when you try it you may not only understand my aberration but join me in the sinful indulgence.

Serves 4–5

1½ cups green sauce	½ cup heavy cream
16-ounce package thin spaghetti	(or evaporated milk)
	½ cup grated Parmesan cheese

I'm going on the assumption you have made and frozen a goodly store of green sauce (if not, see page 163). Cook your spaghetti according to the directions on the box. Drain. Add the green sauce and heavy cream. (You may, if you like, substitute evaporated milk if you have no heavy cream available. It has happened to me on more than one occasion, and could happen to you, that you will receive a family demand for this course on short notice, which is how I discovered that evaporated milk works fine. If you're lacking both heavy cream *and* evaporated milk, add a few tablespoons of regular milk. The addition of the milk or cream, which I originally did not use in the recipe, binds the *pistou* and spaghetti, and makes it lighter . . . well, less heavy.)

Serve, with freshly grated Parmesan cheese on the side.

Chilled Melon, with Mint Leaves and Lime Juice

In cooking, as in much of life, it's the little things that count. Despite the long name of this dessert, it's the marvel of nature's melon that accounts for 80 or 90 percent of the quality here. The mint leaves and the lime, however, raise it that extra degree, both in appearance and in taste.

Serves 4–5

1–2 cantaloupes (or 1 honeydew melon)
2 tablespoons finely chopped mint leaves
1 lime

I prefer to remove the melon rind. It is easier to eat that way. Cut into slices an inch or two wide. Top with mint leaves, and over the platter squeeze the juice of the lime. Chill and serve.

SMALL DINNER PARTIES
(UP TO EIGHT)

Any meal should be a time of respite and repose, a pause in the day's often hectic activities. Its role is not only to satisfy hunger and slake thirst but also to bring people closer together and serve as a means of promoting conversation and conviviality. Of all meals, dinner, I feel, is the privileged one most able to accomplish this social task: it is (or should be) the most relaxed meal of the day; it comes at the end of the day, when the mind and body are ready to unwind and enjoy.

I have learned that dinner parties fall into two main categories: intimate and large. There is just no in-between. Each has its virtues and shortcomings. Here we shall deal with small dinner parties, which I define as those with a minimum of four people and a maximum of eight.

Let me try to explain my philosophy of numbers. During my youth in France and in my early married life there, no dinners ever exceeded five or six people, including the hosts. It was customary to have another couple to dinner, or even one close friend. Coming to America, I was so dazzled by many aspects of the American Way of Life that I followed the example of many of my New York friends and tended to "produce" dinners for ten or fifteen people. Eight was considered a small dinner. But ultimately there was something unsatisfying about these evenings. How many times have I heard people saying to one or more of their fellow guests as they were leaving: "It was so nice to see you. I'm sorry we didn't get more of a chance to talk." Such an evening seemed self-defeating. Our dining room table seated no more than eight comfortably, so when the guest list exceeded that number either we had to set up two or three smaller tables—which had the disadvantage of immediately splitting up the evening into two or three groups—or serve buffet style—which has always been anathema to me, and to be avoided at all costs unless there is no other choice. The image of people sitting in helter-skelter fashion around the living and dining room, balancing their plates of fine food on their laps, struck me as the antithesis of what a dinner ought to be.

Thus we began to reduce the size of our dinners. More and more frequently we stressed the number four. First of all, to invite only another couple is a very simple way of saying to them that they are special to you, and generally they will respond to that tribute. Four people sitting around a table is an assurance that everyone will be truly talking to one another. There will be one conversation, not several. Six people, we have found, is still fun, but even here the dinner often tends to divide itself into two groups—either two and four or three and three—which can be most distracting, especially if you feel you are missing what is going on in the other group. It is as though one were having two small dinners simultaneously. In spite of all the above, there are times when for whatever reasons you find you have to have six to eight people. And it can work. All I am saying is that after experimenting through the years we have found four ideal.

To which I am sure many people will retort: "But I'm much too busy to invite only two or three friends at a time. It would mean that I would have to give two or three times as many dinner parties." But one of the prime purposes of this book is to show that it is both possible and natural to give as many small dinner parties as you want without strain.

Be that as it may, your experience may be different from mine; you may have found the number six or eight ideal, as we have found four. Whatever the magic number, the menus and recipes that follow have been among those that have proved most successful and pleasurable in my own home.

TEN PREPARATORY STEPS

The key to a successful and enjoyable dinner party, I have found, is for me to be so prepared, therefore relaxed, that the guests will feel it was all done with such ease that they can truly relax and enjoy as well. There's nothing more distressing and disturbing for guests than to keep "losing" their host and hostess as they disappear, either singly or jointly, into the recesses of the kitchen for various periods of time prior to and during dinner.

To avoid this, I have always prepared my dinners well in advance, either the day before or the morning of the dinner. All the menus that follow have the advantage of letting you sit with your guests in leisurely fashion throughout cocktail time, for the simple reason that everything has been done—the soup is simmering, the oven has your main dish bubbling—so that at most you may have to disappear for five minutes prior to calling people to table.

Here are ten steps whose goal is to put you in your living room with your guests and keep you out of the kitchen during the hour before your dinner is served:

1. One or two days before, decide on your menu; check what you have on hand, make a list of what you must buy, both in the way of food and in the way of wine, liquor, and accessories (candles and so on).

2. Shop the day before. Thus, if you run into any unforeseen problem, you still have time to find your missing ingredient elsewhere, or if necessary switch your menu without panic.

3. Cook. After completing the cooking of the various dishes, be sure to put each in its appropriate serving dish, cover with lid or equivalent (wax paper, foil, plastic wrap), and refrigerate. The day before a dinner I cook my main dish, my hors d'oeuvre or my soup, and the dessert if it involves baking. Everything except the side dishes. For pies: I bake the crust the morning of the dinner party to ensure crispness of dough. Also, some hors d'oeuvres are served raw and must be prepared the same day, for freshness.

4. The night before (unless, of course, you're having two dinners on successive nights; in which case, read: "the morning of . . ."), set your table, considering each detail in the light of your planned menu. That includes, in addition to setting the table itself, preparing the sideboard or equivalent area with all the accessory serving dishes and implements that cannot or should not go immediately on the table (cheese dish, dessert plates, and such). This will eliminate your having to traipse endlessly back and forth from table to kitchen for each new course.

5. Set up your bar (by which I mean a separate area reserved for that use) the night before as well. (I do.) Put the appropriate number of cocktail glasses face down; take out your pitcher for water; a pitcher if needed for martini mixing; the ice bucket (ready but empty); your decanters or bottles of liquor; your mixers. This may be carrying anticipation to the extreme; however, if as is the case with most people you have a busy day outside the home, how pleasant

and reassuring to return not only to a completely set table but also to a set-up bar.

6. That morning: if you are using a frozen casserole, begin defrosting before you leave for the day. If boiled vegetables are planned as side dishes, peel and prepare for cooking. (I actually cook them in the morning, then refrigerate before I leave for the day, which means they have only to be warmed prior to serving that night. I know this is totally unorthodox, and many of you may frown at this suggestion. However, I have found there is absolutely no loss of freshness or flavor, and the peace of mind gained from having one more element of the dinner out of the way is well worth it to me.)

7. That morning: wash and separate your salad leaves, and immerse in cold water for the day. (The salad will be dried and put in the salad bowl that night, some time before dinner, but only mixed just prior to serving.)

8. That morning: dry cheeses, such as cheddar, Gruyère, and Vermont cheese, can be placed on the cheese tray, covered with foil. Soft cheeses (such as Camembert, Brie, and Coulommiers) must wait until cocktail time before being set free. They tend to be "runny" when left out of the refrigerator too long.

9. That morning: set coffee and tea cups on a tray, together with lemon, sugar, and spoons; place brandy and liqueur glasses on the same tray and put in the living room (or wherever you plan to serve coffee and after-dinner drinks).

10. That morning: put your bread in a baking dish, covered with a damp towel to keep from drying, and place in the oven (unlit!) before leaving for the day. Earlier, I urged you to use several individual butter minicups to cut down on table traffic. Fill them now, cover, and refrigerate.

Leave for work . . . and return home that evening to be a guest at your own dinner party.

One last tip. I have been going on the assumption that most of you, like me, have no one to help serve or clean up at your party. Since a certain amount of mess will have been created in your living room during predinner drinks (dirty glasses, dirty ashtrays, and such) which will be unpleasant to return to after dinner, I have made it a habit to hide an empty tray close by which I use to scoop up this early debris as people are making their way to the table.

The following menus, taken from among those I have used most successfully through the years, derive from the more or less classic French order of courses with which I grew up. Each menu consists of from four to six courses, for the French believe in the principle that eating is a sensual pleasure and that each course should both be a pleasure in itself and contribute to the overall effect. As you will see, these multicourse menus will take you no more time to prepare than most meals you are used to—and often far less. Finally, I have always found that presenting food aesthetically is no trouble, while at the same time it is fulfilling both for the person presenting the meal and for those who receive it. The classic order is: Soup *or* hors d'oeuvre (purists will cry: "Soup *and* hors d'oeuvre," but I disagree) ; main course, featuring either meat or fish, with appropriate side dishes; salad; cheese or cheeses; dessert. I am going on the assumption that coffee (or tea) and brandy will be served after every meal, and therefore will avoid repeating them with each menu.

MENU 1

The entire menu may be prepared up to two days ahead of time. If you choose to do so, all you will have to do the evening of your dinner is to light your oven about 10 minutes before calling your guests to table, and heat up the "anchovy boats" for 5 to 7 minutes. Put your veal in the oven to heat at the same time. The 20 minutes or so that it takes the veal to heat will give you ample time to enjoy your first course.

Barquettes au beurre d'enchois
(Anchovy boats)

Médaillon de veau, provençale
(Medallion of veal Provence style)

Salade de cresson et laitue
(Watercress and Boston lettuce salad: see pages 47–50)

Fromage de Brie
(Brie cheese)

Poires châtelaines
(Poached pears with pineapple slices,
Curaçao, glazed with orange marmalade,
and decorated with blanched almonds)

Wine: Rosé de Provence (chilled)

Anchovy Boats

This is a light, elegant hors d'oeuvre which consists of a pastry shell stuffed with a creamy mixture whose basis is butter, anchovy, and parsley. It is served hot, and literally melts in your mouth.

The "boats" should be shaped like barques and are made from *pâte feuilletée,* or puff pastry (see page 39). If you have made some in advance, remove one batch from the freezer several hours before using (or put it in the refrigerator for the day). Roll out on a floured board, making a narrow strip (about 3 to 4 inches wide), about ½ inch thick. Cut the dough into 2-inch sections (each section will become a barque). Pinch both ends, to form the prow and the stern. With your knife, make an incision—not going all the way through—in the dough parallel to the sides of the boat, thus:

This is the "lid" which will, in baking, puff out. You will later remove it with a knife, leaving a well for your anchovies. After that, the lid will be replaced. Transfer to baking sheet.

Preheat the oven to 400°. Bake the boats for 10 minutes, then lower oven to 350° and bake for another 15 minutes. When puffy and golden brown, remove, and let cool.

While your boats are baking, make your anchovy butter as follows:

Serves 6–8
- 3-ounce can anchovies
- 2 sticks sweet butter, softened
- 1 cup freshly chopped parsley
- ½ cup grated Swiss cheese
- 1 egg yolk (optional)

Mash all ingredients in a bowl with a fork until well mixed. When your boats are cool, fill each one with roughly a tablespoon of the paste. (If desired, sprinkle additional grated cheese on top before covering with lids.) Set aside until a few minutes before serving. It will take 5 to 7 minutes to warm them up in a preheated 350° oven; this can be done while you're lighting candles and calling people to the table.

NOTE: If I have been unable to convince you to make your own *pâte feuilletée,* or if that aspect of the recipe deters you, don't despair: There are excellent frozen patty shells on the market which will serve as a more than adequate substitute. If you use them, however, bear in mind that they are roughly twice the size of the homemade boats. Therefore, you will need only one per person, as opposed to two or slightly more if you make your own. In any event, assuming you start from your own prefrozen pastry or use the Pepperidge Farm patty shells, the preparation time should not exceed 15 minutes, exclusive of baking time.

Medallion of Veal Provence Style

The essence of Provence cooking is its generous use of herbs and vegetables of the region such as tomatoes, eggplant, and zucchini. Not to mention garlic. Although the following recipe calls for veal, given the spiraling cost of that meat, I have tried experimenting with frozen turkey roll, which is far less expensive. It may not have the charm of the veal flavor, but nonetheless I have found it a most satisfactory substitute, particularly in a case such as the present recipe, which calls for a sauce preparation.

Serves 6–8

½ stick butter
½ cup cooking oil
3-pound boneless veal roast
 (or frozen turkey roll)
Salt and pepper
1 eggplant
2 zucchini

4 tomatoes
½ cup chopped fresh parsley
1 teaspoon basil
1 teaspoon thyme
2 cloves garlic, finely chopped
2 cups dry vermouth

Melt butter and ¼ cup oil in *cocotte* (Dutch oven), add roast, and brown on all sides (browning will take about 15 minutes). Season with salt and pepper, put *cocotte* into a preheated oven at 350°, and cook for an hour and a half, or until tender. (To check for tenderness, insert fork into meat: the texture must be soft, and the color gray rather than pink.) Remove from oven and let cool. (When using a turkey roll, bake frozen roll per instructions on the box. Cool before slicing.)

While roast is cooling, peel eggplant and slice. Ditto zucchini and tomatoes. (If you don't like the skin of the tomato, immerse in boiling water for a split second and peel.) Sauté vegetables together in remaining oil. Add herbs and garlic. Cook for 10 minutes.

Slice roast into 12 to 15 slices, and arrange slices at the bottom of a Pyrex or other casserole dish. Remove vegetables from pan with a slotted spoon, and cover layer of meat. Combine the juice of the meat and the vegetable juice, and add vermouth. Pour over the casserole. This dish is now ready to be warmed up in the oven (350° for 20 minutes) prior to serving.

NOTE: If you prefer, you can warm it up for as much as an hour, or roughly the time you spend over drinks, at 200°.

Poached Pears with Pineapple Slices

After a relatively substantial meal to this point, *poires châtelaines* comes as a refreshing and light dessert.

Serves 6–8
6 pears
2 tablespoons vanilla extract
1 cup sugar
1 quart water
1 can pineapple slices

½ cup Curaçao
½ jar (¾ cup) orange marmalade
4-ounce package blanched almonds

Peel pears. Cut into halves, removing cores. Add vanilla and sugar to the water, and bring to a boil. Reduce flame, add pears and cook gently for 10 minutes. Remove pears from syrup. Open can of pineapple slices and drain, reserving juice. Place slices on a serving platter. Mix pineapple juice with Curaçao and pour over slices. Place pears face down over pineapple slices. Melt orange marmalade in a saucepan over a low flame; when it has become liquid, pour over pears, thus forming a glaze. Decorate with blanched almonds. Refrigerate until dessert time.

MENU 2

The soup, lamb, turnips, and soufflé can all be prepared one to two days ahead of time. (Yes, even the soufflé, since it's cold.) The meat and the turnips will need about 20 minutes to heat in the oven, at 300°; the soup, no time at all.

Soupe aux fanes de radis
(Radish-leaf soup)

Agneau à la bourguignonne
(Lamb Burgundy style)

Navets farcis
(Stuffed turnips)

Salade de laitue
(Boston lettuce salad: see pages 47–50)

Fromage de chèvre
(Goat cheese)

Soufflé de pamplemousse
(Cold grapefruit soufflé)

Wine: Côtes du Rhône

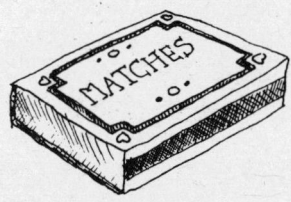

Radish-Leaf Soup

Radishes, one of the least expensive of all vegetables, offer an added and generally unsuspected bonus: the leaves. It may appear strange to you, but those somewhat prickly, seemingly unfriendly radish tops can be turned into an absolutely delicious soup. They have a tartness that is a cross between the flavor of asparagus soup and watercress soup. It's also virtually guaranteed to intrigue your guests, as well as please their palates.

Serves 6–8

2 bunches (3–4 cups) radish leaves
½ stick butter or margarine
2 tablespoons flour
2 cups water or stock
½ cup heavy cream
1 egg yolk
Salt and pepper

Wash leaves thoroughly. In a pot, melt butter, add leaves, and stir for about 3 minutes. Sprinkle flour on leaves, and add water or stock gradually. (Remember: previously frozen beef or chicken stock can always be advantageously substituted for water in any soup recipe. If not available, add a couple of bouillon cubes to your water.) Let simmer for 8 to 10 minutes. Let cool. Blend. At serving time, mix cream and egg yolk and add to soup. Season to taste. Heat and serve.

NOTE: This soup is also delicious cold.

Lamb Burgundy Style

Serves 6–8

½ cup shortening, margarine or peanut oil
3 pounds stewing lamb
Salt and pepper
3 cloves garlic, finely chopped
1½ cups finely chopped parsley
2 cups red wine (Burgundy or substitute)
½ stick sweet butter

Heat shortening in Dutch oven. Add lamb and brown. When brown, reduce flame and add salt, pepper, garlic, and 1 cup of the parsley. Add Burgundy, cover, and let simmer for 30 minutes. Preheat oven to 350° and put *cocotte* in to cook for an hour. Just prior to time of serving, mix butter with remaining parsley, mashing it with a fork. Transfer lamb to serving platter, and top with parsley butter. As it melts over the meat, it will impart a typically "French" accent to your dish.

Stuffed Turnips

Turnips tend to be considered rather low down in the vegetable hierarchy. They also, I find, are generally an acquired taste. I grew up hating turnips, which seemed to be about the only vegetable available to me and other French children growing up during the German Occupation. In France, too, the word for turnip—*navet*—is used to describe any artistic disaster, serving the same sad role as "lemon" does in America. How lowly the turnip is considered is borne out by the fact that it is, with the carrot, the only vegetable poor Vladimir and Estragon have left in their possession in Beckett's *Waiting for Godot*.

Despite that unfortunate beginning, I discovered only as an adult that turnips are not only a fine side dish but indeed a delicacy. That is, they can be made into delicacies. One such is the following.

Serves 6–8

8–10 turnips	6 slices stale bread, cubed
¼ cup sugar	1 cup finely chopped parsley
2 medium-sized onions, chopped	Pepper and salt
½ stick butter	1 cup bread crumbs
2½-ounce can deviled ham	

Wash turnips. Remove stems. Scoop a hole in the stem end. (Save scooped centers in plastic bag for tomorrow's soup!) Blanch the turnips by cooking for 15 minutes in water seasoned with a teaspoon of sugar and salt. Drain. Place turnips upright in buttered casserole dish. Sprinkle each turnip lightly with sugar (which will remove the slightly bitter taste). Sauté the chopped onions in butter in a frying pan until they are transparent, add deviled ham, bread, parsley, pepper, and salt, and stir for 3 minutes. Fill the hollow of each turnip with the stuffing. Cover with bread crumbs and a dot of butter. The dish is now ready for baking in the oven at 350° for 20 minutes.

Cold Grapefruit Soufflé

This is an elegant dessert whose presentation in the hollowed-out grapefruit halves is especially attractive.

Serves 6

6 eggs, separated	½ cup sugar
Juice of ½ lemon	4 grapefruit
1 stick sweet butter	Candied violets or dark jelly

Separate the eggs. By hand, or using an electric mixer, mix the egg yolks, lemon juice, butter, and sugar. Squeeze juice of one grapefruit, add to the mixture, and transfer to a double boiler. With a whisk, beat this mixture until it reaches a custard consistency. Beat egg whites until stiff. Wash the remaining grapefruit, dry, and cut in half. Scoop out sections of fruit, discarding any seeds, and add them to the custard, then fold in the beaten whites. Now scrape out the residue in the grapefruit shells and fill the shells with the soufflé.

Chill. Top with candied violets if available. Otherwise, a dab of any dark jelly, such as raspberry, will do.

MENU 3

The preparation, as well as the cooking, of this menu can be made the morning of or the day before the dinner (as for the marquise, *it is imperative it be made a day in advance). Your vegetable and your main dish can be heated in a low oven (about 300°) for roughly 20 minutes, so put both in just before beginning your cold first course.*

Mousse au cognac
(Mousse-pâté with cognac)

Poussin Quasimodo
(Cornish game hens Quasimodo)

Riz aux petits pois
(Rice and peas)

Salade d'endives
(Endive salad: see page 150)

Fromage de Camembert
(Camembert cheese)

Marquise au chocolat
(A heart-shaped chocolate mousse)

Wine: Beaujolais-Villages (preferably chilled)

Mousse-Pâté with Cognac

There are almost as many pâtés as there are chefs, and one of the pleasures for a cook who has fiddled and puttered in the pâté field is to come up with his or her own invention. Years ago, in a little *auberge* in Dordogne, the chef served a mousse that literally awed me. I had a good idea of the ingredients, but not of the proportions.

When I got home I made various efforts to recapture that mousse. Some were close to the original, all were good, but it was not until one day after more than a dozen tries that I found one that seemed to me the equal of the Dordogne pâté. It takes only about 15 minutes to make.

Serves 6–8
- 1 pound chicken livers
- 3 sticks butter (or 12 ounces chicken fat)
- 1 clove fresh garlic
- ½ teaspoon paprika
- ½ teaspoon thyme
- Salt and pepper
- ½ cup cognac (if not available, substitute rum or bourbon)
- 8-ounce package cream cheese
- Parsley and tarragon sprigs

In a frying pan, gently sauté the chicken livers in the butter over a low flame. (I personally use chicken fat, because it lends a better flavor.) Stir with a wooden spoon and let simmer for 7 to 8 minutes. Add garlic, paprika, thyme, salt, and pepper, and pour into blender. Add cognac and cream cheese. Blend until smooth. (You may have to stop the blender and stir contents to make certain the mixture is properly reaching the blender blades.) Pour the contents into a bowl. Chill. Don't be concerned if the contents appear too liquid at this stage: the mousse becomes firm as it chills. It's a good idea to make the mousse the day before planned use.

When ready to serve, empty the mousse onto a platter, reshape with a knife, generously crown with sprigs of parsley, and add fresh tarragon if available.

Serve with toast, triangled or quartered. Keep warm by covering toast with a napkin and serve in wicker basket. Melba toast is a good substitute.

To make it very French, I advise a jar of French *cornichons* (pickles), served in an earthenware bowl. The purpose of these French pickles is essentially to counterbalance the richness of the mousse. Whenever I can't find the imported *cornichons,* I have found that I can get the same effect by adding half a cup of wine vinegar to a small jar of sour pickles. Don't serve dill pickles; their personality is too strong for the delicacy of the mousse. The value of the *cornichons,* in this context, is their astringency.

Cornish Game Hens Quasimodo

This is a dish more common to the inns of France than to the urban restaurants. My own preference for a side dish with Cornish game hen is rice and peas. However, *pommes allumettes* (ultra-thin French fries) are also recommended.

Serves 6–8
- 5 slices bacon, diced
- 1/3 cup cognac
- 4 Cornish game hens
- 2 teaspoons dried tarragon
- 1 stick butter
- 2 tablespoons flour
- 1 cup dry white wine
- Pepper and salt

Soak the diced bacon, preferably a day ahead of time, in cognac. Wash the Cornish game hens. Pat dry. With a sharp knife, make about 10 incisions throughout breast and back of each hen. Remove bacon from cognac. Drain. Insert bacon in incisions, adding a dab of tarragon with each.

Melt butter in Dutch oven. Brown Cornish game hens gently over low flame (this should take roughly 12 to 15 minutes maximum). Sprinkle flour over the hens, then gradually pour over them the white wine and leftover cognac. Stir, adding pepper and salt to taste, cover, and cook over a low flame for 40 minutes. Ready for serving.

Rice and Peas

Serves 6–8
- 1 cup rice
- 1 package frozen green peas
- 1 stick butter
- Pepper and salt

Cook rice according to instructions on box. Ditto green peas. Mix in a pretty little casserole dish. Add butter, season to taste and cover. Warm up in the oven at the same time you warm your main course.

Marquise au Chocolat

A first cousin of the famous *mousse au chocolat,* the *marquise* will be the aristocratic conclusion to any fine meal. While the former is generally served in a soufflé dish and the *mousse* spooned out to the individual plates, the *marquise* makes its entrance perched on a stand or cake dish. Although it contains no flour whatsoever, it looks for all the world like an elegant cake. (Very rich. . . .)

Serves 6–8

- 8 ounces sweet chocolate
- ½ cup granulated sugar
- 1 tablespoon Grand Marnier
- 1 teaspoon orange extract
- 1½ sticks sweet butter, softened
- 4 egg yolks
- 4 egg whites, beaten stiff
- 1 cup heavy cream
- ¼ cup confectioner's sugar
- ½ chocolate square for shavings

In a double boiler, melt the 8 ounces of chocolate with the granulated sugar, the Grand Marnier, and the orange extract, stirring with a wooden spoon. Let it cool for a few minutes. Add the butter, and the egg yolks one by one. Fold in the egg whites. Pour mixture into a buttered heart-shaped mold (any other mold will do). Leave overnight in the refrigerator. When ready to serve, whip the cream, adding the confectioner's sugar. Unmold the cake and decorate the top with the cream and chocolate shavings.

MENU 4

You can conceive and prepare this entire menu a day or two ahead of your planned dinner. The fresh vegetables can sit chilling in your refrigerator; the meat actually gains by a second "cooking"; and as for the dessert, for best results it needs firming time, so it too profits from advance preparation.

Légumes Côte d'Azur
(Fresh vegetables dipped in vinaigrette sauce)

Rôti de porc aux poires, flambé
(Flaming pork roast)

Salade de cresson
(Watercress salad: see pages 47–50)

Plateau de fromages
(Cheese tray)

Crème bavaroise au kirsch sans oeufs
(Five-minute Bavarian cream)

Wine: St. Émilion

Fresh Vegetables Dipped in Vinaigrette Sauce

A few years ago my husband and I were taken to a very good, fashionably small restaurant in the hills overlooking Cannes. The patron took our order for the main dish, adding that he was taking care of the hors d'oeuvre. A few minutes later he proudly brought to our table a rounded cork tray (cork trees are local to the region) on which was piled an array of brightly colored raw vegetables, beautifully arranged. A perfect still life. Along with it came a bowl of aromatic vinaigrette. It was truly a food "happening," a collective, participatory event in which all four of us compared notes as we tried the various vegetables. We carved our own pieces of avocado, cucumber, mushroom, raw fennel, green peppers, and baby artichokes and dipped them or not in the vinaigrette.

I have since used this as an hors d'oeuvre for many of our dinners. Though it requires no great culinary ability, it is a joyful opener which invariably gets an ovation from my guests and puts them in a good mood for whatever follows.

The vegetables you use will of course depend on the season and the region of the country you live in, but the beauty of the dish is that the same effect can be obtained with a wide variety of raw vegetables. Here is a basic list, which you can vary as climate or fantasy dictates:

Serves 6–8

- 2 green peppers
- 1 basket cherry tomatoes
- ½ pound mushrooms
- 2 Belgian endives
- 2 cucumbers
- 1 bunch radishes (red or white)
- 6 carrots
- 1 avocado
- 1 bunch celery
- 1–2 turnips

Wash all vegetables carefully. Peel carrots and turnips, leaving stems for decoration. Wipe mushrooms with damp kitchen towel (or wash if the mushrooms are particularly sandy). Cut radish roots, leaving stems. Separate celery stalks, but serve full length. Leave all other vegetables whole.

Make your vegetable arrangement according to your artistic tastes and inspiration, combining colors and textures as you will. Insert between vegetables, here and there, as many kitchen knives as you have guests. Serve, and enjoy, with the following vinaigrette:

2 shallots, finely chopped
1 cup chopped fresh parsley
2 tablespoons Dijon mustard
1 teaspoon thyme
1 teaspoon tarragon
1 teaspoon basil
½ cup wine vinegar
⅓ cup lemon juice
2½ cups olive oil
2 cloves garlic, chopped
Salt and pepper

Combine all ingredients. Although in its original incarnation, the *patron* of the restaurant served us a single bowl of vinaigrette to share, I have decided that the dish works even better if each person has his or her own minibowl of dressing.

Serve with warm French bread.

Flaming Pork Roast

Any flaming dish tends to be thought of as spectacular, and indeed it adds an element of the festive to any dinner. It may or may not really add to the flavor of the dish being flamed, but it unquestionably enhances the occasion. The trouble is that too many cooks think that any flaming dish entails a big production. It doesn't.

Serves 6–8
3–4-pound loin pork roast, boned
2 onions, quartered
1 cup raisins soaked in water
1 teaspoon thyme
½ teaspoon nutmeg
Pepper and salt
4 pears, peeled and quartered
½ cup heavy cream
 (or evaporated milk)
Juice of ½ lemon
½ cup rum

Heat up Dutch oven over medium flame for 2 to 3 minutes. Sprinkle salt in it, then brown roast evenly on all sides. (This will take about 15 minutes.) The roast, even lean, will have rendered its own fat (pork always does). Add onions, and cook until transparent. Drain the raisins, add them with thyme, nutmeg, pepper, and salt, and stir. Cover. Cook in an oven at 350° for one and a half hours. Remove meat. Place Dutch oven on stove over medium flame, add pears to sauce, and let simmer for 10 minutes. Add cream, and stir.

Slice roast, and put slices in sauce. Return pot to oven to warm at 180° for whatever time it takes for drinks and hors d'oeuvres.

To serve, place slices on a platter, surround with a crown of pears, sprinkle lemon juice on top, and cover with sauce. Warm up the rum in a saucepan for 10 seconds. Place platter in center of table. As unobtrusively as possible, bring in saucepan of heated rum. Light (still in the saucepan), and pour quickly over the platter.

The more usual accompaniment for pork is, of course, apples. The pears, raisins, and rum, however, give the pork a new "aroma."

NOTE: If fresh pears are unavailable, use canned pears. But drain them of their syrup to avoid oversweetening, and squeeze a few more drops of lemon over them for added tartness.

Five-Minute Bavarian Cream

The usual Bavarian cream, which I have often made, calls for eggs. But not long ago a New York friend introduced me to this eggless variation, which is faster to make and, I think, just as good.

Serves 6–8
1 envelope gelatin
1 cup heavy cream
1 cup sour cream
½ cup Kirsch
½ cup sugar
1 pint raspberries (fresh or frozen)

Dissolve gelatin in a half cup of cold heavy cream. Heat up remaining heavy cream, but do not boil. Mix into sour cream, dissolved gelatin, Kirsch, and sugar. Pour into a heart-shaped (or other-shaped) mold. Cover and refrigerate.

To unmold, immerse for 10 seconds or so in hot water and turn over onto serving platter. Top with raspberries and serve.

MENU 5

This entire meal can be prepared and cooked in advance. The rillettes *will keep under refrigeration up to 10 days. The ducks can be roasted (and the apples baked) a good day ahead of your scheduled dinner, and actually arranged on an (oven-proof) platter, ready to be heated just before serving. Ditto the mashed potatoes, which will be placed in their casserole dish. As for the dessert, both the pastry shells themselves and the lemon-custard filling can be done any time convenient before your dinner: they should, however, be assembled —a matter of two minutes—just before your guests arrive.*

Rillettes
(*Pork pâté*)

Canard à la Normande
(*Duck Normandy style*)

Purée de pommes de terre gratinées
(*Mashed potatoes au gratin*)

Salad de laitue
(*Boston lettuce salad: see pages 47–50*)

Plateau de fromages
(*Cheese tray*)

Tartelettes au citron
(*Lemon tartlets*)

Wine: Châteauneuf-du-Pape

Pork Pâté

This is one of the most popular pâtés you will find in France. In every town and village, however tiny, throughout the country, you will inevitably find the four culinary cornerstones: the *boulangerie/pâtisserie*, the *charcuterie/boucherie*, *épicerie*, and *bistro*. (In the cities, you will find these four cornerstones on every other block.) In every charcuterie you will find *rillettes*. In fact, it is so popular that it has a connotation of being a people's pâté and, for that reason, will rarely if ever be found on the menu of any state dinner. Too bad for the visiting heads of state and their entourage, for it is, in my opinion, one of the most delicious of all pâtés. It's almost always the first thing I order in a restaurant whenever I go back to France.

Because of the presumed difficulty in making *rillettes*, and because of its ready accessibility in France, no French person would ever dream of making it. Nor until recently had it been exported. I missed *rillettes*. Whenever I took the plane back from France I would invariably come armed with a few *baguettes* of French bread, an assortment of cheeses that would drive my fellow passengers mad, some Normandy butter ... and *rillettes*. But what to do in between? Necessity being the mother of invention, I determined to make my own. The cookbooks were no help. Those that had a recipe for *rillettes* struck me as so long and complicated as to discourage even the most willing. But after a number of efforts, I came up with the following recipe which, while long by the standards of this book, still takes only 10 to 15 minutes' preparation time, the rest being cooking time, during which you can of course be doing other things.

Rillettes have a unique texture and taste. However, they vary slightly, for there are as many different *rillettes* as there are charcuteries. A charcutier in Trouville with whom I became friendly explained to me that the slight differences derived from the fact that each charcutier used in his *rillettes* the small "crumbs" of ham that accumulated in the course of a normal day's slicing. Being thrifty, he would add them to the pork meat: but ham remains of course optional.

Serves 6–8

- 1 pound pork meat, cubed (any inexpensive, even fat, cut of meat will do)
- 1 pound bacon ends or scraps
- ½ pound fatback
- 4 bay leaves
- 6 medium-sized onions, chopped
- ½ teaspoon thyme
- 1 tablespoon salt
- ½ teaspoon pepper

I recommend that you not go to the expense of buying a lean cut of pork for *rillettes*. Into a Dutch oven, put the pork, bacon, and fatback, and cook over a medium flame for about 10 minutes, that is until the fat becomes transparent. Add bay leaves, onions, thyme, salt, and pepper, and stir with a wooden spoon. Do not cover. Let simmer on low flame for 3 hours, stirring occasionally. I suggest that you set out to make your *rillettes* in the evening when you plan to be home anyway, or at any other time when you'll be available to the kitchen for a short stretch of time, without obviously having to be glued there.

Most classic French recipes for *rillettes* call for cooking for 6 to 8 hours. The reason for this is that by the end of that time the meat will have become soft enough to mash with a fork, or a mashing device, which was what the French charcutiers did with it. Thanks to my blender, I have been able to cut it back to 3 hours. Remove bay leaves (save them), then transfer your cooked meats, two ladlefuls at a time, from Dutch oven to blender. Blend at low speed, and pour into an attractive ceramic or other bowl. Cover and refrigerate. By the following morning the fat will have surfaced to form a white film over the top. Replace the bay leaves as decoration, and serve in the crock with French bread or crackers.

Duck Normandy Style

Normandy is famous for its dairy products and its apples and apple products, from cider to calvados. Whenever you see any dish *à la normande* it is likely to be prepared with cream or some form of apple. In the recipe that follows, I combine both.

Serves 6–8

- 2 4–5-pound ducks
- 6 apples, whole, cored and unpeeled
- 1 lemon, sliced
- 1½ cups light cream
- ½ cup stock
- ½ cup calvados (or applejack)
- Pepper and salt

In a roasting pan roast both ducks in an oven preheated to 350°, for one hour. In a second pan, bake 4 apples at the same time. Remove roasting pans from oven and scoop out excess fat from ducks with a ladle—there will be a lot, since duck renders a great deal of fat when cooking—leaving 3 or 4 tablespoons in the bottom of the pan. Quarter the two remaining apples and place evenly around the ducks. Place lemon slices over both ducks. Return to the oven for 20 minutes. Remove from oven and stir into the sauce the cream and stock. Carve the ducks, season with salt and pepper, and arrange with the sauce on an oven-proof platter (or large casserole dish), again crown with quartered apples and top with lemon slices. Place the baked whole apples at the four points of the compass.

All the above can be done either the morning of your dinner, or even the day before. To reheat, place the covered ovenproof platter in your oven at low temperature (150–200°) while you are having cocktails.

Just prior to serving, warm up the calvados for a few seconds in a saucepan, then ignite, quickly pour over the four apples, and serve. (The four apples will appear, however briefly, like four flaming torches: a lovely effect.)

Mashed Potatoes au Gratin

Serves 6–8

- 8–10 medium-sized potatoes
- ¾ cup warm milk
- 1½ sticks butter (or margarine)
- Pepper and salt
- ¼ cup bread crumbs
- ½ cup grated cheese (Swiss or cheddar)

Peel and quarter the potatoes. Add to a saucepan, cover with salty water, and cook until tender, 20 to 25 minutes after water has come to a boil. Drain. Add warm milk and one stick of butter, and beat with whisk until smooth. (Use electric mixer if you prefer.) Season with pepper and salt to taste. Transfer the mashed potatoes to a casserole dish, cover with bread crumbs and cheese, dot generously with remaining butter, and bake for 20 minutes.

Lemon Tartlets

Serves 6–8

¾ cup strained lemon juice
Grated zest of 1 lemon
1 cup sugar
2 tablespoons flour
3 tablespoons sweet butter
4 egg yolks
8 baked pastry tartlet shells

Into the top part of a double boiler put all the ingredients (with the notable exception of the pastry shells). Beat with a whisk for about 10 minutes, or until mixture thickens. Remove from heat and let cool. Pour into pre-baked pastry shells.

MENU 6

Do this entire menu, if you can, the day before. Your stuffed leaves will require 20 minutes (at about 300°) prior to serving. Even the rice can be cooked earlier and set in the oven along with the main course, to heat up.

Potage Choisy
(Cream of parsley soup)

Petits paquets de salades farcis
(Stuffed salad leaves)

Riz
(Rice)

Salade d'endives
(Endive salad: see page 150)

Plateau de fromages
(Cheese tray)

Tarte aux prunes
(Plum tart)

Wine: Médoc

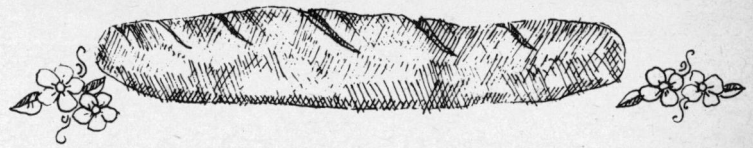

Cream of Parsley Soup

Most French cooks, including me, use parsley primarily for garnishing and seasoning. Rare is the dish that doesn't call for a handful of freshly chopped parsley, to give it its final touch of fresh country flavor.

It also could be classed as a staple "health food." In fact, when one researches a little into the widespread use of many foodstuffs and eating habits, one often finds health reasons at the basis of many customs. Parsley, for instance, is rich in iron; its roots are reputedly good for liver and kidney problems. In France, where every other citizen seems to be suffering from a mild or not so mild form of *mal au foie*—liver trouble—the use of parsley is almost self-explanatory (*O les bons vins!*).

Here is a dish in which parsley moves from the wings to center stage, to take its place as a full-fledged first course.

Serves 6–8

1 stick butter
2 bunches fresh parsley, chopped (approximately 3 cups)
4 cups water
Pepper and salt
4 medium-sized potatoes, peeled and chopped
1 tablespoon butter to top

Melt butter in a kettle. Add parsley, reserving 2 tablespoons for decoration. Stir for 2 minutes. Add water, pepper, and salt. Add potatoes. Bring to a boil, cover, reduce flame, and continue cooking for 15 minutes. Pour contents into the blender, and blend until you have a smooth, creamy consistency. (If the blender won't hold all contents of the kettle, blend in two stages.) Return contents to the kettle, heat until the soup is piping hot, top with the remaining parsley, and add a *noix* of butter (a piece of butter the size of a walnut). Serve, preferably with hot, crisp French bread.

Stuffed Salad Leaves

Serves 6–8

1 pound veal	Pepper and salt
½ pound pork	1 head escarole
1 egg	¼ cup cooking oil
3 tablespoons uncooked rice	½ stick butter
½ teaspoon sage	2 cups beef or chicken stock
½ teaspoon rosemary	½ cup heavy cream
1 teaspoon tarragon	

Grind the veal and pork. If you do not have a meat grinder or Moulinex, cube meats and blend a little at a time. It will do the trick and take 8 minutes to blend. Put ground meat in a bowl. Add the egg, rice, herbs, and pepper and salt to taste. Knead for a minute or two until all the ingredients are properly amalgamated. Separate the leaves of the escarole, washing each leaf separately and thoroughly. Cook leaves in boiling salty water for 2 minutes. Drain. Cool. Place a salad leaf on your table or counter, and in the center place about a tablespoon of the meat mixture (the larger the leaf the larger the stuffing). Fold salad leaves tightly, as you would a package you were wrapping.

In a Dutch oven, heat oil and butter, place packages carefully side by side, and brown evenly on both sides (when done on one side, turn them with a spatula). This should take no more than 10 minutes. Add stock. Cover Dutch oven, and place it in the oven at 350° for an hour.

At serving time, add heavy cream.

Endive Salad

Endives have soared so much in price that they tend to be in the luxury gourmet department. However, the rest of this dinner is so reasonably priced that the endive indulgence here is, to my mind, fully warranted. Even if the endives—and you will need from eight to ten for this salad—strike you as exorbitant, the total dinner cost will be well within bounds.

Wash and cut endives into 1- to 1½-inch pieces, dry well, and place in a salad bowl over ⅓ cup vinaigrette dressing (page 46). Toss just before serving.

Plum Tart

This is as classic as apple tart.

Serves 6–8

Dough for 1 pie crust
(see page 39)
1½ pounds plums
½ cup sugar
3–4 cookies (plain vanilla, sugar, or butter), crumbled
1 tablespoon vanilla extract
½ stick sweet butter
½ cup apricot jam

Roll out the dough and line a buttered, 9-inch pie mold. Wash, halve, and pit the plums. Put in a bowl and cover with ¼ cup of the sugar. Line the pie crust with crumbled cookies (their purpose is to soak up the juice). Arrange halved plums in tight rows, neatly, in full overlapping circles. Cover with remaining sugar and vanilla extract. Dot with butter. Preheat the oven to 350°, and bake for 45 minutes. Remove from the oven.

In a saucepan over low flame, melt the apricot jam for a minute or two until liquid, and pour over the entire surface of the plum tart. This will impart to the tart its final, *pâtisserie* glaze.

Refrigerate until serving time.

MENU 7

Do make the pot-au-feu a day before your planned dinner. It will serve a dual purpose: (a) it will be done, and (b) the fat from the meat will rise to the surface and enable you to degrease the broth. You can even poach your marrow and stuff your brioches in advance. As for the hazelnut soufflé, since it's a cold one, it's almost essential that you do it far enough ahead so that it has plenty of time to set.

Bouillon avec brioches à la moelle
(*Broth with marrow-stuffed brioches*)

Pot-au-feu
(*Boiled beef and vegetables, French style*)

Plateau de fromages
(*Cheese tray*)

Soufflé aux noisettes
(*Cold hazelnut soufflé*)

Wine: Nuits-Saint-Georges

Broth, Boiled Beef and Vegetables, French Style

Pot-au-feu is as French as the Eiffel Tower. In the country, farmers and peasants eat the dish in a soup plate, that is, the broth, meat, and vegetables are combined. City dwellers have generally turned pot-au-feu into two courses, first the broth, then the meat and vegetables.

Reasonably inexpensive, this dish requires no lengthy presence in the kitchen. (This may well account for its popularity in France, despite the prevailing myth of the number of hours the French cook spends in the kitchen each day.) It originated in the country, but spread to every town and city. The farmer's wife was able, having started to cook the pot-au-feu earlier in the day, to return to the field to do her daily share, then return at dusk with a ready-made supper, as delicious as it was hearty.

Today, it has become part and parcel of the current culinary tradition, cutting across all classes. This dish appears at least three times a month on the tables of most French families, from fall to summer. Of all the dishes of French cuisine, pot-au-feu best symbolizes the home, the family—so much so that you will rarely see a French person ordering or eating it in a restaurant.

Sharing a pot-au-feu with a French family may seem rather ordinary to the non-Frenchman, who might in his mind equate it to inviting someone home to share stew or pot roast. But there is a difference: pot-au-feu, being a private, home dish, is to a privacy-minded Frenchman something to be shared *only* with his family, or with those he admits to his *foyer*. French people, it should be remembered, have a sharp sense of privacy. Houses in the country (and sometimes in the suburbs) are surrounded by high stone walls. Frenchmen are slow to open up their homes to new friends. Thus, if you are invited into a Frenchman's home for dinner, you know you have passed all sorts of esoteric, Gallic tests. If, in addition, you are served pot-au-feu, consider it a declaration of real friendship.

In America, I have been served dishes calling themselves pot-au-feu in a number of homes, and invariably they have differed from the French dish in several ways. First of all, they tend to be overly generous, with three or more meats offered, and a variety of vegetables. The French are a bit more parsimonious, and more sober. What seems to have happened is that a number of traditional French dishes, all relatives of pot-au-feu, have been assimilated into a single dish parading under that name. One is: *la potée campagnarde,* or *potée bretonne,* whose meat dish is ham or fresh pork. It is accompanied by cabbage, carrots, and potatoes.

Another is: *poule au pot,* which consists of boiled chicken, served with carrots, leeks, and boiled rice on the side, and accompanied by *sauce suprême* (a white sauce made with flour, lemon juice, chicken broth, and one egg yolk).

In America, I have been served a dish in which beef, pork or ham (or sausage), and chicken have all been served at the same time. I found it delicious, but at the risk of being called a purist, the traditional pot-au-feu consists of beef only. This recipe serves six to eight most generously; you should have some left over for the next day; or if two or four extra guests arrive unannounced, you can provide for them adequately.

Serves 6–8

- 1 pound short ribs beef
- 3–4 pounds bottom round or chuck
- 1 pound beef soup bones
- 4 quarts water
- 1 large onion, pricked with 3 cloves
- 1 clove garlic
- 6–8 whole peppercorns
- 2 tablespoons salt
- 1 bunch fresh parsley, chopped
- 3 sprigs fresh dill
- 1 bunch celery, including leaves
- 3 bay leaves
- ½ teaspoon thyme
- 12 carrots
- 2 turnips
- 2 parsley roots (if available)
- 2–3 leeks
- 2 pounds marrow bones, washed
- 1 cup fresh peas (if in season)

Take the biggest kettle you own. Put the meat and soup bones into the kettle. Cover with water. Add the onion, garlic, peppercorns, salt, chopped parsley, dill, celery leaves (when washing celery, remember not to discard the leaves; each precious celery leaf imparts an important aroma to the pot-au-feu), bay leaves, and thyme. Bring to a boil, reduce flame, cover, and let simmer for an hour and a half. A foam will have formed on the surface which should now be skimmed with a spoon. Add all remaining vegetables—carrots, turnips, parsley roots, leeks, and celery stalks—and the marrow bones. Cook for 20 minutes, add the peas, and continue cooking for another 10 minutes.

The pot-au-feu is now ready for serving, after the following procedure which will produce for you your first course, that is the beef broth, accompanied by brioches stuffed with the marrow.

There are very good, already prepared brioches on the market. If like me, however, you prefer to make your own, see page 41. Whichever course you choose, remove the tops of the brioches. Fish the marrow bones out of the kettle. With a small spoon scoop out the marrow into a bowl, add pepper and salt to taste, mash with a fork, then fill the hollows of the brioches with the marrow. Replace lids. Brioches are now ready for warming (10 minutes at 250°) just prior to serving. When they are warm, remove to a napkin-covered basket, pour bouillon from the pot-au-feu into a soup tureen and serve. (Your soup tureen will hold only from about one-third to a half of your pot-au-feu liquid; the rest will be keeping your main dish hot while you eat the first course.)

For the pot-au-feu itself: on a large serving platter, arrange the meat in the middle and crown it with the vegetables. Serve with the following:

Mandatory: each guest, or every two guests, should have a small bowl of coarse salt; a small bowl of prepared mustard; a bowl of pickles.

Optional: Horseradish sauce. Pot-au-feu does not necessarily call for this sauce, but I find it enhances the dish. Mix together 1 cup heavy cream (whipped), ½ cup sour cream, and a 4-ounce jar of horseradish.

Another option, which I have tried and enjoyed, is the Italian version, which calls for a vinaigrette. Use the standard vinaigrette (see page 46), and add 4 shallots, finely chopped, and 1 cup finely chopped parsley.

Each guest can pour vinaigrette over pot-au-feu, more or less generously, according to taste.

Personally, I find that a dinner featuring pot-au-feu can do without salad. The pot-au-feu being rather light (yes, despite all those ingredients! The boiling does the trick), it does not need a salad, whose role generally is to complement the richness of the preceding course.

But if you feel that no meal is complete without a salad, by all means serve one. If you do, however, I suggest you resist the temptation to serve your pot-au-feu with the vinaigrette.

Cold Hazelnut Soufflé

Serves 6–8
4 eggs
1 cup sugar
2 teaspoons vanilla extract
½ teaspoon almond extract
1 cup hazelnuts, ground in the blender
1 package gelatin
1 pint heavy cream
Whole hazelnuts or candied violets (optional)

Separate the eggs. In the top of a double boiler stir the yolks with the sugar, vanilla, and almond extract, until mixture thickens. Remove from flame. Add ground hazelnuts. Dissolve gelatin in ¼ cup of cold water, and add. Whip the egg whites; then whip the heavy cream until stiff. Fold together with hazelnut mixture, and place in a soufflé dish. Cover and refrigerate. When ready to serve, you can if you like decorate with a few whole hazelnuts or candied violets.

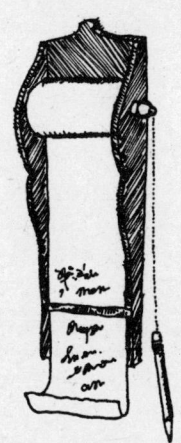

MENU 8

Everything in this menu—except tossing the salad and flaming the apples—can be done a day in advance, and will gain from so doing. Allow 20 to 30 minutes for heating your main course (350° oven); ditto for the turnips.

Soupe royale—"Varsovie"
(Chilled soup, Polish style)

Jambon en croûte
(Ham in pastry crust
with frosted grapes)

Navets au gratin
(Turnips au gratin)

Salade de betteraves et d'endives
(Beet and endive salad: see page 99)

Fromage Gourmandise aux noix
(Gourmandise cheese with walnuts)

Pommes flambées
(Flaming apples)

Wine: Fleurie (Côte de Beaune)

Chilled Soup, Polish Style

This member of the cold-soup family is as elegant as it is easy to prepare. It takes but minutes to put together.

Serves 6–8

- 2½ cups yogurt
- 1 cup heavy cream
- 1 cup stock (beef or chicken)
- 1 cup beets, diced
- 2 cups beet juice
- 4 hard-boiled eggs, diced
- 1 cucumber, diced
- Juice of ½ lemon
- 2 bay leaves, crushed
- 1 tablespoon dry dill
- 1 cup leftover meat (any meat), cubed, or 1 cup shrimp, diced
- Pepper and salt

In a bowl or soup tureen mix all the ingredients. Chill for at least two hours. Serve cold.

NOTE: A seafood variant of this soup can be made by substituting a cup of clam juice for the stock and a cup of diced shrimp for the cubed meat.

Ham in Pastry Crust

Serves 6–8

Dough for two 9-inch pastry crusts (see page 39), or brioche dough (see page 42)
3–5 pounds canned ham or a 6–7-pound pre-cooked cured ham, boned
2 egg whites
1 pound grapes
½ cup granulated sugar

Any dish that is served wrapped in pastry inevitably creates an aura of *haute cuisine* and prompts a gratifying response. Lest you should worry about the added step of having to make a pastry crust, let me hasten to reasure you. First of all, I hope that by now I may have convinced you of the importance of making several pastry crusts at a time and freezing those you do not use immediately. If you have, take from the freezer two plastic bags, each containing enough dough for the equivalent of a 9-inch pie and leave dough to defrost on the counter or in the refrigerator if it is a particularly hot day. This should be done the morning of the day *before* your planned dinner. That evening, while you're fixing your own dinner, fit into one of your time interstices—no more than 5 minutes will be needed—the rolling out of the now soft dough. Roll out, on a floured board, into two equal-size rectangles about one-eighth inch thick. In one of the two rectangles, draw with the point of a knife a number of X's, thus:

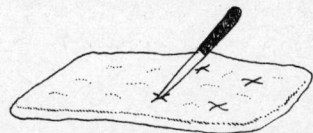

These X's will serve as vents to allow the steam of the ham to escape in cooking without bursting the crust. If you have opted to use a canned ham open the can of ham. Remove the ham jelly and discard. (The reason for using canned ham is that it is already boned and shaped, easy to cover with dough.) If you use a cured ham, be sure it is pre-cooked. Place the ham in the center of the unmarked rectangle. Lift the one with the X's carefully and lay it over the ham. Cut off any excess, that is overlapping, dough. Pinch edges to seal. With the excess dough, form a ball and roll out again. With a knife, cut out leaf shapes, or any shape your fancy dictates, to be added as decoration to the top of the crust. (If you want to skip this step, simply take the ball of leftover dough, return to a plastic container, and refreeze.)

Mix one egg white with a tablespoon of water, brush the top of the crust, then add decoration and brush again. Bake in preheated oven at 350° for 45 minutes, or until golden brown. Transfer to a platter and serve as is or, for a more festive touch, dress as follows:

Crown the ham with frosted grapes, white, dark, or preferably both. Here is how you frost the grapes (it is these little extra "secrets" of *haute cuisine* that will earn you the reputation of chef, so the little added effort is really worth it). Wash grapes and remove stems. Place a lightly beaten egg white in a small bowl. Add grapes. Stir with a spoon to make sure all the grapes have been covered. Remove the grapes from the bowl and place on a surface covered with granulated sugar (a cookie sheet or a piece of wax paper will do nicely). Shake to ensure grapes are coated thoroughly. Let stand for at least 2 hours. By then the egg white will have dried and the sugar will adhere properly.

Turnips au Gratin

Serves 6–8

2 cups stale bread	4 ounces grated Swiss cheese
1 cup milk	1 stick butter or margarine
2 hard-boiled eggs	½ teaspoon nutmeg
2 pounds turnips	Pepper and salt

Soak the bread in milk. Peel the hard-boiled eggs. Peel the turnips, and cook them in a quart of boiling, salty water for 10 minutes. Drain. In the blender, put the eggs, the bread and milk, half the grated cheese, half the butter, the nutmeg, pepper, and salt. Blend at high speed for 1 or 2 minutes. Cut the turnips into halves, arrange in a casserole dish, cover with the blended mixture, top with the remaining cheese, and dot with the remaining butter. Bake for 15 minutes, and serve.

Flaming Apples

Serves 6–8

8 apples (peeled, whole, and cored)	1 cup sugar
	¾ cup rum

Poach apples in boiling water for 10 minutes. Drain. Place sugar in a soup plate or a bowl, and roll apples in it until well coated. Arrange apples on a dessert platter. Warm the rum in a small saucepan, ignite, and pour over apples. Bring to table flaming. (The apples may also be poached ahead and served cold.)

MENU 9

Everything in this menu can be done in advance and kept in the refrigerator. You'll need about 25 to 30 minutes to heat up your roast (at 300°).

>*Pain de crevettes aux pistaches*
>(Shrimp pâté with pistachios)
>
>*Rôti de veau sauce citron*
>(Roast veal with lemon sauce)
>
>*Petits pois à la française*
>(Green peas, French style)
>
>*Salade de laitue*
>(Boston lettuce salad: see pages 47–50)
>
>*Fromage au poivre*
>(My pepper cheese)
>
>*Crème d'abricots au four*
>(Apricot cream loaf)
>
>Wine: *Vouvray* (chilled)

Shrimp Pâté with Pistachios

Serves 6–8

- 3 pounds shrimp
- 5 slices stale bread, soaked in water
- 1 egg
- 1 green pepper, diced
- 1 teaspoon Worcestershire sauce
- 1 stick butter, melted
- ¼ cup heavy cream
- ¼ cup dry vermouth
- ½ cup chopped parsley
- Pinch of dry mustard
- Pepper and salt
- 1 cup pistachio nuts
- 1 lemon, sliced

Cook shrimp in boiling, salty water for 3 minutes. Shell. Grind them in the blender, a handful at a time. Squeeze water out of bread. In a large bowl, put all the ingredients, including the blended shrimp, but reserve half the pistachio nuts and the lemon slices. Knead with fingers until well mixed. Press mixture into a buttered loaf pan (any long, narrow pan or tin). Bake in a preheated oven at 400° for 15 minutes. Cool. Unmold. Place on a serving platter and garnish with remaining pistachios. Surround loaf with lemon slices. Serve with melba toast or buttered, thinly sliced toast.

Roast Veal with Lemon Sauce

Serves 6–8

- ½ stick butter (or margarine)
- ¼ cup cooking oil
- 4–5-pound boned veal roast (loin or rump)
- Pepper and salt
- 2 teaspoons tarragon (fresh or dried)
- 2 lemons
- ½ cup chicken or beef stock
- 6 medium-sized onions, coarsely chopped
- ½ cup heavy cream (or evaporated milk)

In a Dutch oven, heat butter and cooking oil. Over medium flame, brown roast on all sides. Season with pepper, salt, and tarragon. Squeeze juice of one lemon and add to the contents of Dutch oven, together with stock and onions. Place slices of second lemon on top of roast, cover, put in preheated 350° oven, and cook for 1 hour and 20 minutes.

When roast is cooked, remove, cool slightly, and slice evenly. Add heavy cream to the meat juice, stirring to make a sauce. Put sliced roast onto a Pyrex or other heat-resistant serving platter, pour sauce over meat, and top with the onions and cooked lemon slices. Cover with foil and refrigerate if you are making it ahead. Also, reserve and refrigerate any excess lemon sauce, which you will also reheat and serve as additional sauce for your guests.

Green Peas, French Style

Green peas traditionally accompany veal and poultry. The following recipe is an integral part of the *cuisine bourgeoise;* curiously, it does call for canned peas, even at the height of the pea season.

Serves 6–8

- 2 17-ounce cans tiny peas
- 2 8½-ounce cans small whole white onions
- ½ cup chopped parsley
- 4–5 leaves lettuce (any kind)
- ½ stick butter
- 3 slices bacon, diced
- 1 tablespoon flour
- Pepper and salt

Open cans of peas (I use Le Sueur, perhaps influenced by the French name of the brand, but also because I have found them to be the closest equivalent of French *petits pois* in America). Pour peas *and* juice into a pretty saucepan (so you can avoid transferring into a vegetable dish, and can serve directly). Open cans of onions and drain. Add to saucepan, together with parsley, lettuce leaves, butter, and bacon. In a cup, combine flour with 2 tablespoons of the pea juice, and add to saucepan. Season to taste. Stir. Over a very low flame, bring to a boil, constantly stirring. This roughly 5-minute simmering will allow the flour to cook and the bacon to become transparent.

My Pepper Cheese

Serves 6–8

8-ounce package cream cheese
1 pint heavy cream, whipped
1 tablespoon prepared mustard
½ teaspoon nutmeg
3 tablespoons peppercorns, crushed

In a bowl, mix all the ingredients, using only 1 teaspoon of the peppercorns. Mash with a fork until thoroughly mixed. Form into desired shape, roll in remaining peppercorns, and place on a serving platter. Serve.

Marvelous cheese dish. Have ice water handy.

Apricot Cream Loaf

If the name of this dessert strikes you as weird, and you are asking yourself how you can make a loaf of a cream, well, you can. Here's how.

Serves 6–8

1½ pounds fresh apricots
 (or 32-ounce can apricots)
1 cup sugar
Juice of 1 lemon
¼ cup Grand Marnier
 (or Benedictine)
½ stick sweet butter
4 eggs
½ cup confectioner's sugar
1 pint heavy cream

Pit and wash fresh apricots, put into a saucepan containing about ½ inch of water, and cook for 10 minutes. (If using canned apricots, drain off half the syrup.) Put apricots and juice in blender, add lemon juice, Grand Marnier, butter, eggs, and sugar, and blend until smooth. Pour into a buttered soufflé dish. Set in a pan of hot water and bake in the oven at 350° for an hour. Cool in refrigerator. When thoroughly chilled, unmold onto a dessert platter. Return to refrigerator. Just before serving, whip heavy cream with confectioner's sugar and cover the apricot loaf. To counterbalance softness, serve with crisp cookies or wafers.

MENU 10

Bouillabaisse and dessert in this menu can both be done ahead of time. The morning of your dinner, scoop off and discard the excess fat from the surface of the bouillabaisse. One slight admonition: for your dessert, although you've made your filling and baked your puffs, wait until an hour or so before your guests arrive to actually fill the puffs, to ensure crispness.

Bouillabaisse de poulet au pistou
(Chicken bouillabaisse with green sauce)

Fromage de chèvre
(Goat cheese)

Petits choux à la crème
(Mini cream puffs)

Wine: Côtes de Provence (chilled)

Chicken Bouillabaisse with Green Sauce

The chicken bouillabaisse creates its own first course, namely a delicious broth.

The word "bouillabaisse" is one of those magic culinary words that evokes pungent aromas and visions of Mediterranean fishing ports or cities. Marseilles, the legendary home of this classic dish, uses various local fish for its ingredients, but throughout the south of France bouillabaisse can be found with certain local variations.

A few years ago while we were summering in Provence, we stopped for lunch in a tiny village. We opted for a bistro where, we learned, the *patronne* did the cooking. There was no written menu, but among her specialties she offered us a "chicken bouillabaisse." The meal was such a success that we went back to her place half a dozen times in the next few weeks, and before the end of our stay the *patronne* had given me her recipe for that dish, which I have adapted for time-saving purposes.

Bouillabaisse, whether fish or chicken, is both the soup and the main dish. When serving any form of bouillabaisse, make sure you set your table with large soup plates, for the meat, vegetables, and juice are all generously served in the same dish, at the same time.

French bread, warm and crisp, mandatory!

Again, as for pot-au-feu, I do not find it necessary to serve salad with this meal. But if you feel differently, by all means serve one.

Serves 6–8
- 6 medium-sized onions, coarsely chopped
- ½ cup olive oil
- 2 28-ounce cans whole, peeled tomatoes
- 1 tablespoon thyme
- 1 tablespoon basil
- 1 teaspoon tarragon
- 1 teaspoon sage
- 1 teaspoon rosemary
- 4 cloves garlic, squeezed or finely chopped
- 2 chickens, cut up
- 2 cups green sauce (following recipe)
- 2 cups chicken broth
- 4 cups dry white wine
- 1½ pounds small potatoes, washed and peeled

In a Dutch oven, sauté onions for about 5 minutes in the olive oil, until they become transparent. Add tomatoes with their juice. Add all the herbs, garlic, chickens, green sauce, chicken broth, and wine. Cover and transfer to oven, baking at 350° for 35 minutes. Add potatoes and continue baking for another 15 minutes. Your bouillabaisse is now ready . . . and your house smells like the scented streets of Provence. Serve as with fish bouillabaisse, that is in a soup plate.

Green Sauce

Our family (with one exception, who shall remain unnamed) is so enamored of *pistou*, as the green sauce is called in French (*pesto* in Italian), that we could literally make a meal of it, with only a loaf of French bread and a glass of wine. In Italy, you find it frequently as a sauce over spaghetti, and in Provence it is used for a wide variety of dishes, from soups to meats. In this book, you will find it as often as I can find a good excuse to use it. But here, in my opinion, it is a must. If you insist on making chicken bouillabaisse without green sauce, you do so at your own risk.

Makes 2 cups
2 cups chopped fresh basil
1½ cups olive oil
1 cup grated Parmesan cheese
4 cloves garlic
Pepper and salt
½ cup walnuts, chopped (optional)

Put all the ingredients in the blender and blend.

If fresh basil is unavailable, my poor-man's substitute for it is: 1 handful fresh parsley (preferably flat-leaved), ½ handful fresh spinach, and 2–3 ounces dry basil. Combine with other ingredients as above, and blend. Add walnuts, if you wish.

Mini Cream Puffs

To me, this comes as a soothing, delicious aftermath to the rather pungently spiced bouillabaisse.

Serves 6–8
1 cup water
⅛ teaspoon salt
1 stick sweet butter
1 cup flour
4 eggs
Confectioner's sugar for sprinkling

Combine water, salt, and butter in a saucepan and bring to a boil. Add flour (not a little at a time but all at once; this is important). Turn off flame and stir quickly with wooden spoon until mixture forms a smooth ball. Beat in eggs, one at a time, until slippery mixture becomes smooth. When all mixed, scoop up by teaspoonfuls and place on an ungreased cookie sheet, spacing the little mounds about 3 inches apart. Bake in preheated oven at 375° for 45 minutes, until puffy and golden.

While puffs are baking, make the filling as follows:

2 pints heavy cream, whipped
1 cup confectioner's sugar
2 teaspoons vanilla extract

Mix all ingredients together. When puffs are cool, remove their tops with a knife. With a spoon fill each of the puffs with cream mixture. Replace their "hats," and sprinkle with confectioner's sugar. Refrigerate until just before serving.

The above quantities should give you about 40 to 50 puffs. That many puffs may seem a trifle too many for eight, but you will be surprised at how fast they disappear.

MENU 11

Everything in this menu can be made a day in advance. The mocha cake must *be, since it needs time to set.*

Salade de poivrons et crevettes
(Shrimp and green pepper marinade)

Veau à la crème d'avocat
(Veal in avocado sauce)

Salade de laitue
(Boston lettuce salad: see pages 47–50)

Gâteau mocha rapide
(Quick mocha cake)

Wine: Blanc de Blancs (chilled)

Shrimp and Green Pepper Marinade

Made in large quantities, this can also be a perfect main course for lunch. As an hors d'oeuvre, portions should be kept reasonable, since what is to follow is quite rich and filling.

Serves 6–8

- ½ pound small shrimp
- 2 cloves garlic, finely chopped
- 1 shallot, finely chopped
- 1 medium-sized onion, finely chopped
- 3 tablespoons olive oil
- ½ teaspoon thyme
- ½ teaspoon ground bay leaves
- Pepper and salt
- 4 green peppers

Cook the shrimp for 3 minutes in salty water to cover. Drain and shell. (I'm assuming you've bought fresh shrimp. If unavailable, frozen shrimp are fine. For cooking, follow package directions.)

In a skillet, sauté garlic, shallot, and onion in the olive oil. Add cooked shrimp, and stir for about a minute. Add thyme and bay leaves, pepper and salt to taste. Wash and dice the green peppers. (If you can find both red and green peppers at your market, buy two of each. The taste will be similar, but your appetizer will be prettier.)

Combine the contents of the skillet with the peppers in a serving bowl. Chill. Serve.

Veal in Avocado Sauce

This recipe calls for 2 pounds of veal. Considering the price of veal, you might want to consider substituting turkey roll (see page 133).

Serves 6–8

2 pounds veal (shoulder is fine)	½ cup dry vermouth
Pepper and salt	1 cup beef broth
1 teaspoon powdered ginger	1 ripe avocado
2 tablespoons oil	Juice of 1 lemon
3 onions, finely chopped	1 egg yolk
1 clove garlic, squeezed	2 tablespoons sour cream
⅓ cup rum	1 cup finely chopped parsley

If you opt for the shoulder cut of veal, ask your butcher to bone it. (The shoulder cut is considerably less expensive than the loin or most other cuts.) Cube the veal in about 2-inch squares. (Your butcher will also cube it if you ask him. Otherwise, it is a cinch to do it yourself.) Season veal pieces with pepper, salt, and ginger. In a Dutch oven, heat oil and sauté meat on both sides over medium flame for about 10 minutes (5 per side). Add onions and garlic. Pour the rum, vermouth, and beef broth into the Dutch oven. Cover, and let simmer for 35 minutes.

Scoop the avocado meat out of its shell. Blend or mash with lemon juice, egg yolk, and sour cream. When your veal has finished simmering, add the avocado sauce and parsley, and continue stirring for 10 minutes. Serve.

Quick Mocha Cake

I always used to associate mocha cake with parties and pastry shops. But in fact even the busiest person can make a mocha cake worthy of the most accomplished *pâtissier*—in no more than 12 to 15 minutes. Here is how:

Serves 6–8

- 2 sticks sweet butter, softened
- 1 cup confectioner's sugar
- 2 tablespoons strong coffee
- 1 teaspoon vanilla extract
- 2 egg yolks
- 1–2 tablespoons Kirsch
- 2 packages ladyfingers
- Walnuts, candied violets, or candied coffee beans

With a mixer, whip the butter, sugar, coffee, vanilla, egg yolks, and Kirsch until you obtain a creamy consistency. Lay out a layer of ladyfingers on a cake platter, covering as much of the platter as you want. With a knife, spread the layer with butter-mocha cream, then place a second layer of ladyfingers, followed by a layer of cream, until all the ladyfingers are used up. Frost the top layer and the sides. Decorate with walnuts, candied violets, or candied coffee beans. Cover with foil or wax paper. Refrigerate for 2 hours or more. Serve, slicing as you would any cake.

MENU 12

Almost everything here can be done in advance with the exception of the two final steps in the preparation of the first and last courses. Finishing the soup will take no more than a couple of minutes. You can keep the main course warm in the oven, at low temperature, during cocktails. But if you do, be sure to cover it with a loose piece of foil, to keep it from drying. With the soufflé you will have to beat the egg whites and fold them in; this should be done just 30 minutes before serving so that the soufflé can be rising in the oven while you are having salad or cheese. Only you can judge precisely when to slip away from the table and put the soufflé in the oven, but you should plan so that your guests will be ready for the soufflé the minute it is ready for them.

Soupe exotique
(Consommé topped with toasted almonds)

Poulet poché aux quenelles aux herbes
(Poached chicken with herb dumplings)

Salade de laitue citron
(Boston lettuce salad with vinaigrette dressing:
see pages 46–50)

***Fromage hongrois maison* (Liptauer)**
(Homemade Hungarian cheese)

Soufflé aux fruits confits
(Candied fruit soufflé with rum)

Wine: Tavel (chilled)

Consommé Topped with Toasted Almonds

The main course of this meal—poached chicken—provides as a dividend a chicken consommé, a soup which is perfectly adequate in itself. However, I have often tried to vary the consommé or dress it up in different ways. Here is one rather exotic variation:

Serves 6–8

2 tablespoons cooking oil
½ stick butter or margarine, plus 1 tablespoon
6–8 slices bread
1 cup blanched sliced almonds
1½ quarts strained chicken broth

In a skillet, over medium flame, heat the cooking oil and ½ stick of butter (or margarine). The reason for using both oil and butter as shortening is that the butter gives the flavor but tends to burn; the oil tempers the burning. Fry the bread slices on both sides. Spread the almonds evenly over the fried bread. Dot the almonds with tiny bits of butter.

Heat the broth in an ovenproof pot. Top the broth with the fried bread slices. Place the pot under the broiler for a minute or two, or until the almonds are toasted. Serve.

Poached Chicken with Herb Dumplings

This is a very light main course—even the dumplings, which ought to be fluffy.

Serves 6–8

- 4–5-pound chicken, quartered
- 2 chicken breasts, cut in half
- 2 onions, peeled and quartered
- 4 cloves
- 2 quarts water
- 3 bay leaves
- 1 teaspoon thyme
- 5 sprigs parsley
- 6 peppercorns
- 3 carrots, peeled, whole
- 1 tablespoon dill
- 3–4 celery leaves
- 4 tablespoons flour
- 2 tablespoons butter
- Juice of ½ lemon

Wash the chicken. (The reason for the extra breasts of chicken is that there seems to be a preference for that part of the chicken and a single chicken would not be quite enough for a dinner of 6–8.) Prick the onions with the cloves. In a large kettle, put all the ingredients except the flour, butter, and lemon juice. Bring to a boil, reduce flame, cover, and let simmer for a good hour. Remove the chicken pieces and place in a casserole dish. Crown with carrots.

In a small saucepan, melt the butter, stir in the flour, and remove from the flame. Dilute with a cup of the broth from your kettle. Stir until it thickens. Add the lemon juice. Pour this sauce evenly over the casserole dish. (You may, if you like, use more than a cup of the broth to make your sauce—up to a cup and a half, I would suggest. It doesn't matter this time if your sauce is liquid. It's the taste that matters.) Place casserole in the oven at 200–250°.

Now the dumplings:

- 2 quarts salty water
- ½ cup finely chopped parsley
- 2 teaspoons dill
- 2 cups flour
- 2 teaspoons baking powder
- 1 teaspoon salt
- 1 tablespoon butter or margarine
- ⅔ cup milk

Bring water to a boil in 2- or 3-quart pot. Reserving half the parsley and some dill, mix all the ingredients in a bowl, kneading with your fingers. Roll the dumpling dough between the palms of your hands, make small balls, and drop them in the boiling water. When they rise to the surface, reduce the flame and cook for 10 minutes. Using a slotted spoon, remove dumplings and place them over the chicken. Sprinkle with dill and remaining parsley, and serve.

Homemade Hungarian Cheese

Serves 6–8

- 8 ounces cream cheese
- 3 tablespoons prepared mustard
- 1 onion, finely chopped
- 2 cloves garlic, finely chopped
- 3 tablespoons caraway seeds
- 1 stick butter, softened
- 2 tablespoons paprika
- Pepper and salt

In a bowl, mash all the ingredients with a fork until well mixed. Transfer to a serving platter, and form into desired shape, be it mound, cone, triangle, or other. Top with additional caraway seeds, and serve. As inexpensive as it is delicious.

NOTE: If you have any leftover Camembert or similar cheese which looks too sad to serve per se, mash it in with the above. It will add its own personal touch.

Candied Fruit Soufflé with Rum

In principle, this is a light dessert, although the candied fruit, not to mention the rum, takes it out of the featherweight category.

Serves 6–8

- ½ cup candied fruit, minced
- 4 tablespoons rum
- ½ stick sweet butter
- 2 tablespoons flour
- ⅔ cup milk
- ½ cup sugar
- ½ teaspoon salt
- 6 egg yolks
- 4 egg whites, beaten stiff

Soak candied fruit in a bowl with the rum while you are preparing the soufflé base. In a saucepan, melt the butter, add the flour and the milk, stir for about 5 minutes, then add the sugar and salt. Remove from stove. To this mixture, add the candied fruits and rum. Add the egg yolks one by one, and stir. All this can be made well ahead, in the morning even, and refrigerated. Fold in the whites just before baking.

Butter an 8-cup soufflé dish, pour the soufflé batter into it, and bake in a preheated 350° oven for 25 to 35 minutes. Serve immediately.

NOTE: In case the time variation above worries you, the reason for it is that ovens vary, no matter what the temperature control says. It doesn't mean that you should keep opening your oven to check. On the contrary, if you do you'll have no soufflé, because continued drafts will deflate it. What I suggest is that at the 25-minute mark or thereabouts, you open the oven just a crack and peek inside. If you see that the soufflé has risen to form a gentle dome above the edges of the casserole dish, and the top is a golden brown, you're fine. If it is not yet domed, and the color is pale yellow, give it a few more minutes.

MENU 13

For this menu there will be a few simple last-minute preparations. Have the stuffed eggs ready but put them in to bake 10 minutes before serving. Plan to cook the filets mignons after your guests have finished the first course—it will take you scarcely 5 minutes. And as for the dessert you will want to flame the tart at the last moment.

Oeufs à la polonaise
(Baked stuffed eggs)

Filets mignons

Crème de coeurs d'artichauts
(Cream of artichoke bottoms)

Salade d'endives
(Belgian endive salad: see page 150)

Fromage de Brie
(Brie cheese)

Tarte normande
(Normandy tart)

Wine: Marqués de Riscal

Baked Stuffed Eggs

This is a recipe handed down from my mother, and why she called it *oeufs à la polonaise* I'm not quite sure, since she's never been to Poland. She claims to have got it directly from Chopin's cook's granddaughter. But maybe that's a Polish joke. Anyway, whatever its origin, it's one of my favorite appetizers.

Serves 6–8
- 4 hard-boiled eggs, unpeeled
- 2 tablespoons cottage cheese
- 1 tablespoon butter
- 1 teaspoon mustard
- 1 teaspoon brandy
- 1 tablespoon chopped chives
- 2 tablespoons finely chopped parsley
- Pepper and salt

Cut the unpeeled eggs in half with a knife (a surprisingly easy procedure). Without breaking the shell, scoop out the insides, and put into a mixing bowl or in the blender (which is faster). Mix or blend all the ingredients and return to each half-egg shell. You will have some stuffing left over. With foil, make as many pseudo-egg shells as you have stuffing for and fill. Place in a casserole dish and bake in a preheated 350° oven for 10 minutes. Serve hot.

Filets Mignons

In contrast to the economy principle which governs most of my recipes, this one, I confess, dispenses with it. But we all deserve a *folie* once in a while, no?

I want to remind you that by buying a whole filet of beef, cutting individual steaks, and freezing them you will not only save money but enjoy better meat.

I assume every American knows as much as or more than I about steaks. Tastes differ, from well done to very rare. All I can say on the subject is to repeat the admonition offered by a New York restaurant noted for its steaks: "The Management Is Not Responsible for Any Steaks Other Than Those Ordered Rare."

Heat a frying pan with salt to very hot, and cook meat 2 minutes or more on both sides.

Cream of Artichoke Bottoms

I am not a partisan of canned artichokes, except as a last-minute addition to pep up a salad. Fresh ones are by far better.

Serves 6–8
- 10–12 artichokes
- 2 quarts salted water
- Juice of 1 lemon
- 1 stick butter
- 2 slices stale bread
- ½ cup heavy cream
- Pepper and salt
- ½ cup chopped parsley

Wash the artichokes and cook in boiling water for roughly 30 minutes. (You know an artichoke is cooked when a leaf detaches easily.) Drain. Remove leaves, and reserve for a later-date hors d'oeuvre. With a kitchen knife, cut off the stems flush to the bottom of the "heart." Scrape off the stringy matter on the top of the hearts. In the blender, put the "hearts," lemon juice, butter, bread, cream, and pepper and salt to taste. Blend until smooth. Transfer to a casserole dish, top with chopped parsley, and put in oven at very low temperature to keep warm until time of serving.

Normandy Tart

This recipe reflects the natural resources of Normandy (except for the bounty of the sea): apples, cream, and calvados.

Serves 6–8
- Dough for 8–9-inch pie crust (see page 39)
- 2½ cups applesauce
- 2 tablespoons sour cream
- 1 teaspoon nutmeg
- 2 eggs, separated
- ½ cup raisins, soaked in water
- ½ cup calvados (or applejack)

Roll out the dough on a floured board. Reserving some trimming, line an 8–9-inch pie mold. Add half a dozen kidney beans or small stones for ballast, then bake for 15 minutes at 350°. Mix applesauce, sour cream, nutmeg, and egg yolks. Beat egg whites until stiff, and fold them into applesauce mixture. When the pie crust is ready, pour in the filling. Cut the crust trimmings into thin strips, and weave them over the filling. Drain the raisins, and place one on each opening of the "trellis." Return to oven and bake for 20 to 25 minutes at 350°.

In a small saucepan, heat the calvados for a few seconds. Ignite, and pour over the pie. Serve immediately.

MENU 14

For this menu, make your soup in advance and refrigerate. Prepare the sauce for your lamb and set aside. The gigot itself, assuming a six-pound roast, will require roughly an hour and a half. So calculate backward. I usually put my gigot in the oven about half an hour before the first guests are due to arrive. The rice can be fully cooked ahead and put in a covered casserole alongside. While people enjoy the gigot, the already baked tart can warm up in the turned-off oven; then it will need only to be caramelized just prior to serving—a matter of a few seconds under the broiler.

Soupe sénégalaise
(Senegalese soup)

Gigot au pastis
(Leg of lamb with Pernod)

Riz
(Rice)

Salade de laitue
(Boston lettuce salad: see pages 47–50)

Fromage de chèvre
(Goat cheese)

Tarte tatin
(Caramelized apple tart)

Wine: Pommard

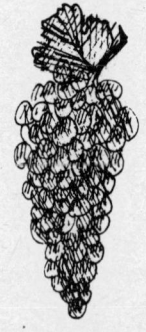

Senegalese Soup

Serves 6–8

- 2 slices stale bread
- 1½ teaspoons curry
- 1 cup heavy cream
- 4 cups beef broth
- Pepper and salt
- ½ cup finely chopped parsley

Blend bread, curry, and heavy cream. Pour into the broth, season to taste, stir, and chill. Serve topped with parsley.

Leg of Lamb with Pernod

Serves 6–8

7-pound leg of lamb, boned and rolled
2 cloves garlic, slivered
2 tablespoons cooking oil
½ teaspoon rosemary
½ teaspoon thyme
Pepper and salt

With the point of a sharp knife, make slight incisions in the lamb, and press the garlic pieces into the slits. Pour the cooking oil evenly over the roast, then sprinkle on the rosemary, thyme, and pepper and salt to taste. Roast in an oven preheated to 350°, allowing 15 minutes per pound, in order for the meat to be pink.

When the gigot is nearly done, make the following sauce:

1 shallot, finely chopped
1 onion, finely chopped
1 tablespoon cooking oil
16-ounce can tomato sauce
½ teaspoon thyme
½ teaspoon crushed bay leaves
1 teaspoon sugar
1 cup Pernod

In a saucepan, sauté the shallot and onion in the oil until they turn light brown. Add the tomato sauce, thyme, bay leaves, sugar, meat juices from the lamb, and ½ cup of the Pernod. Transfer to a sauce dish.

When your gigot is cooked, remove from the oven and place on warm serving platter. Pour the remaining Pernod into a soup ladle, heat briefly over a flame (you may use the table candle), ignite, and pour over the lamb. Serve immediately, with sauce on the side.

Recommended side dish: boiled rice.

Caramelized Apple Tart

This tart is currently very much à la mode in France, most of the top restaurants and inns featuring it on their menus. What it is, really, is a glorified apple tart, rich in butter and caramel. Also, the apples do not have to appear in the classic geometric arrangement of the *tarte aux pommes,* because the caramel will cover and conceal the apples.

The standard recipe for it would frighten away most home chefs. It's rather long, complicated, and involves numerous skillet and saucepan transfers. My recipe is a simplified adaptation which I think loses nothing and can be done in one operation.

Serves 6–8
Dough for a 9-inch pie crust
  (see page 39)
6–8 apples, peeled and sliced
1 stick butter
⅔ cup sugar
4 tablespoons water
2 tablespoons vanilla extract

Roll out dough and line pie pan. Fill crust with sliced apples, and dot with half the butter. Now make your caramel sauce. In a saucepan, melt the sugar with the remaining butter, the water, and the vanilla, stirring constantly with a wooden spoon, until golden brown. Remove pot from stove, and quickly (to prevent setting) pour over the apples. Place in the oven at 350° for 45 minutes. When the pie is baked, place it under the broiler for a few seconds to brown the caramelized topping. Serve hot.

MENU 15

Here, for gastronomic as well as planning reasons, I recommend full preparation of this menu a day or even two ahead of your dinner. The choucroute will actually gain in flavor and texture by reheating. As for the sherbet, it will keep for several days in your freezer.

Consommé

Choucroute de Transylvanie
(Transylvanian choucroute)

Salade de cresson
(Watercress salad: see pages 47–50)

Sorbet de poires à l'alcool
(Pear sherbet with pear brandy)

Wine: Muscadet (chilled)

Consommé

The main course here is rather hearty. Therefore, broth is a good opening. You can serve either chicken or beef consommé, depending on what you have on hand in your freezer.

Transylvanian Choucroute

Alsatian choucroute garnie is better known than the following recipe, which is my mother's. The former variety uses only pork meat and a variety of sausages. The secret to the Transylvanian recipe is the addition of lamb, paprika, caraway seeds, and sour cream. While this is a trifle richer, it is also, in my opinion, a little more succulent.

Serves 8 (with leftovers)
- 4 tablespoons bacon fat
- 1½ pounds pork, cubed
- 2 pounds stewing lamb, cubed
- 4 onions, chopped
- 2 shallots, chopped
- 4 pounds sauerkraut
- 2 tablespoons paprika
- 1 tablespoon caraway seeds
- 2 tablespoons juniper berries (optional)
- 2 cups white wine
- 1 clove garlic, minced
- Pepper and salt
- 4–6 knockwursts
- 1–2 white sausages (if available)
- ½ cup finely chopped parsley
- 2 cups sour cream
- 10–12 boiled potatoes

Melt the bacon fat in a Dutch oven, and brown the pork for 10 minutes. Add the lamb, onions, and shallots. Place sauerkraut in a colander, rinse under cold, running water, and drain. Add to Dutch oven, together with paprika, caraway seeds, juniper berries if you have them, wine, garlic, pepper, and salt. Stir well, cover pot, and bake in the oven for 2 hours at 300°. The knockwursts and white sausages need only 15 to 20 minutes of gentle steaming on top of the choucroute before the end of the two hours of cooking. Mix the parsley in the sour cream, top the choucroute, and serve, with crown of boiled potatoes.

You will note that this menu skips cheese. I consider the heartiness of the main course such as to make the cheese unnecessary. I sometimes even omit the salad with this menu, but that grave decision I leave up to you.

Pear Sherbet with Pear Brandy

The first time I had this dessert several years ago in a small, unpretentious, but excellent Left Bank restaurant in Paris, I loved it so that I have re-created it many times. It is a perfect dessert after a hearty main course: aromatic, unusual, refreshing, and above all light. This dessert must be made either the day before or the morning of your dinner. If you have any left over, it keeps well in the freezer, just like ice cream.

Serves 6–8

- ½ cup granulated sugar
- 12-ounce can pear nectar (or 16-ounce can pears in syrup)
- 4 ripe pears, peeled, cored, and quartered
- Juice of 1 lemon
- 2 egg whites, beaten stiff, with a pinch of salt
- ½ cup confectioner's sugar

In a saucepan, stir together the granulated sugar and pear nectar, add the pears, bring to a boil, reduce flame, and cook for 10 minutes. (If you are using canned pears, omit the ripe pears, sugar, and nectar; simply use pears and syrup.) Pour the contents of the saucepan into blender, add lemon juice, and blend. Pour the fruit purée into a bowl and place in the freezer.

In a double boiler, mix the beaten egg whites and the confectioner's sugar, and cook for 8 to 10 minutes, stirring with a wooden spoon. Freeze this "meringue" for 30 minutes. Remove both bowls—fruit purée and meringue—from the freezer. By now the contents of both bowls will have set sufficiently to prevent them from separating when mixed. Combine the contents of both bowls into one, and return this new mixture to the freezer. You should allow 3 to 4 hours of freezing time (better yet: make it the day before).

Now your sherbet is ready to be spooned into long-stemmed glasses, which I do well before the guests arrive, and returned to the freezer.

For this dessert you will need a syrup—the final touch which separates a good from a divine dessert:

- ½ cup sugar
- ⅔ cup water
- 1 cup pear brandy

In a small saucepan, cook the sugar with the water for 10 minutes over a medium flame until it thickens a little. Add brandy, and refrigerate. At time of serving, pour generously over each portion.

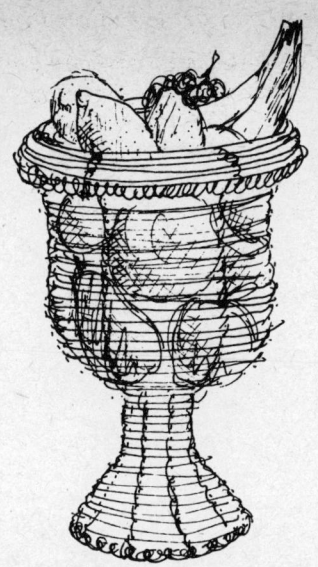

A FEW TIPS ON ENTERTAINING

Recognizing that in cooking and entertaining, as in any art, there are no hard and fast rules, I nonetheless feel that the most liberated cook, the most open host or hostess, needs certain concepts and guidelines with which to operate.

If some of what follows—which I list more or less at random—strikes a sympathetic chord, then perhaps you may want to heed the advice or take the tip. If it does not, then pass on. This "list" simply reflects my own experience, my own trials and errors, my own reflections and observations.

Heavy drinking and gourmet cooking mix like oil and water. Sorry. And if that sounds moralistic, it's not. It's gastronomic. The fact is that if you and your guests linger over drinks—heavy drinks—from 7 to 9:30 or even 10, as I've often seen happen in dinner parties, there's really little point of sitting down to a fine meal.

This is not to imply that cocktails are out: all I suggest to any host or hostess is that you plan to call your guests to table no more than an hour after their scheduled arrival, and that you not, in an act of overgenerosity, ply them with several cocktails before dinner.

Similarly, don't overload your cocktail table with too many or too rich appetizers. I'm an advocate of appetizers with drinks, but to my sorrow I've sometimes served, or seen others serve, a variety of dips, pâtés, and sausages, which guests have nibbled at so eagerly that they have probably exceeded their calorie count before they arrive at table and can have little appreciation of the dinner itself.

Down with background music! One of the goals of having people to dinner is to create intimacy. To fill the "background" with music not only distracts but also makes that intimacy virtually impossible. If you have music to fill the void, you'll inevitably find your guests raising their voices to overcome it, which both drowns the music and destroys the atmosphere. Music is to be listened to, not to be used as a crutch. I admit that this is one of my pet peeves—and of all the music that offends, the most offensive to me is classical "background" music. I have eaten in restaurants where all conversation is impeded by the intrusion of Handelian trumpets or Mozartian strings; while I know the intention is good, the effect is disastrous.

Intimacy is one thing; darkness is quite another. Despite all the energy crises real or threatened, proper lighting is needed to dine by. I am an advocate of candles for every dinner; what I am against is eliminating all but a single candle by whose flickering light you can see neither the food you are served nor the people you are with. The impulse is right; it's the degree that is wrong, and I suspect that the misunderstanding derives from the "cave effect" created by far too many restaurants.

Don't invite haphazardly: give some thought to your guest mixture. Remember, I'm going on the theory that to invite people into your home is a special gesture, an effort at intimacy; basic to it is making at least an educated guess that the assembled company will enjoy one another. On this point, after some less than successful evenings, I have come to the conclusion that two factors should be borne in mind: first, build on a nucleus of people you know, or suspect, like one another. It is far easier, and more comfortable, to integrate new acquaintances into an already comfortable group. What I tend to do, when four to six (at the most) are coming to dinner, is to invite perhaps two or three new "friends"; and, so far as I can guess or intuit, I invite people who I hope will have something in common.

If the above seems irritatingly simplistic, just think back to the last time you entered a room full of people you didn't know and with whom you found you had little in common. The strain is often excruciating.

Remember to bridge the gap. Simply introducing people to one another, and letting nature take its course, is not enough. Place the person being introduced, with a word about who and what he or she is and does. If in their work or lives people have points in common, it's a good idea to make that known to those concerned. It will often spark a conversation and establish an early contact.

Don't space your guests as far apart as possible. Within the limitations of your living room and furniture, physical proximity is a positive agent.

Be with your guests as much as possible. While a brief pre-dinner foray in the kitchen is inevitable, a host or hostess who constantly disappears, either during cocktails to make the meal or during the meal to hurry to and fro a dozen times, will destroy the feeling of ease you obviously want to create. Your guests will feel guilty at all the work they're putting you to. I'm going on the assumption throughout this book that you have no one to help you. But your best help is your head—that is, your advance planning. Of

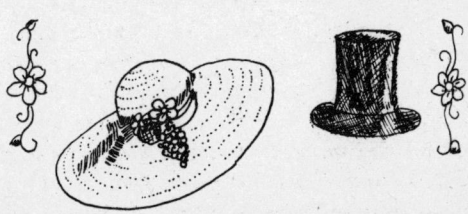

course you're going to have to make a few trips to the kitchen, to remove plates and bring on new courses. But with good planning you can keep such forays to a minimum (see pages 128–130 on planning).

If you can help it, decline anyone's offer to help. If your guests are thoughtful, they will undoubtedly be solicitous. But remember, it's their night out. If your planning is good, there will be an effortless quality to your serving which will automatically eliminate the need for their assistance.

Don't set your table at the last minute or, worse yet (I've seen it happen), after your guests arrive. It creates a feeling of hysteria that will transmit itself to all present. Even if, for space reasons, you have to, try to have everything ready on a tray and do it as discreetly as possible. But in any case start figuring out what extra plates, glasses, or serving utensils you're going to need—beyond the initial settings—before you're at table (see pages 128–130 on planning).

Don't mismatch your menu. At the risk of sounding chauvinistic, I must stress that one of the things that makes the French cuisine special is the delicate balance. You may serve people a five-course meal, but if it has proper equilibrium you will be able to enjoy each course separately and the meal as a whole.

Let's be specific:

Don't serve a creamy gratinéed first course (such as *coquilles St. Jacques*) followed by a creamy gratinéed main dish (such as moussaka, gnocchi, or the like). Similarly, avoid a succession of fried dishes, or a succession of heavy dishes, such as pâté (which implies bread and perhaps butter) followed by, say, cassoulet or a meat pie, with as a concluding act a rich chocolate cake.

Bear in mind the necessity to vary weight, texture, and even the color of your courses, and focus on your "star" course. It will probably be your main course, but not necessarily; there will be times when the dessert may be your *pièce de résistance,* and you'll work back from there—and plan accordingly.

Don't ladle out soup into your guests' plates before calling them to table. If it's a hot soup, it will be lukewarm by the time everyone begins. And even if it's a cold soup, serving the soup is part of the ceremony of eating. Ladling from a soup tureen right at the table is a lovely "dinner act."

With a fish course, feel free to serve any vegetable you like—as long as it's boiled potatoes, topped with butter and fresh parsley (and don't ever forget quartered lemons, on a separate dish, no matter how you've prepared your fish).

Put your thoroughly washed and carefully dried salad into the salad bowl before the meal, but do not toss. You will have first put your dressing at the bottom of the bowl, but let the salad rest there on top until serving time. Otherwise it will wilt and lose its crispness.

Don't keep your cheeses in the refrigerator until serving time. They need to "breathe" at room temperature for at least an hour or so, to bring out their full flavor. If you're worried about the overpowering fragrance that some good cheeses impart, cover with a glass dome or foil.

Don't rush your meal. Dinner should be lingered over, savored, appreciated. Each course in a thoughtful meal is a solo; give it its due.

Above all, don't go by the book—and that includes this book. Take from the book what pleases and strikes your fancy. Rules and regulations are made to be broken, or at least bent. But first of all you have to know the "rules" before you can break them properly. One rule, however, from which you shouldn't deviate under any circumstances is:

Don't arrive more than half an hour late when you've been invited for dinner. Better yet, arrive on time.

If punctuality in arriving is important, so is it in departing. Many guests feel they will offend their hosts if they leave too early. Obviously, I do not subscribe to the "eat-and-run" school, but to my mind a reasonably early departure is better than a late one. Everyone will have to define personally what "reasonably early" means, but for me it is anywhere from an hour to an hour and a half after the end of dinner.

Don't forget to thank your host or hostess, or both, the day after the party. There are many ways of thanking, from a phone call to a written note to a bouquet of flowers. The only unpardonable sin is silence.

LARGE DINNER PARTIES AND BASHES

Despite all my proselytizing for the small, intimate dinner, I know very well there will be times when for a myriad of reasons you will have to think of entertaining in large numbers. What I call large dinners range from eight to thirty guests; beyond that, you're into the bash.

In the early years of my entertaining life, I gave my share of large dinner parties—and probably more than my share. There were many reasons for it, not the least of which was ignorance. But there was also the fact that as a transplanted Frenchwoman, I was trying in many ways to adapt to America, and the large dinner party seemed, in contrast to France, the standard rather than the exception. But more and more I began to feel that I should follow my own convictions rather than simply adopt others' customs, and one of my increasing convictions was that large dinner parties were often self-defeating. If, as I believed, the basic intent of a dinner is to further cement relationships or get to know someone better, then by definition large dinners are frustrating, for by their very nature they are fragmented and generally superficial. Hosts and guests alike, intimidated by the sheer numbers, feel obliged to "circulate"—and soon circulation replaces communication. Then there's the noise factor: often the decibel level reaches such astounding proportions that you have literally to shout to make yourself heard. Considering all the so-called normal assaults on all our systems in the course of any given day, who needs this added irritant during what ought to be a relaxing evening?

Finally, large dinner parties are always more work than anticipated —unless, of course, you have a battalion of helpers. But in this day and age, who does? It's not so much the work of preparation, which I've managed to reduce to reasonable proportions, but the work *during* the dinner itself. What the hosts are really doing in a large dinner party is a supercatering performance. And that's exhausting. Ask any waiter. And to my mind for a dinner party to be good and fun, the hosts simply cannot be overwhelmed with the sheer mechanics, but should be free to enjoy the evening themselves.

The conclusion I've come to is that if your evening must exceed twelve to fifteen people, perhaps it's better to move up—at least numerically—and give a cocktail party.

All this said, since there are occasions when you feel you must give a large dinner party, here are a few suggestions, based on my own experiences, that might prove helpful.

If at all possible, I highly recommend a sitdown dinner as opposed to a buffet. You can either gather all your tables together and cover them with tablecloths to make one large festive banquet board, or set up as many smaller tables as you need or have, perhaps seating four to six at each table. At least this arrangement has the advantages of being intimate within the confines of each table, and comfortable.

However, many people simply do not have the space for the above. This leads inevitably to my least favorite means of entertaining:

The buffet dinner, also known as the "lap dinner" or "balancing-act buffet." It may be justifiable for a spontaneous get-together, but the idea of actually planning such a barbaric event strikes me as nonsensical. Ah, those evenings, holding the glass of wine while trying to keep the dish of very liquid *boeuf bourguignon* sufficiently horizontal to keep your new velvet suit intact! To my mind, the whole problem is to *limiter les dégâts*—keep the disaster to a minimum. Here are a few ideas:

Decorate your buffet table as brightly and inventively as possible. A basket of fresh vegetables or fruit, or a bouquet of flowers, is a good beginning. Don't forget the tablecloth; it's so much nicer. Also lighted candles.

A cold buffet is easier to handle than a hot one, from the guests' point of view as well as the hosts'.

The day before, or the night before, your dinner party, prepare your various cold platters on their serving dishes, fully garnished (that is decorated as required with lemon wedges, tomatoes, olives, hard-boiled eggs either sliced or crumbled in a mimosa effect, pimiento, anchovies, and so on. For instance, any fish platter must have lemon wedges, and can optionally be further dressed with any one of the other ingredients mentioned above. Veal also calls for lemon wedges. Parsley goes for literally everything. Watercress is welcome on any meat platter. Remember, for these two greens, that even if you prepare your buffet a day ahead as I recommend, you must keep your watercress and parsley in cold water until just prior to serving. Keep your platters refrigerated and sealed to prevent drying.

Always set the buffet table the night before or at the latest the morning of the party (minus the food, of course). I can't overemphasize the importance of this perhaps seemingly minor point. It has a soothing and reassuring effect, which is based on reality. With your buffet set, and your platters in the refrigerator, you can cope with any emergency that might keep you away from the house or the kitchen that day.

Also in the morning, go through the following checklist:

- Empty your ice trays and fill a plastic container or bag. Then refill and repeat, as required. If you're having more than twelve, consider buying a bag or two of ice.
- Check your liquor supply and see if anything is lacking. If it is, get it right away. Don't wait until evening.
- Ditto on the mixers: soda, quinine water, and the rest. I recommend having ginger ale or fruit juice available for those who don't drink.
- Check your wine supply. Allow a minimum of one bottle for every four guests. If you're serving white wine, refrigerate the anticipated number of bottles, plus two. Same for rosé. Same for Beaujolais or any nonvintage domestic wine. Red wine of the Bordeaux family should be served at room temperature, and uncorked about an hour prior to serving. Read my husband's wine-chapter for more suggestions.
- Scatter a fair number of bowls of nuts and chips for predinner nibbling.
- Don't ignore the ashtrays.
- Inspect your coat closet. Make room for your guests' coats, and supply the necessary amount of coat hangers. Unless you prefer stacking coats on a bed. I don't.

Having said that a cold buffet has distinct advantages over a hot one, I want to add that a hot buffet cannot be ruled out. There are dozens of recipes in this book that will serve admirably for hot buffet dinners.

But by far the most important thing to remember about preparing any meal, be it large or small, is to eliminate anxiety insofar as is humanly possible and preserve the "fun" element of entertaining.

What has always helped me to accomplish this is my training as a performer: one is ready for the critics six weeks before "opening night." Mentally, one learns to think of every detail in advance, from the artistic to the trivial. No surprise element should be capable of destroying the "good works" of this preparation.

Obviously, you don't have to have been a performer to do this. Anybody can plan in advance. It's all a question of getting used to the idea. Once you have, I can guarantee you that your dinner parties will be more enjoyable, not only for your guests but above all for you.

There are many reasons you may want or have to give a very large party: anniversaries, birthdays, business bashes, farewell parties, and so on.

Whatever the reasons for such a gathering, you should not let the sheer numbers involved make you think of it as an "invasion" or even as an intolerable burden. If I am against the oversized dinner party because the numbers tend to fragment and stifle real communication, with a bash the numbers can—and often do if you bring the right attitude to the affair—create an effervescence and feeling of gaiety.

What is a bash? A lot of people. I have given parties for twenty, and I have given parties for two hundred. Invariably, the latter is better. It is hardly any more work, while just a little more expensive. The potential problem with a party of twenty is that the people don't—or won't—relate, and no electricity is generated. I've also been to bashes that were dull as dishwater, but I think without question that your chances for success are far greater with a bash than a small cocktail party.

Two important factors, to my mind, are space and light. In general, I've found that a smaller space is better than a larger. I've been to big parties in ballrooms and artists' lofts, where the thousands of square feet create vacuums and distance. Therefore, if you worry that your apartment may not be big enough to accommodate a large crowd, be reassured: your seeming lack of space may actually be a plus factor. Remember, too, when you glance down your guest list that suddenly seems to have grown to gigantic proportions, that not all those people are going to arrive and depart at the same time. Bashes, like the ocean, have tides, and there will come a point when you'll wonder if you can fit another person in, but in my experience this will not be the case for very long: both the first hour and the last will be relatively warm and comfortable.

Light: there are two schools of thought. Bright lights. Or dim lights (but not to the point of darkness, as I've sometimes seen practiced, presumably in an effort to create atmosphere). Take your pick. I personally prefer bright lights, in the right dosage, for large cocktail parties.

I have found, too, that if you're giving a strictly business party, it's a good idea to dot the assemblage with a fair number of your good friends. It will bring an added warmth and joy to what might be an otherwise stiff occasion.

What follows are some suggestions and concrete tips which I have found helpful in my planning and which you may find equally so.

Generally speaking, a cocktail party is not a dinner party. Therefore, the food element should be kept to a minimum, that is "finger food," in just sufficient quantities to be circulated with ease on platters among the guests. The "food" here is not meant to feed, but simply to accompany the drinks.

Here roughly is what I have found necessary in the way of beverages for a cocktail party of 100 people, predinner, meant to last two hours.

LIQUOR

5–6 fifths of Scotch	1 fifth sweet apéritif wine
1 fifth of bourbon	(or sherry)
2 fifths of gin	1 gallon of red wine
2 fifths of vodka	1 gallon of white wine
1 fifth of dry vermouth	

These quantities will vary to some degree from season to season, of course. In the winter, larger quantities of Scotch seem to be consumed than in warmer weather (the quantities given above are for a winter cocktail party). In summer, I recommend decreasing the amount of Scotch to 3 or 4 bottles, and increasing the vodka and gin by a bottle or two. Also in summer, I often make a fruit and rum punch, or sangría.

In our own experience, more and more people are drinking wine and sangría in winter as well as summer.

Sangría

Here is my recipe for sangría. The quantities indicated will vary according to number of guests, the length of the party, the outside temperature, and the general thirst of those present. However, the following is what we used for a recent cocktail party of about fifty, which ran for between three and four hours. Of those present, it turned out that about three-quarters opted for sangría.

In addition to the following, other sliced fruits are welcome depending on availability and personal preferences. Thus in various of my sangrías I have also used sliced peaches, sliced bananas, seedless grapes, strawberries, sliced apples.

2 gallons red wine (Spanish or domestic)
1 bottle Curaçao
8-ounce can frozen orange juice
2 bottles club soda
Ice (equivalent of contents of four ice trays)
6 oranges, washed and sliced in their skins
6 lemons, washed and sliced in their skins

Mix all the ingredients in any container large enough to hold them, be it a kettle, roasting pan, or whatever. Then transfer to a punch bowl for actual serving, as required.

I think you'll be surprised how many people will choose sangría (or any other "punch" you decide to make) rather than hard liquor, but you must nonetheless have sufficient mixes on hand in case the choice goes the other way. For the amount of liquor called for, you should plan on the following:

MIXES

8–10 quart-size bottles of club soda
6–8 quart-size bottles of quinine water
2 six-packs of Coca-Cola
2 six-packs of diet sodas
1–2 quart-size cans of V-8 juice
1 quart of orange juice

EQUIPMENT

1 small cutting board with 6 lemons
1 sharp knife
1 dish cocktail onions
1 bottle Tabasco sauce
1 large pitcher of water
65 pounds of ice cubes
150 plastic glasses
100 cocktail napkins
Mixing spoons
Towel (for the bartender)
Wastebasket for the "empties"

FINGER FOOD (budget)

3 packages of carrots, peeled, washed, and cut in strips
2 quart baskets of cherry tomatoes
4–6 green peppers, washed and cut in strips
1 cup coarse salt
2–4 packages of radishes, washed and trimmed
4 large packages of potato chips
3 large packages of pretzels
2 one-pound cans mixed nuts
8 cups of dip (see page 195)

This "finger food on a shoestring" ought not to cost you more than twelve to fifteen dollars. Ridiculous for a party of that size. And yet the number and variety of "nibbling dishes" placed and passed around will suffice for its purpose. If you would like to upgrade your finger food a notch or two, you may want to add one or more of the following:

1 cheese tray, with any number of your favorite cheeses, or perhaps just one large Brie. Or any one of my homemade cheeses (see pages 68, 80, 161)
1 large bowl of guacamole, surrounded by tortilla chips (see page 100)
1 large dish (or two or three smaller ones) of homemade pâté, surrounded by melba toast or crackers (see pages 138 and 145)
1 platter of assorted cold cuts, with sliced bread or crackers

Or you may want to go a degree or two further and offer tartar steak, some delicious Middle Eastern "eggplant caviar," *hummus* (also Middle Eastern), or one of any number of sour-cream dips.

Tartar Steak

Here is what you will need for your tartar steak, which should take you no more than 10 minutes to prepare.

2 pounds round steak, ground
1 medium-sized onion, minced
2 cups finely chopped fresh parsley
½ cup prepared mustard
2 egg yolks
Juice of 1 lemon
½ cup olive oil
½ cup Worcestershire sauce
Pepper and salt
Parsley sprigs

In a bowl, mix all the ingredients except parsley sprigs, shape into any attractive form, decorate with parsley, surround with rye bread, and serve.

The French, who doubtless brought this back from Lebanon, call it *caviar d'aubergine*. You will note that some recipes call for baking your eggplant in the oven, but the authentic, Middle Eastern method is to char it over an open flame, which adds a distinctly smoky flavor to the dish.

Eggplant Caviar

2-pound eggplant
1 cup olive oil
2 cloves garlic
1 onion, chopped
Juice of 1 lemon
Pepper and salt
Garnish: green pepper, onions, lemons, tomatoes

Place your eggplant directly over your gas burner (if you have an electric stove, you're out of luck; light oven and bake). When you see the skin cracking, it's time to turn it and repeat the process until all sides are shriveled and look frightful. Set aside on a plate to cool. When the eggplant is cool, strip off the charred shreds of skin, discard, and put the pulp into the blender. Add all the other ingredients except the garnish, blend to creamy consistency, and serve. When I serve this at table as an hors d'oeuvre, I crown my serving bowl with sliced green pepper, quartered onions, quartered lemons, and quartered tomatoes.

Like the eggplant caviar, I serve *hummus,* or "chickpea dip," both as a party canapé and as a first course for dinners.

Chickpea Dip

16-ounce can chickpeas
2 slices stale bread, soaked in milk
1 cup olive oil
Juice of 1 lemon
2 cloves garlic
½ cup sour cream
1 tablespoon crushed dried red pepper

Open the can of chickpeas, pour into a colander, rinse under cold water, and drain. Put all the ingredients except the dried red pepper into the blender and blend to creamy consistency. Pour into a serving bowl, top with the dried red pepper, and serve with pieces of sliced French bread, or Arabic flat bread.

There are as many sour-cream dips as there are chefs. Here are a couple, one plain and one fancy, that I like.

Plain Dip

16 ounces sour cream
2 tablespoons dill
Pepper and salt

Mix and serve, crowned with any number of crisp, raw vegetables such as: flowerets of cauliflower, strips of red or green pepper, turnip slices, zucchini slices, cherry tomatoes, celery stalks, or carrot strips.

Olivia's Dip

16 ounces sour cream
4-ounce package cream cheese
½ pound cooked shrimp, chopped
Juice of ½ lemon (or more to taste)
2 tablespoons Worcestershire sauce
1 small onion, minced
Pepper and salt

Mix and serve crowned with crackers (the rice variety lends itself well to this dip, since it is delicate).

These are only some suggestions of course; use one or more, or all if you like, depending on your allotted budget. But at the risk of being repetitious, I maintain that a six-to-eight cocktail party is not a dinner party, and the light "nibbles" on my first list are really all you need.

There is another type of cocktail party, the "from nine o'clock on" party that presumes you have already had dinner. Nonetheless, since these parties tend to go on often until the wee hours, it is customary to bring out more substantial offerings around midnight. For this, I would suggest that any variety of the above-mentioned food, plus others of your choice, are called for.

But I have also found that at these later parties, following the meat and/or cheese nibbles, some form of sweet, be it fruit or pastry, and coffee are often appreciated.

Remember, too, for these late-night parties, you're going to need a goodly supply of forks, knives, and spoons, as well as plates. Paper plates and plastic utensils are in order, unless you have a friendly neighbor or collection of neighbors who can supply you with the real item.

If your party is smaller, say fifty people or so, you can think of offering a wider variety of canapés than for the very big bash, since you do not have overwhelming numbers to contend with and can therefore broaden your culinary spectrum without going bankrupt, or without working yourself to death.

No matter what your numbers, I urge you to calculate what you can comfortably spend—beyond the basic sum you'll have to spend for liquor—and plan it from there. The point is, most people, when thinking of giving a bash, automatically assume it's going to cost them several hundred dollars. Nonsense. If you want to, you can throw any bash for a hundred for between a dollar and a dollar-fifty per person—and that includes the bartender(s). (Tip: you don't need to resort to the most expensive catering or bartending services. Very often, local colleges and universities maintain lists of students who are ready and willing to do the job.)

Last but not least, if you exceed fifty people, I urge you to rent two coat racks the day before your party.

And speaking of the day before: *all* your preparations should be completed the day before the party. That includes your liquor delivery, your food preparation, your supplies and utensils. Then you too will enjoy your party, as much as your guests will.

LEFTOVERS
(THE SQUIRREL COMPLEX)

The French are notorious for being thrifty. But thriftiness can take many forms, both positive and negative. The French, doubtless because of their incurable pleasure complex, have made a virtue of it, at least in the culinary realm. (Maybe they're so ashamed of their apparently inherent stinginess that they cover it by often producing minor miracles from nothing.) I save everything—or almost everything—and I strongly urge you to do the same: as you will see, you may be able to turn it into a soup, a soufflé, a sauce, or a casserole. In fact, I'm convinced that some of the most famous and fanciest dishes were born of the necessity to turn out epicurean feasts with only leftovers to go on.

My family views my habit of saving virtually everything—meats, vegetables, prepared salad (perhaps the most outrageous aberration of all), all kinds of bread, gravies, and soups—as yet another proof that I'm a French lunatic still suffering from the vestiges of the postwar-hunger obsession. Maybe I am. But I've always had a great deal of fun cooking with leftovers. It may simply be the challenge. Or in an age of rampant inflation, when waste seems sinful, it may be a matter of economics. But whatever the underlying reason, here, category by category, are my "leftover recipes."

BEEF

Steak: Beef is expensive, especially the better cuts that you will serve originally as steak: sirloin, porterhouse, tenderloin (fillet), and such.

Therefore, it is assumed you will buy carefully, closely calculating your needs. And yet there will nonetheless be times when you will find yourself with some leftover steak. If your eyes were considerably larger than your appetites, and you find yourself with enough left over for another steak dinner, consider yourself lucky. However, there is a slight problem: it will be somewhat difficult to serve steak rare or medium rare, since you're starting with partially cooked meat. If for your first dinner you cooked your meat very rare, you still have a fighting chance; otherwise, you'll have to do the best you can, realizing that even in the worst of all possible worlds a well-done steak is better than no steak at all (or is it?). Anyway, the whole question is to keep the damage to a minimum. This you can help by getting the rest of your dinner ready to serve, including warming the plates. It will help, too, to have the steak out at room temperature for a while before cooking; not only will it improve the flavor but it will make the chances of a cool center less likely. Then sprinkle salt in a preheated skillet and cook the steak briefly, no more than a minute or two on each side.

If you have reserved some of the meat juice from the previous serving, add it, once you have turned the steak to the second side, for extra flavor. Your steak may not be as sizzling hot as you like it, but you can still hope to have it relatively rare: better rare and warm than hot and overdone.

Another method of re-serving steak as such is as an open sandwich.

Open Steak Sandwich

Serves 4
½ stick butter
4 slices bread

Cooked steak, thinly sliced

In a skillet, melt the butter, and fry bread on both sides. Set bread on warm plates. In the same skillet, sauté the sliced steak very quickly—no more than a minute a side. (No shortening or salt is needed; the skillet is sufficiently lubricated.) Arrange steak over the fried bread and serve.

Beef Stroganoff

If you're not in the mood for two successive nights of steak with its ensuing risks, here is a dish for almost any palate. To serve four, you will need a good pound to a pound and a half of leftover steak.

Beef stroganoff is especially good served with boiled rice. If you choose this for the side dish, start cooking your rice a good 10 minutes before the stroganoff, so that the rice will be ready at the same time as the meat.

Serves 4

- ½ stick butter
- 1 onion, finely chopped
- ¼–½ pound mushrooms, washed, dried, and sliced
- ½ lemon, squeezed over mushrooms
- ¼ teaspoon nutmeg
- Pepper and salt
- Cooked steak, very thinly sliced (and pounded with a wooden mallet or rolling pin for thinner results)
- ½ cup sour cream
- ⅔ cup heavy cream

In a skillet, over a medium flame, melt the butter and brown the onion. Stir in the mushrooms with lemon juice, nutmeg, pepper and salt, reduce flame to low, and cook for 5 minutes. Add the meat, cook for another 3 minutes, then stir in the creams and let simmer for 2 more minutes. Pour onto a warm platter and serve.

Steak à la Chinoise: If the 10 minutes it takes for stroganoffing your leftover steak is still more time than you have available, here are several Chinese-inspired dishes I have used when I hardly had any time at all. (None will take much over 5 minutes.) These dishes will all be served with a side dish of boiled rice, which should be started about 15 minutes before you cook any of the following.

Snow Pea Steak

Serves 4

- 1–2 cups cooked steak, thinly sliced
- 2 tablespoons soy sauce
- 1 teaspoon sugar
- 1 teaspoon wine (red or white)
- 1 tablespoon cornstarch
- 2 tablespoons water
- Pepper and salt
- 1 pound snow peas (or young peas in pods)
- 4 tablespoons cooking oil

When you arrive home, or roughly half an hour before dinner time, mix meat, soy sauce, sugar, wine, cornstarch, water, and pepper and salt to taste (mix well so that the meat will marinate). Set the table, and start your rice cooking. Wash the peas. When the rice is almost cooked, heat the oil in a skillet, add the peas, and cook for 3 minutes.

Pour the full contents of the bowl into the skillet, stir for a minute or 2, then serve.

Pepper Steak

Serves 4

- 4 tablespoons cooking oil
- 1–1½ cups cooked steak, cut into very thin strips
- 3 green peppers, cut into ½-inch strips
- 1 scallion, chopped
- 1 clove garlic, minced
- ½ teaspoon each pepper and salt
- 2 tablespoons soy sauce
- 1 cup stock or water
- 2 tablespoons cornstarch

Begin cooking rice to serve with meal. In a skillet, heat the oil. Brown the meat for one minute, add peppers, scallion, garlic, pepper and salt. Stir. Reduce flame. Cover, and simmer for 10 minutes. In a cup, blend the soy sauce, water or stock, and cornstarch, then pour into skillet. Stir for 2 minutes and serve.

Steak and Cucumbers, in Soy and Lemon Sauce

Serves 4

- 1½–2 cups cooked steak, cut into very thin slices
- ¾ cup cooking oil
- 2 tablespoons cornstarch
- Pepper and salt
- Juice of ½ lemon
- 1 onion, finely chopped
- ½ cup stock or water
- 3 cucumbers, peeled and sliced

About half an hour before dinner, place the meat in a bowl together with ½ cup of the oil, cornstarch, pepper, salt, and lemon juice. Begin cooking rice to accompany the meal. Heat the remaining oil in a skillet, sauté the onion until it is light brown, add the meat (reserve the marinade), and stir for 2 minutes. Pour the marinade in, add the stock or water and cucumbers, stir for an additional 5 minutes over a low flame, and serve.

Steak and Kidney Pie

If the original steak was not all that tender to start with, or if the leftover piece is not the best part of the steak, you might want to try this English recipe—but only if you like kidneys. This dish can be made well ahead of time. If you're going to serve it a day after you make it, refrigerate and heat up in the oven about half an hour at 350°. If you want to keep it for several days, it can be frozen. You can take it straight from the freezer to the oven and bake it for 45 minutes. (NOTE: If you freeze this or any other dish, and plan to bake it without thawing, do not use Pyrex, but ceramic or tin. The sudden change in temperature from freezer to oven can, and usually does, shatter Pyrex.)

The following standard English recipe calls for a deep-dish filling covered with what amounts to a biscuit dough. However, I have sometimes Frenchified it by using a regular pie crust both to line the deep dish and to cover the filling. I prefer it, and it makes the pie stretch even further.

First make the filling:

Serves 5–6

2 lamb (or beef, or pork) kidneys	1 tablespoon Worcestershire sauce
2 tablespoons butter	Pepper and salt
1 medium-sized onion, sliced	1 tablespoon flour
1 (or more) cups cooked cubed beef	1 cup boiling water

Wash the kidneys under cold, running water. With a sharp knife peel off the skin that covers them, then slice kidneys in half. Discard all fat. Rinse and cube. (NOTE: This cleansing process is an imperative step. I personally take one additional step, which consists of immersing the kidneys for whatever time I have available—from half an hour to a full day—in a bowl of cold water to which has been added 3 tablespoons of vinegar.) Pat dry with a paper towel.

In a skillet, melt the butter and sauté the onion until golden. Add beef and kidneys, reduce flame, and stir for 3 to 5 minutes. Add Worcestershire sauce and pepper and salt to taste. In a cup, blend flour and water and pour into skillet, stirring for an additional 2 minutes, until mixture thickens. Transfer contents of skillet into buttered ovenproof dish, then make your dough:

2 cups flour	⅔ cup milk
1½ teaspoons baking powder	1 teaspoon salt
2 tablespoons butter	

In a bowl, mix all the ingredients, working them together lightly with the tips of your fingers until properly blended into an elastic dough (this should take only 3 to 4 minutes). Roll dough onto a floured board to roughly the dimension of your dish. Place over the filling, and pat gently so the dough is flush against the meat mixture. Prick with a fork, making tiny vents for the steam to escape through. Bake in 450° oven for 12 to 15 minutes. Serve.

NOTE: A mixed green salad is recommended as the only side dish you will need.

Cold Steak

People sometimes forget, perhaps because it's so obvious, that leftover steak can be re-served cold. It makes an excellent meat platter for a lunch, or a summer dinner.

Cooked steak, sliced thinly
1 bunch watercress, washed and dried

1 hard-boiled egg, sliced
Pepper and salt

Since the meat has been refrigerated since its original incarnation, make sure you leave it out for at least half an hour before serving; the steak will then regain its full flavor. On a bed of watercress, arrange the meat slices. Decorate with egg. Over the platter, grind fresh pepper. Salt to taste.

As a side dish, I suggest a cold vegetable, such as broccoli salad in a vinaigrette sauce, green bean salad, or sliced tomatoes with basil. Red cabbage shredded and served in vinaigrette is also good and crunchy with cold meats.

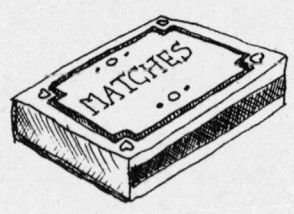

Roast Beef: The problems of re-serving roast beef are roughly the same as those that apply to steak. By slicing your remaining roast beef, you can use it as the basis for all the preceding leftover steak recipes. But in its original cooking, roast beef creates generous and distinctive pan juices which should be put to good use. One of the best, and certainly easiest, re-servings of roast beef is:

Sliced Roast Beef

Pan juices   Roast beef, thinly sliced

In a skillet, heat the pan juices over a low flame for a minute or so. Add the meat, cook for no more than 2 to 3 minutes, then serve immediately.

NOTE: Don't bother turning your slices, since the immersion in the pan juices will do the job.

Sliced and Baked Roast Beef

Pan juices   Roast beef, thinly sliced

Preheat your oven to 350–375°. Pour pan juices into a casserole dish, add meat, and bake for 10 minutes. For those who insist on rare roast beef, this dish is not recommended. Even the preceding recipe is borderline, but can pass in a pinch.

Cold Roast Beef Served with (Homemade) Mayonnaise

In France, *rosbif froid mayonnaise* features frequently on charcutier and buffet tables in restaurants. It's a late-night favorite available to theater- or party-goers even if the kitchen is closed.

Serves 4–6
Lettuce leaves   1–2 cups homemade mayonnaise
Roast beef, thinly sliced   (see page 46)

Here I would like to stress again, for those who still may be intimidated by the thought of making their own mayonnaise, that it is really very easy and eminently well worth the (small) effort (see page 46).

On a bed of lettuce leaves place the meat slices, decorating as you wish with dabs or mounds of mayonnaise. Serve.

An elegant side dish I recommend for this is raw tomatoes stuffed with *macedoine de légumes* (cooked mixed vegetables served cold and combined with mayonnaise).

Raw Tomatoes with Cooked Mixed Vegetables Served Cold

Serves 4–6
6 medium-sized tomatoes
1-pound can mixed vegetables
½ cup mayonnaise

Wash the tomatoes, cut off the tops, scoop out pulp, and reserve for a future leftover. Open can, wash the vegetables in colander under cold, running water, and drain. In a bowl, mix the vegetables well with mayonnaise, fill the hollowed-out tomatoes, and serve.

Another lovely way of serving cold roast beef is as *boeuf en aspic*—beef in meat jelly.

Beef in Meat Jelly

Serves 4–6
3 carrots, peeled and sliced
1 cup water
1 teaspoon thyme
1 clove
1 bay leaf
Pepper and salt
Roast beef, thinly sliced
2 scallions, finely minced

½ jigger brandy
1 envelope gelatin
1 cup white wine or sherry
Juice of ½ lemon
1 teaspoon tarragon
Juice of the roast (if any)
4 parsley sprigs
1 can boiled onions, drained

In a saucepan, cook the carrots with the water, thyme, clove, bay leaf, pepper, and salt for 15 minutes, covered. Drain the carrots. Place the meat slices evenly on a serving platter. Arrange the carrots decoratively on top of or around the meat. Sprinkle the scallions over the meat and carrots. In a bowl, mix the brandy and gelatin. In a saucepan, bring the wine to a boil and pour over the gelatin, then add the lemon juice, tarragon, and roast juices. Season to taste. Chill for half an hour, by which time it should have begun to thicken but can still be poured to cover the meat and carrots. Refrigerate. Decorate with parsley and onions, and serve.

Another cold variation, especially useful when you have only a smattering of roast beef left over, is *salade de boeuf à la russe*—Russian beef salad. This is my mother's recipe.

Russian Beef Salad

Serves 4–6

Roast beef, diced
1 can mixed vegetables, rinsed and drained
1–2 dill pickles, cubed
1 onion, finely chopped
1 apple, cored, peeled, and cubed
1 large pickled herring (or two small), diced
3 tablespoons hot mustard
1 cup sour cream
1 tablespoon vinegar
1 teaspoon sugar
Pepper and salt
2 hard-boiled eggs, quartered
8-ounce can beets, drained and diced
1 teaspoon dill

Mix all the ingredients, with the exception of one of the eggs, half the beets, and the dill, in a salad bowl. Toss until thoroughly mixed. Decorate with the remaining egg and beets. Sprinkle with dill. Serve. Delicious with dark pumpernickel bread and butter.

If you have even less meat left over than you require for Russian beef salad, which means practically none, think chef's salad, stretching the roast beef with ingredients as follows.

A Sort of Chef's Salad

Serves 4–6

Roast beef, cut in thin strips
½ cup ham or bologna, cut in thin strips
½ cup diced Swiss or American cheese
2 hard-boiled eggs, quartered
½ Spanish onion, grated
1 small iceberg lettuce, shredded
1 handful spinach leaves, thoroughly washed and drained, then chopped
1 teaspoon prepared mustard
⅓ cup vinegar
1 cup oil
Pepper and salt

Mix and toss all the ingredients in a salad bowl and serve. Excellent for lunch, or for picnics.

You can serve your leftover beef in various hot guises. Needless to say, all of the following can also be made from scratch.

Here's one so elegant and so disguised no one will ever suspect it came from a leftover, if indeed that is the source of the meat. Despite its long and impressive-sounding name, it is still an easy dish to make: *paupiettes de boeuf braisées, à la crème et au porto.*

Rolled Stuffed Beef with Cream and Port Wine

Serves 4–6

½ cup mushrooms, washed and finely chopped
1½ sticks butter
1 onion, minced
1 cup finely chopped parsley
½ cup green olives, finely chopped
Juice of ½ lemon
2½-ounce can deviled ham
6 or more thin slices roast beef
¼ cup cooking oil
1½ cups port wine (or sherry)
1 pint heavy cream

In a skillet, sauté the mushrooms in half a stick of butter for 5 minutes. Add onion, and stir for another 5 minutes until golden. Transfer to a bowl and add parsley, olives, lemon juice, and deviled ham. Mix with a fork. Take a spoonful of this filling and place on each slice of meat. Roll and close with a poultry pin (or tie with a string). In a skillet, heat the remaining butter and the cooking oil. Place the *paupiettes*—the rolled meat slices—and brown on all sides over a medium flame. Add the port and cover. Reduce flame to low and cook for 15 minutes. Add the cream and stir for 2 minutes. Serve.

Paupiettes are good with boiled rice, or mashed potatoes, whichever you prefer.

If you have as much as 4 to 6 good slices of roast beef left over, here's a relatively rich but savory dish I've tried with good results: *côte de boeuf gratinée.* If you're starting from scratch here, get a couple of ribs of beef, at least half an inch thick.

Casserole of Beef Gratin

Serves 4–6

½ cup mushrooms, washed, dried, and minced
1 hard-boiled egg, mashed
1 clove garlic, minced
½ cup finely chopped parsley
¼ teaspoon thyme
8–10 slices bacon
1 tablespoon olive oil
Pepper and salt
1 large onion, quartered
2 bay leaves
4–6 thick slices cooked beef
1 cup stock
⅓ cup red wine
⅔ cup bread crumbs
1 cup grated Swiss cheese
2 tablespoons butter

In a bowl, combine the mushrooms, egg, garlic, parsley, thyme, one slice of bacon finely chopped, oil, and pepper and salt to taste. Line an ovenproof dish with three bacon slices, then cover with beef slices. Arrange onion and bay leaves around slices of meat. Spread the contents of the bowl over the slices of meat. Cover with the remaining bacon slices. Mix stock and wine, and pour into the dish. Mix bread crumbs and cheese, then cover the bacon slices, dot with butter, cover with lid (or foil), and bake at 350° for 45 minutes. Remove lid and continue baking for another 10 minutes, or until top is golden and crisp. Serve.

A suggested side dish is thin vermicelli with butter and chopped parsley.

It may seem sacrilegious, but there are a number of classic dishes that can be concocted from your leftover roast beef if only you are prepared to grind it. For example, there is: *galettes de boeuf frites aux fonds d'artichauts.*

Beef Croquettes with Artichoke Hearts

Serves 4

4 artichokes	1 cup bread crumbs
⅔ stick butter	Pepper and salt
1 onion, finely chopped	1 egg white, lightly beaten
1–1½ cups ground cooked beef	2 tablespoons cooking oil
1 whole egg	½ cup finely chopped parsley

Cook the artichokes in boiling water for 30 minutes.

In a skillet, melt a tablespoon of the butter and sauté the onion until golden. In a bowl, mix meat, whole egg, onion, half the bread crumbs, and pepper and salt to taste. Shape into round or cone-shaped patties, and dip them into the egg white, then into the remaining bread crumbs.

In a skillet, melt the remaining butter and the oil, and fry the croquettes until they are golden brown. Remove them to a warm serving platter. By now your artichokes should be ready. Strip them of their leaves, reserving for later use. Remove the choke (or thistle), and discard. In the same butter you've used to fry the croquettes, sauté the artichoke hearts for a minute or two. Garnish the croquette platter with the artichoke hearts, sprinkle with parsley and serve.

NOTE: In many recipes that call for artichoke hearts, the presumption is that the canned variety will be used. I regret to say that I do not so presume: please take the trouble to cook your own artichokes rather than resorting to the canned equivalent. It will be well worth your culinary while, in taste, texture, and even expense if the season is right.

Let's suppose now the "leftover" worst, that is that in probing the lower depths of your refrigerator you come across two or three dried-out, tired-looking pieces of roast beef from some prior festive occasion. Tired maybe, but still edible. But what can you do with them? Think crêpes: more specifically, *crêpes farcies à la viande.*

French Pancakes with Meat Filling

Crêpes—French pancakes—are a source of endless culinary possibilities, one of the most creative and seductive methods the French cook has contrived to present a seemingly endless variety of fillings—many of which derive from leftovers. (For the batter and way to make crêpes, see page 76.) For this recipe, make 8 to 10 crêpes, and set aside.

Serves 6–8

- 1 tablespoon cooking oil
- 1 small onion, finely chopped
- 1 cup ground roast beef
- 1 tablespoon tarragon
- ½ cup finely chopped parsley
- 2 hard-boiled eggs, mashed
- Pepper and salt
- ½ cup grated Swiss cheese
- ½ stick butter
- Bread crumbs (optional)

In a skillet, heat the oil and sauté the onion until golden brown. Combine in a bowl with beef, tarragon, parsley, eggs, pepper, and salt. Fill each crêpe with 1½ tablespoons of the mixture. Roll and set the crêpes in a casserole dish, side by side. Sprinkle cheese evenly over the crêpes. Dot with butter. Bake at 350° for 15–20 minutes, then serve.

Here is another variation on the same theme. Proceed to make your crêpes and filling as above. Here, however, instead of rolling the individual crêpes and placing them side by side in the casserole dish, the ingenious plan is to make them into a "cake." To do this, lay a crêpe flat on the bottom of your casserole dish, brush with melted butter (or pour a light film of butter over the crêpe), spread the meat mixture, then alternate crêpe and meat mixture until you top the entire "cake" with a crêpe. Over the top pour the remaining butter. Sprinkle with cheese and bread crumbs, and bake at 350° for 20 minutes. To serve, cut in the manner of any cake.

NOTE: You can add a Russian touch to this dish by serving in a bowl a cup or so of sour cream mixed with a tablespoon of dill, which each person can dot in whatever quantity desired on top of the "cake."

Another solution for your leftover roast beef is to turn it into a beef stew. Normally, of course, beef stew is made from lesser, cheaper cuts of beef, and for this reason people often look down their noses at stew. Don't: a good stew has its rightful place in any cook's repertory. And if you choose to call it *boeuf bourguignon* rather than stew you'll immediately eliminate the opprobrium. (*Boeuf bourguignon* is the proper title, despite what you see on most menus in America, or in most cookbooks, which insist on calling it *boeuf bourguignonne*. "Boeuf" being masculine, it has to be "bourguignon." Or it can be called *boeuf à la bourguignonne*.) If, therefore, you have four or more slices of leftover roast beef whose condition is judged somewhat less than presentable for re-serving in its original guise, try this:

Boeuf Bourguignon

Serves 4

2 tablespoons bacon fat
2 slices bacon, cut up
3–4 slices cooked beef, cubed
3 onions, coarsely chopped
1 tablespoon flour
1½ cups red wine
½ teaspoon thyme
½ teaspoon tarragon
Pepper and salt
¼ pound mushrooms, washed and dried
Juice of 1 lemon
½ cup finely chopped parsley

The proportions of the meat, mushrooms, and wine can easily be varied according to what you have on hand without this dish suffering any loss.

In a Dutch oven, heat the bacon fat, cook the bacon until transparent, add the meat, reduce flame, and brown the pieces on all sides. Add onions and cook until they become transparent. Sprinkle in flour, stir in the wine, add thyme, tarragon, pepper, and salt. Cover. Let simmer over low flame for an hour. Needless to say, you don't need to stay glued to your stove during that hour. You should, however, check the Dutch oven once or twice to make sure nothing is burning or that too much of the liquid has not evaporated. If it has, add a little water or wine, as much as half a cup, and continue simmering.

Meanwhile slice the mushrooms, and squeeze the lemon juice generously over them to keep them white. Add them to the stew 15 minutes before the end of the hour's cooking time.

Just prior to serving, add your parsley.

NOTE: If you're starting your Burgundy-style beef from scratch rather than from leftovers, use bottom round, rump, or even chuck. Allow about a pound for every four people to be served.

Beef Stew: As there are second-generation immigrants, second-generation computers, and so on, so are there second-generation leftovers. Take, for example, the Burgundy-style beef you've just made, or any other beef stew: what do you do with leftovers of leftovers, with, for example, a cup or two of leftover stew? You can do several things. For one, any soup will benefit mightily from the addition of a cup or two of stew. In Austria and Hungary, where stew parades as goulash, one of the most common soups is goulash soup, which very often—and probably originally—comes from leftover goulash.

Goulash Soup

Serves 4

- 2 onions, finely chopped
- 1 tablespoon bacon fat
- 2 teaspoons paprika
- 1 tablespoon flour
- 1 teaspoon caraway seeds
- ½ cup tomato paste
- 1 quart water
- 1 cup goulash or stew
- 3 cooked potatoes, cubed

Sauté the onions in bacon fat until they turn light brown. Add the paprika, flour, caraway seeds, tomato paste, water, and goulash or stew. Stir, add the potatoes, and let simmer for about 10 minutes. Serve.

As hearty as it is tasty, this "peasant" dish makes a meal in itself.

Any omelet will benefit from the addition of some leftover stew: it will turn plain omelet into *omelette à la viande*—meat omelet—in no time at all.

Meat Omelet

Serves 4

1 cup beef stew (or other kind of meat stew)
2 tablespoons milk
4 eggs
½ stick butter

Heat the stew in a saucepan for 5 minutes or so prior to cooking the omelet. Add a teaspoon or two of water if necessary to keep the stew from sticking to the saucepan.

Mix the milk and the eggs. In a 9-inch skillet, over a low flame, melt the butter, then cook the egg-milk mixture, lifting the edges gently to let as much of the liquid cook as possible. When it is firm, but still "wet" on top, fill the center with the stew. Turn off the flame, fold the omelet in half, and slide it off onto a warm serving platter.

Pot-au-feu: This boiled meat-and-vegetable dish (see page 152) is just as good reheated as it was the first time around. Nonetheless, if you don't want to serve it again in the same form, here are several sauces you can use, each of which will change the character.

Cold Pot-au-Feu Sauce Rémoulade

Remove the meat and vegetables from the pot-au-feu broth. Slice, and arrange neatly on a serving platter, with the meat in the center and the vegetables forming a crown. Now make the following sauce:

Makes 2 cups

1½ cups homemade mayonnaise (see page 46)
2 tablespoons hot mustard
Juice of ½ lemon
2 pickles, finely chopped
1 teaspoon tarragon
1 teaspoon chervil
Pepper and salt to taste

Mix all the ingredients together in a bowl. Pour generously over the meat. Dot the vegetables with same. Put the remaining *rémoulade* sauce in a gravy bowl and serve on the side.

Cold Pot-au-Feu Sauce Ravigote

The same dish can be varied by serving with a *ravigote* sauce:

(The Squirrel Complex)

Makes 1½ cups
- 2 shallots, finely chopped
- 1 tablespoon capers, finely chopped
- 1 onion, finely chopped
- ⅓ cup dry, white wine
- ½ cup finely chopped parsley
- 1 teaspoon anchovy paste
- Juice of ½ lemon
- 1 hard-boiled egg, mashed
- 1 cup mayonnaise (see page 46)

In a saucepan, cook the shallots, capers, onion, and wine for 12 minutes over a low flame. Let cool for a few minutes, then pour into a bowl. Mix with the remaining ingredients. Dress the meat and dot the vegetables as in the preceding recipe. Serve the balance in a gravy bowl.

Cold Pot-au-Feu Sauce Aïoli

This zesty garlic-mayonnaise sauce is used in a wide variety of southern French dishes. Southern Frenchmen will go to almost any lengths to serve garlic in one form or another: aïoli is one of the better excuses.

Makes 1½ cups
- 1 egg yolk
- 1 cup (or slightly more) olive oil
- 1 whole egg
- 6 cloves garlic
- Juice of 1 lemon
- 2 slices bread
- Pepper and salt

Put egg yolk into blender, then trickle in half the oil. Blend for a few seconds, until of creamy consistency. Add the whole egg, garlic, lemon juice, bread, pepper, and salt. Blend for less than a minute, at high speed, trickling in remaining oil. (NOTE: If your sauce turns out too thick—if it's butter consistency, it's too thick—add 1 teaspoon of water and stir.)

If you don't have a blender, you can do the same with a mixer, which will take you more or less 8 to 10 minutes. If you don't have a mixer, you can still make aïoli sauce with a whisk, or fork, in a mixing bowl. It will take a little longer, perhaps up to 20 minutes.

Pour sauce over meat, dot vegetables, and serve remainder in a sauce boat.

Pot-au-Feu with Watercress Sauce

If you like the taste of watercress, I highly recommend this variation.

Makes 1½ cups
- ½ bunch watercress, thoroughly washed
- 1 cup homemade mayonnaise (see page 46)
- Pepper and salt

In the blender, purée the watercress. Pour out into a bowl and mix with the mayonnaise. Add pepper and salt to taste. Pour sauce over meat, dot vegetables, and serve remainder in a sauce boat.

In cooking, presentation is always important, and here's a way you can turn your leftover pot-au-feu meat into a dish as tasty as it is elegant. The French call it *gâteau de boeuf haché,* which translates roughly as:

Ground Boiled Beef Pie

Serves 4–5
- 1 cup (or more) ground boiled beef
- 2 slices bread, soaked in water
- 1 onion, minced
- 1 tablespoon oil
- 1 slice ham (optional)
- 3 slices bacon, cut in small pieces
- 1 egg
- ½ cup finely chopped parsley
- 1 tablespoon brandy
- 1 teaspoon thyme
- Pepper and salt
- ½ cup bread crumbs
- 1 cup green olives, pitted and sliced

In a bowl, place all the ingredients except the bread crumbs and half the olives. Mix thoroughly with your fingers (the mixture is too thick for the mixer). When well blended, transfer it to a buttered pie mold. Top with bread crumbs and bake for 30 minutes at 375°. Then top with remaining olives, bake for another 5 minutes, and serve, preferably with the following sauce:

Tomato and Mushroom Sauce

Makes 1½ cups
- 1 tablespoon olive oil
- 1 small onion, chopped
- ¼ pound mushrooms, washed and sliced
- 8-ounce can tomato sauce
- Pepper and salt

In a saucepan heat the oil, and sauté the onion until light brown. Stir in mushrooms, cook a few minutes, then add tomato sauce, and pepper and salt to taste. You can either pour the sauce directly over the pie, or serve on the side.

This leftover pie creation with sauce can also be served cold, as a leftover-leftover.

Boiled beef: There is one delicacy that actually has to be made from already boiled beef: it's the Russian piroshki, which are small pastries filled with meat.

Piroshki can be made in several ways, and the sizes and fillings can vary according to whim, taste, or availability of leftovers. They can be deep-fried as well as baked; they can be filled not only with boiled beef but also with cabbage, or chicken. They often accompany the traditional Russian soup, borscht, but they can just as well serve as an appetizer by themselves. For large dinners they will enhance any buffet. Tailored small, they make a perfect cocktail hors d'oeuvre.

For piroshki, I generally use my cream cheese and butter dough, because it is quick and reliable.

Piroshki with Beef Filling

Serves 4–5

Dough for one 9-inch crust (see page 39)
1½ cups ground boiled beef
1 onion, finely chopped
2 hard-boiled eggs, mashed
1 tablespoon bacon fat
⅓ cup beef broth
1 teaspoon dill
Pepper and salt
1 egg yolk mixed with 2 tablespoons water

Prepare dough, then put in refrigerator to chill. In a bowl, mix all the remaining ingredients except egg and water mixture. Remove your previously prepared dough and roll out on a floured board. With a glass, cut out circles, the size depending on your intended use. Put a dab of meat, from one teaspoon to one tablespoon, on one-half of the circle of dough, fold over the second half, and seal tightly by pressing the edges with your fingers. Brush egg and water mixture over each piroshki, to glaze. Bake for 25 minutes in an oven preheated to 350°. Serve hot, or warm.

L A M B

Leg of Lamb (*gigot*): Leg of lamb, as opposed to roast beef or steak, can be eaten a second time around without any real loss of flavor. Assuming (hopefully) you've started with French-style leg of lamb—

gigot—your leftover will obviously lose some of its rareness in the reheating. But since most people, with the exception of the French, eat and enjoy leg of lamb well done, perhaps that should prove no problem. To re-serve gigot, preheat your oven to 400° and cook your leftover roast for 15 to 20 minutes in an ovenproof dish.

Cold Leg of Lamb

The texture and the flavor of lamb is such that it does not require a side sauce when served cold. Simply slice and serve. Good with it are any of the following: green bean salad; cold cauliflower salad; tomato salad with basil and feta cheese; arugula salad; potato salad.

Feta cheese, a Greek goat cheese, brings to mind another prime leftover candidate: the Middle Eastern specialty, moussaka. Keep this possibility in mind even if you have as little as three or four slices of leg of lamb left. You can stretch your lamb by adding a half pound or so of ground beef.

Rice is generally served with moussaka. Before starting to make your moussaka, put your rice on to cook, the quantity depending of course on the number of people to be served. When the rice is cooked (no Minute rice, please! There is a limit to time-saving), add butter and salt and pepper to taste. Top with parsley and, to obtain the "Greek" touch, add half a cup of pine nuts (pignolia).

Moussaka I

Serves 5–6

- 1/3 cup olive oil
- 1 large eggplant, peeled and cubed
- 1 onion, finely chopped
- 1 teaspoon thyme
- 1 clove garlic, minced
- 1/2–1 pound cooked ground lamb
- 1/4–1/2 pound ground beef (optional)
- 1 teaspoon mint leaves, crushed
- Salt and pepper
- 1 1/2 cups white cream sauce (see page 46)

In a skillet, heat the oil over a low flame. Stir in the eggplant until it turns light brown. Add the onion, and stir until also light brown. Add thyme and garlic. With a slotted spoon, remove and transfer to a casserole dish. In the same skillet, sauté the meat for about 3 minutes. Add mint and salt and pepper to taste. Spread meat layer over the eggplant-onion mixture, then pour cream sauce over to cover the top. Bake in the oven for 18 to 20 minutes at 350°.

NOTE: If you have more than 2 cups of cooked lamb, adjust your other ingredients accordingly and make several alternate layers. This increased quantity does not affect the cooking time.

Moussaka II

This variation of moussaka will taste virtually the same as the preceding one, but is more decorative and festive in its presentation. Here you do not discard the skin of the eggplant but use it to line the charlotte mold in which the moussaka will be cooked. When it's unmolded onto a serving platter, you have a satiny-purple, cakelike dish.

Serves 6–8

- 2 eggplants
- 4 tablespoons olive oil
- 2 onions, finely chopped
- 1 clove garlic, minced
- 2 cups cooked leg of lamb
- ½ pound ground beef (optional)
- 3 eggs
- 2 cups stale bread
- 1 teaspoon thyme
- 1 teaspoon oregano
- Pepper and salt
- Parsley and tomatoes

Wash and halve the eggplants lengthwise. Place them face down in a baking dish containing an inch and a half of water. Bake for 30 minutes at 375°. Remove eggplants from oven, and scoop out pulp, being careful not to tear the skin. Butter a 1–2-quart charlotte mold (or any ovenproof dish; the charlotte dish will simply give a more decorative look to it) and line with eggplant skins, overlapping edges of mold. (You may have to make incisions in the skin to make it fit the mold.) In a skillet, heat the oil, sauté the onion until light brown, add garlic and eggplant pulp, and cook for 5 minutes. Transfer the contents to a mixing bowl and mix with lamb meat (or lamb and beef combined), eggs, bread, thyme, oregano, pepper, and salt. Combine, kneading with your fingers until well blended. Spoon mixture into mold. Fold the eggplant skins over the mixture, then cover with a double thickness of foil.

Place the mold in a roasting pan containing an inch or so of water, and bake for an hour at 350°. Unmold onto a warm serving platter, and garnish with small bouquets of parsley and tomato "roses" (to

make a tomato rose, peel the tomato with a sharp knife or potato peeler—in a spiral motion).

Again, serve with Greek-style rice as in preceding recipe.

NOTE: Moussaka can be prepared in advance and frozen. If possible, thaw in the morning for use that evening. But you can take it directly from the freezer to the oven, if you have cooked it originally in a ceramic or metal mold. Remember, however, that if you have cooked it in a Pyrex dish, do *not* transfer directly: Pyrex can literally "explode" when subjected to sudden sharp changes of temperature.

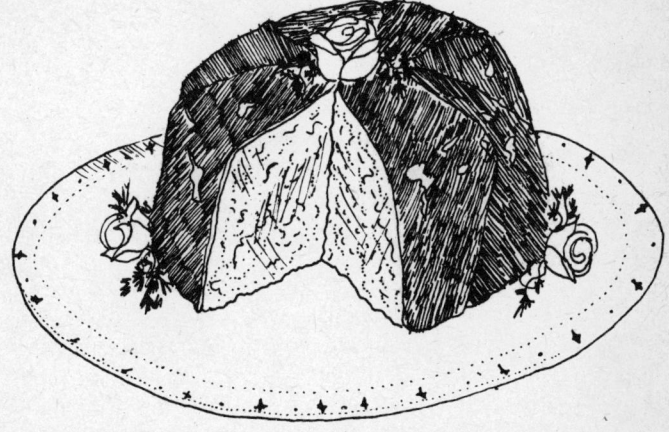

This dish gains added savor if served with yogurt sauce—which can also be served to good advantage with little lamb pies.

Yogurt Sauce

Makes 1 cup sauce
1 cup plain yogurt
1 teaspoon mint leaves
Juice of ½ lemon
½ clove garlic, squeezed
Pepper and salt

In a bowl, mix well all the ingredients. You can either pour the yogurt sauce directly over the pies before serving, or serve it on the side.

Lamb is the staple meat in most Middle Eastern countries. Therefore, not surprisingly, a number of leftover lamb dishes derive from that area. As festive and fun as moussaka are:

Little Lamb Pies

The dough generally used for this is a yeast dough, similar to pizza pie crust. I prefer my own puff paste, or cream cheese and butter dough.

Serves 6

- Dough for one 9-inch pie crust (see page 39)
- 1 cup onion, finely chopped
- 1 package pine nuts or ½ cup
- 2 cups ground lamb
- 1 tomato, chopped
- 1 green pepper, chopped
- 1 cup finely chopped parsley
- Juice of ½ lemon
- 2 tablespoons wine vinegar
- 1 tablespoon tomato paste
- Pepper and salt

Prepare dough. In a bowl, mix all the remaining ingredients, kneading with your fingers until you have a smooth paste. Roll out your dough onto a floured board, until dough is about ⅛ to ¼ inch thick. Line several small tart molds with the dough, and fill as you would for any pie. Put in the oven and bake for 30 minutes at 350°.

NOTE: If you do not have tart molds, you can use cupcake molds, or you can cut out circles of dough, using a glass, and place a mound of filling on the center of each, leaving a rim of dough to prevent spilling. Place on cookie sheet, and bake as above.

Still in the Middle East, if you have a fair amount of leftover leg of lamb—at least a pound or more—try *ragoût d'agneau à l'orientale*, which translates as:

Lamb Stew Middle Eastern Style

Serves 4–5

- ⅓ cup olive oil
- 2 tablespoons butter
- 4 onions, quartered
- 1 small eggplant, unpeeled and cubed
- 2 tomatoes, washed and quartered
- 1 clove garlic, minced
- 1 green pepper, diced
- 1 pound (or more) cooked lamb, cubed
- 2 cups beef or chicken stock
- ½ teaspoon saffron
- ½ teaspoon thyme
- Pepper and salt

This dish, like many Middle Eastern dishes, is served with rice as a side dish. Therefore, I recommend that before you proceed with the preparation of your meat you start cooking your rice. To add flavor to your rice, chop finely four scallions and add to the rice when cooked.

In a skillet, heat the oil and butter. Sauté the onions until light brown, add the eggplant, and cook over a medium flame until the eggplant pieces become transparent (about 10 minutes). Now add tomatoes, garlic, green pepper, and meat. Transfer to ovenproof dish and add stock, saffron, thyme, pepper, and salt. Cook in the oven for 40 minutes at 350°.

Yogurt sauce (see page 219) is also highly recommended as an accompaniment to this lamb stew.

If you're a turnip lover, as I am, try *mouton aux navets:*

Lamb with Turnips

Serves 4
1½ sticks butter
2 pounds turnips, peeled, quartered, washed, and rolled in sugar
1-pound (or more) piece of cooked lamb
¼ cup brandy
1–2 cups beef broth
Pepper and salt

In a skillet, heat the butter; sauté the turnips over low flame for 8 to 10 minutes, until they are golden brown on the outside and soft inside. Put your piece of meat in a casserole dish. Heat brandy in a saucepan, ignite, and pour over the meat. Add broth to the casserole dish. Season to taste. Place turnips around the roast. Cook in the oven for 35 minutes at 350°. Serve.

Although originally it applied to game, *salmis* is the culinary term in French for any meat cooked and served in pieces, generally in some kind of spicy sauce. You can make the gastronomic delight, *salmis d'agneau, sauce piquante,* with only half a dozen slices of leftover lamb. Here again, start cooking your rice side dish first.

Lamb in a Spicy Sauce

Serves 6

- 2 tablespoons butter
- 3 shallots, finely chopped
- 1 clove garlic, minced
- 2 tablespoons flour
- 2 tablespoons vinegar
- ½ cup white wine
- 1 cup beef broth
- Salt and pepper to taste
- 5–6 pieces cooked lamb, in 2-inch cubes
- 3 sour pickles, minced
- ½ cup finely chopped parsley

In a skillet, melt the butter. Sauté the shallots and garlic until golden brown. Add the flour, vinegar, wine, and broth. Season to taste. Stir until mixture thickens. Place lamb pieces in a casserole dish. Cover with the sauce, place in the oven, and bake for 25 minutes, at 350°, then sprinkle pickles and parsley over the top. Return to the oven and cook for another 5 minutes. Serve.

Agneau aux citrons, noix et oignons verts probably takes longer to say than to prepare. There are certain ingredients which might seem disparate at first glance but which, when married, add to each other's flavor or special taste.

Lamb in Lemon Sauce with Scallions and Walnuts

Serves 4

- ⅓ cup olive oil
- 2 cups cooked cubed lamb
- 1 onion, sliced
- ½ lemon, sliced
- 1 bunch scallions, washed and cut into 1-inch pieces
- ½ cup walnuts
- Pepper and salt
- 1 cup water
- 2 egg yolks
- Juice of 1 lemon
- ½ cup heavy cream

In a Dutch oven, heat the olive oil, and sauté the meat for 5 minutes. Add onion, lemon slices, scallions, walnuts, and pepper and salt to taste. Add water, cover, and cook over a low flame for 35 minutes. Uncover. Mix egg yolks, lemon juice, and cream in a bowl, and pour into Dutch oven. Stir and serve.

To make the lamb in lemon sauce especially festive, try serving it with *quenelles de farine*—plain dumplings.

Dumplings

Serves 4–5
- 2 quarts water
- 2 cups flour
- 2 teaspoons baking powder
- ½ cup milk
- ½ teaspoon sugar
- ½ teaspoon salt
- ½ cup finely chopped parsley

Place water in a kettle to boil. In a bowl, mix all the remaining ingredients to form a smooth dough. This should take no more than 5 minutes. With your hands, form little balls and drop them in boiling water. Let them rise to the surface, reduce flame, and let simmer for 10 to 12 minutes. Remove with a slotted spoon and place either on a serving platter or, if you are not ready for dinner, directly on top of the simmering lamb.

Another fun dish using lamb leftovers is *boulettes surprise*—surprise lamb patties. I believe this dish is Russian in origin, although I've eaten it both in France and in other Mediterranean countries. The surprise is a hidden hard-boiled egg inside each patty.

Surprise Lamb Patties

Serves 4–5
- 1–2 cups cooked ground lamb
- 1 onion, finely chopped
- ⅓ cup finely chopped parsley
- 1 cup bread crumbs
- 2 eggs
- 1 teaspoon thyme
- Pepper and salt
- 4–5 hard-boiled eggs, peeled
- ½ cup oil

In a bowl, mix lamb, onion, parsley, half the bread crumbs, one raw egg, thyme, and pepper and salt to taste. Cover each hard-boiled egg with the meat mixture to form a patty. Dip patties in the second raw egg, lightly beaten, then finally in the bread crumbs to coat. In a skillet, heat the oil. Fry patties until brown on all sides. Drain on a paper towel.

Rice is a good side dish. But even better, and more festive, is a mixture of sliced red radishes and sour cream.

Equally festive is *brioche méridionale,* which was served me for the first time in one of those tiny, unpretentious restaurants that so often come up with unexpected marvels: this one was a few miles outside Aix, which was why I baptized it "méridionale," or "southern style."

Lamb and Vegetables in Brioche

Serves 6–8

- 1 brioche dough (see page 42)
- 1/3 cup olive oil
- 2 finely chopped onions
- 2 hot Italian sausages
- 1 small eggplant, peeled and cubed
- 1 zucchini, cubed
- 1–1 1/2 cups ground lamb
- 4–5 tomatoes, peeled and halved (or a 1-pound can, drained)
- 1/2 cup bread crumbs
- 1 green pepper, diced
- 1 clove garlic, squeezed
- 1 cup finely chopped parsley
- 2 tablespoons basil
- 1 teaspoon thyme
- 1 teaspoon oregano
- Pepper and salt
- 1 egg yolk mixed with 2 tablespoons water

I assume you have on hand some brioche dough in your refrigerator, or thawed from your freezer. If not, prepare dough (see page 42).

In a skillet, heat the oil, and sauté the onions until light brown. Force the sausage meat out of its skin and add to onions, and cook over a low flame for 10 minutes. Add the eggplant and zucchini, stir, and cook for another 8 minutes. Add all remaining ingredients except egg and water mixture.

You're now ready to roll out your brioche dough. On a floured board, roll out dough to about 1/2-inch thickness. Divide it into two roughly equal rectangles. Lift one and place on a buttered cookie sheet. Using a slotted spoon (to drain excess juices) place the meat and vegetable filling on the bottom dough. Cover with second rectangle, and seal all around by pinching tightly with your fingers. Brush with the egg and water solution, to glaze. Bake for 50 minutes at 350°. Serve.

Part of the fun of cooking with leftovers is to make something out of almost nothing. And the more chic the presentation under these "leftover" circumstances, the better. If ever you find yourself with only two or three slices of leftover lamb, one way to deal with the slimness of your pickings and still dine gourmet is to serve *petits ragoûts d'agneau individuels*. For this you will need several small ramequins, that is, ovenproof casserole dishes large enough for a single serving.

Lamb Stew in Ramequins

Serves 8

2 tablespoons olive oil
1–2 cups cubed cooked leg of lamb
16-ounce can boiled onions, drained
2 cloves garlic, minced
1 teaspoon thyme
Pepper and salt
4–5 potatoes, sliced
1 carrot, sliced
1 cup red wine
16-ounce can white beans
½ cup finely chopped parsley

In a skillet, heat the oil and sauté the lamb for 2 to 3 minutes. Add the onions, and brown for 5 minutes. Add the garlic, thyme, and pepper and salt to taste. Spoon into the small casserole dishes, making sure to divide the meat and onions more or less evenly. Add potatoes and carrots, again more or less proportionately. Pour in the wine. Add any juice from the skillet, then seal each casserole dish with a piece of foil. Bake for an hour and a half at 300°. Ten minutes before the end of cooking time, divide the beans and parsley among the ramequins. Serve.

There is nothing very original about the next recipe, but since we're dealing with leftover lamb, this is one of the best and most called-for uses: curried lamb. There are of course literally dozens of recipes for curried lamb, and you may have your own favorite. In which case, move on. The following, however, is one I have used and liked, since it is quite simple and delicious.

Curried Lamb

Serves 4–5

1 clove garlic, minced
2 onions, finely chopped
2 tablespoons cooking oil
1–2 cups cubed cooked lamb
1 apple, peeled and cubed
2 cloves
1 tablespoon cumin
1 tablespoon coriander
½ teaspoon chili powder
½ teaspoon curry powder
Pepper and salt
½ cup red or white wine
1 cup finely chopped parsley
1½ cups shredded coconut
½ cup peanuts
3 slices bacon, fried and crumbled
Chutney (optional)
2 tablespoons sour cream

In a Dutch oven, sauté the garlic and half the onions in the oil until brown. Add meat, apple, cloves, cumin, coriander, chili, curry, and salt and pepper to taste. Stir in the wine. Add half the parsley. Cover and cook over a low flame for one hour. (If you choose, you may transfer the Dutch oven into the oven and cook for the same length of time at 350°. The advantage is that your curry won't burn, which is a possibility, however slight, when your Dutch oven is directly over the flame.)

While the curry is cooking, prepare your side dishes: one of coconut, one of peanuts, one of chopped parsley, one of onions, and one of fried, crumbled bacon. If you have it on hand, add a sixth bowl: chutney.

Twenty minutes before your curry is cooked, boil enough rice for your number of guests. Stir sour cream into Dutch oven. The curry can be served directly over the rice, or on the side, as preferred.

A whole stuffed cabbage has many virtues. For one thing, it is a complete meal in itself. It's extremely economical, cabbage being, still today, one of the least expensive vegetables on the market. And it's a most attractive dish to present. Although I've classed it under "lamb," it can just as well be made with beef.

Called in French *choux entier, farci*—whole stuffed cabbage—preparation of this dish requires several steps, and looks far more complicated than most of the recipes in this volume. Do not let this deter you, however: preparation time should not exceed 30 to 40 minutes, and the dish can be prepared in advance.

Whole Stuffed Cabbage

Serves 5–6

1 large green cabbage	½ cup finely chopped parsley
2 cups ground cooked lamb (or beef)	¼ teaspoon thyme
	¼ teaspoon rosemary
1½ cups cooked rice	Pepper and salt
1 clove garlic, squeezed	6 tablespoons butter
1 egg	1 onion, minced
15-ounce can tomato sauce	Chopped parsley for garnish

Wash the cabbage under running water. Trim outer or damaged leaves. In a large kettle, place 2 quarts of water and 1 teaspoon of salt. Bring water to a boil, put in cabbage, and blanch by cooking for 10 minutes. Drain. Cut off the top of the cabbage and set it aside. With a sharp knife, hollow out the inside of the cabbage, leaving a shell about an inch thick. Chop up the hollowed-out leaves and set aside.

In a bowl, mix the meat, rice, garlic, egg, half the tomato sauce, parsley, thyme, rosemary, and pepper and salt to taste. Stuff the cabbage shell with two-thirds of this meat mixture, using the remaining third to slip in between the outer leaves. Put the cabbage "cap" back on. Around the approximate equator of the cabbage, tie a string to hold it together. Place the stuffed cabbage in a buttered, ovenproof dish.

In a small skillet, heat half the butter and sauté the onion until light brown. Add the remaining tomato sauce and ½ cup of water, stir, and pour over the cabbage. Cover with foil and bake for one and a half hours at 325°. Baste every 20 to 30 minutes.

About half an hour before your stuffed cabbage is cooked, in a skillet melt the remaining butter and sauté the chopped-up cabbage leaves over a low flame until they are "blond." Season with thyme and pepper. Cover and let simmer for 25 to 30 minutes.

Remove the stuffed cabbage from the oven, cut off the string, surround with the sautéed cabbage leaves, sprinkle with parsley, and serve.

PORK

Unlike beef, but similar to lamb, pork loses nothing of its flavor or texture when served a second time in its original form. Thus roast pork, for example, can be reheated at 300–325° for half an hour and served again to full enjoyment. If your roast pork is refrigerated, it is easy to skim the fat off the gravy, and then you are ready to make any of the following variations with your *rôti de porc reservé*—leftover pork.

Leftover Roast Pork with Stewed Prunes

Serves 5–6

1–1½ pounds roast pork	8-ounce can boiled onions
1 pound stewed prunes	Pepper and salt

In an ovenproof dish place your cooked roast pork. Surround meat with the stewed prunes, including juice. Drain the onions of their liquid, and scatter among the prunes. Add salt and pepper to taste. Cook for 25 to 30 minutes in a preheated 325° oven. Serve.

Leftover Roast Pork with Cream Sauce

Serves 4

1–1½ pounds roast pork	2 tablespoons water
1 pint light cream	Pepper and salt

In an ovenproof dish place roast pork. Skim pan juices, if any, and add cream, water, and salt and pepper to taste. Cook for 25 to 30 minutes in preheated 325° oven. (If you happen to be in the kitchen during the cooking, you can baste it once or twice, but it is not essential.)

Leftover Roast Pork with Mustard Sauce

Serves 4

1–1½ pounds roast pork	Juice of ½ lemon
3 tablespoons prepared mustard	Pepper and salt
1 pint light cream	

Place meat in an ovenproof dish and skim pan juices. In a bowl, mix well the pan juices and the remaining ingredients, and pour over the roast. Cook 25 to 30 minutes in a preheated 325° oven.

Leftover Roast Pork with Sliced Apples

Serves 4

1–1½ pounds roast pork	½ teaspoon nutmeg
1 stick butter	Pepper and salt
2–3 apples, peeled, cored, and sliced	

Cook pork and skimmed pan juices in a preheated 325° oven for 25 to 30 minutes. If the liquid is scant, add a tablespoon or so of water (or white wine, if the spirit moves you). About 10 minutes before the roast is ready to serve, in a skillet melt the butter, sauté the apples, and sprinkle nutmeg and pepper and salt to taste. Add contents of the skillet to the pan juices at the time of serving.

Roast pork can also be served cold to good advantage. It makes an excellent summer meal, and is a good dish to feature among several meat platters at a buffet.

Cold Roast Pork

Slice leftover roast pork. Skim the fat off the cold pan juices, which will be jellylike. Spoon out the jelly and scatter it around the sliced meat. Decorate with sprigs of parsley, and serve, preferably with a cold salad. One of the following would make a good complement: broccoli with oil and vinegar dressing; tomato salad with oil and vinegar dressing; green and red peppers thinly sliced, served with the same dressing; green bean salad, same dressing; cucumber salad, with a sour cream and dill dressing.

Another fun way to utilize to good advantage your leftover pork is to go Chinese. For a cold pork dish as appetizer try:

Chinese Cold Pork Snacks

Serves 6–8

- 4 tablespoons cooking oil
- 1–1½ cups ground roast pork
- 1 clove garlic, minced
- ½ cup water
- 2 tablespoons sherry (or white wine)
- Pepper and salt
- 1 tablespoon cornstarch
- 2 tablespoons soy sauce
- ½ cup cooked green peas
- ½ cup almonds
- 1 head iceberg lettuce

In a skillet, heat half the oil, brown the meat and garlic for 2 minutes, then add half the water, the wine, and pepper and salt to taste. Cook over a low flame for 5 minutes. In a cup, mix the cornstarch with the soy sauce and remaining water. Pour into the skillet. Add peas, and stir until mixture becomes translucent. (Some people may wonder about the term "translucent": actually, when you add the cornstarch, even diluted, it will give the mixture a cloudy look. When the cloudiness disappears, you know your cornstarch is properly integrated and cooked.) Transfer the contents of the skillet to a serving platter.

In the same skillet, heat remaining oil and roast the almonds for about 5 minutes, stirring constantly. Grind in the blender, then sprinkle over the meat. Surround the meat mixture with lettuce leaves. Serve. Part of the fun of this dish is in the eating: take a lettuce leaf, fill with a spoonful of meat mixture, balance carefully, and eat.

If you're after a main dish rather than an appetizer, and still want to think Chinese, here are three Oriental pork recipes you might like to try:

Pork in Tangerine, Ginger, and Gin Sauce

Serves 4–5

- 1 tangerine
- 4 slices pork roast, cut into strips
- 1 cup sherry
- 2 scallions, washed and chopped small
- ½ teaspoon ginger
- ½ teaspoon soy sauce
- 1 teaspoon aniseed, crushed
- ½ teaspoon cinnamon
- 4 cloves
- 1 tablespoon cornstarch
- 2 tablespoons gin
- Salt and pepper to taste

Grate the tangerine rind, then squeeze the juice. Place both in a skillet, along with the rest of the ingredients, and cook over a low flame for 8–10 minutes. Serve.

Sweet and Sour Pork

Serves 4–6

- 2 cups cooked cubed pork
- 2 tablespoons soy sauce
- 1 egg, slightly beaten
- ½ cup cornstarch
- ½ cup cooking oil
- 2 carrots, peeled and thinly sliced
- 1 onion, finely chopped
- 1 green pepper, cut into strips
- 1 cup water
- 5 tablespoons vinegar
- ¼ cup brown sugar
- 13-ounce can crushed pineapple
- 1 tablespoon raisins
- 2 tablespoons sherry
- 2 tablespoons gin
- Pepper and salt
- ½ lemon, sliced

In a bowl combine the pork with the soy sauce and egg. Let sit for 30 minutes. Remove the meat from the bowl, and put into a brown paper bag. Pour the cornstarch into the bag. Shake (just as though you were making southern fried chicken), until the pork cubes are well coated with the cornstarch. Remove pork and reserve cornstarch.

In a skillet, heat the oil and fry the meat until it's brown and crisp. (NOTE: A tip on how to ensure it *will* be brown and crisp is to leave the meat alone for 3 or 4 minutes, without shaking the skillet or turning over with the spatula. I know the temptation is to stir because of the fear of burning. But don't: reduce your flame, allow the meat to sizzle as indicated above, and only then turn over with a spatula.) Remove meat with a slotted spoon, and drain on a paper towel.

In the same skillet, sauté the carrots, onion, and green pepper for 2 minutes. Mix the cornstarch with the water, vinegar, brown sugar, pineapple, raisins, sherry, gin, and pepper and salt to taste. Pour mixture over the vegetables. Add the lemon slices. Stir until the mixture thickens.

Now put the cooked meat back into the skillet, and stir for 2 minutes. Serve.

Chinese Pork with Water Chestnuts and Mushrooms

Serves 4

- 4 slices cooked pork
- ½ cup dry sherry or white wine
- ¼ cup soy sauce
- 2 tablespoons cooking oil
- 1 onion, sliced
- 1 green pepper, cubed
- ¼ pound fresh mushrooms, washed, dried, and sliced
- 1 small summer squash, sliced
- 8-ounce can water chestnuts, drained and sliced
- 4-ounce can pimiento, chopped
- 2 tablespoons cornstarch
- ¼ cup cold water

Place the pork slices in a bowl, and cover with the wine and soy sauce. Marinate for half an hour. Remove the meat from the bowl.

In a skillet, heat the oil and sauté the meat for 2 minutes on each side. Remove the meat. In the same skillet, sauté the onion until transparent. Add the green pepper, mushrooms, squash, and wine-soy sauce marinade. Stir for 3 minutes over a low flame. Add the water chestnuts and pimiento. Cook for another 2 minutes.

In a cup, blend the cornstarch with 1 tablespoon of the water, then pour into skillet. Add the remaining water, and cook for an additional 2 to 3 minutes. Serve.

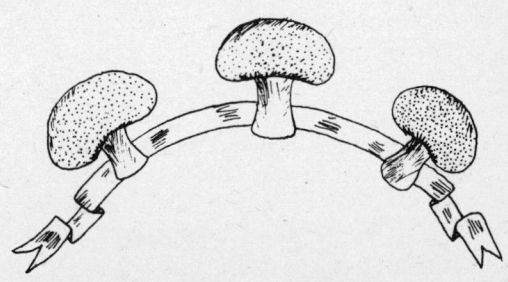

Here's an Alsatian specialty that turns leftover pork into a delicious, hearty meal, especially recommended for a cold winter's night—and for people with strong culinary constitutions: this recipe involves sauerkraut, and if that basic ingredient is not to your taste, move on. In Alsace, it's known as *porc en choucroute*.

Pork with Sauerkraut

Serves 4–5

- 1½ quarts sauerkraut
- ½ stick butter
- 6 juniper berries (optional)
- 2 cups white wine
- Pepper and salt
- 2 slices bacon (preferably thick)
- 4 frankfurters
- 3–4 slices pork roast
- 6–8 small boiled potatoes

In a colander, rinse the sauerkraut under running water. In a Dutch oven, melt the butter, and add the sauerkraut and the juniper berries if you like the taste. Stir. Pour in the wine, and season to taste. Over the sauerkraut lay the bacon slices, frankfurters, and pork. Cover, and continue cooking for 20 minutes.

At serving time, decoratively add the boiled potatoes.

Here is a recipe straight out of the French *cuisine bourgeoise*—which translates roughly, though literally, as "middle-class cooking." It reminds one forcibly of how the French middle class eats: *tranches de porc farcies aux pruneaux et aux oignons*.

Stuffed Sliced Pork

Serves 4–5

- 1–1½ pounds roast pork
- 1 cup dried prunes, minced
- 1 stick butter
- 1 onion, finely chopped
- 1 cup bread crumbs
- 1 egg yolk
- ½ cup finely chopped parsley
- Pepper and salt

I'm assuming here that you have enough leftover pork roast (hopefully boned and rolled) that you'll be able to cut fairly thick slices. The reason for this is that you'll want to make an incision in each slice for your stuffing. If, however, you don't have enough meat left over for thick slices, you can still make this dish, although for thin slices I recommend covering them with the stuffing. Or you can put stuffing between two thin slices and reconstitute the roast.

Cover the prunes with boiling water and let stand for 5 minutes. Drain.

In a skillet heat the butter and sauté the onion until it is light brown. Combine bread crumbs, prunes, onion, egg yolk, parsley, and pepper and salt to taste in a mixing bowl, using a wooden spoon or fork. Make a deep incision in your meat slices (assuming they're thick) and insert a spoonful of the stuffing in each. Arrange in an ovenproof dish, add a bit of water to keep the meat from sticking or burning, and cover with foil. Bake for 30 minutes at 350°.

HAM

Ham is a most versatile meat, used in a myriad of ways in cuisines throughout the world. There are literally hundreds of recipes from virtually every region and country calling for a handful or only a slice or two of ham. One can go on almost endlessly, therefore, on the subject of ham-as-leftover. Another virtue of ham is that it offers a dual possibility when it comes to leftovers: on the one hand, the ham itself; and on the other, the ham fat. Before baking or cooking any ham in its original incarnation, I always remove the fat and store it separately for later use. You can use ham fat in making your own sausages (if you've never done it, you should try it); for making pâté; for cooking lentils or beans, to moisten and impart flavor; for making *rillettes;* or, to take a page from the Austrian repertoire, to make that marvelously hearty dumpling called *specknödle*. This is basically Tyrolean, though it has spread throughout Austria, and even beyond: served with broth, it makes a meal in itself. Or it is sometimes served in lieu of a meat dish, generally garnished with sauerkraut.

Austrian Bacon Dumplings

Serves 4

½ cup diced ham fat
2 cups cubed stale bread
1 tablespoon bacon fat
1 medium-sized chopped onion
¼ cup milk

½ cup flour
2 tablespoons tarragon
½ cup chopped parsley
Pepper and salt
1½ quarts broth

In a skillet, cook the ham fat until it turns light brown. Remove. In the same skillet, fry the bread cubes until well toasted. Transfer to a mixing bowl. Add the tablespoon of bacon fat to the skillet and sauté the onion until it becomes light brown, then transfer to bowl and mix with the ham fat, bread, milk, flour, tarragon, parsley, pepper and salt (go easy on the salt, since the ham and bacon fat already provide a fair amount of salt to start).

Roll the mixture into balls, shaping them with your hands. Bring broth to a boil. Drop dumplings into the boiling broth, reduce flame, and let simmer for 10 to 12 minutes. Serve broth and dumplings together.

If you're in the mood for an especially abundant meal, try this variation: melt 2 tablespoons of butter in a Dutch oven, and sauté 2 minced onions until light brown. Add 2 pounds of sauerkraut, a tablespoon of paprika, and pepper and salt to taste. Cook for 45 minutes, covered, over a low flame. Transfer to a serving platter, top with the dumplings, and serve.

NOTE: If your sauerkraut tends to stick to the bottom of the Dutch oven, add a little broth or white wine to lubricate, a tablespoon at a time as required.

Ham is almost always an essential ingredient for making pâté, or terrine. Depending on what pâté you make, you will of course need several different meats. Here's one pâté I often make: illogically, the French call it *pâté de veau et jambon en croûte*. It does indeed contain veal and ham, but it also has pork and beef liver, and just why the French ignore the last two meats is anybody's guess. If you own a blender, use it to grind your meats. (NOTE: Remember to put in a little at a time; it does a better job; otherwise use a meat grinder, or even a fine-bladed knife.)

Veal and Ham Pâté in Pastry

Serves 8

Dough for two 9-inch crusts (see page 39)
2 shallots, finely chopped
2 tablespoons bacon fat
2 cups ground ham
1 slice veal, ground
1 slice beef liver, ground
1 slice pork meat, ground
2 eggs
5 slices stale bread, soaked in milk
4-ounce package cream cheese
3 tablespoons brandy
1 teaspoon thyme
1 clove garlic, minced
1 cup finely chopped parsley
Pepper and salt
2 bay leaves

For the pastry, prepare your favorite pie crust and place in refrigerator to chill. I lean toward either my puff paste dough or cream cheese and butter dough. You will need approximately the amount of dough normally required for two one-crust pies, since you have both a bottom and a top, as for an American apple pie.

In a skillet, sauté the shallots in bacon fat until they turn light brown. Then add them to the ground ham, veal, liver, and pork in a bowl with one egg, the soaked bread, cream cheese, brandy, thyme, garlic, parsley, pepper and salt, and stir until the mixture has turned into a smooth paste.

Roll the dough in a large rectangle on a floured board, then divide into roughly equal halves. Place one half in an ovenproof dish, or even on a cookie sheet. Remove the filling from the mixing bowl and place it in the center of the bottom rectangle. Top with bay leaves. Make a series of short crosses or incisions with a sharp knife in the second rectangle, to vent the steam, then lift the dough onto the pâté, to cover. Seal top and bottom rectangles by pinching the edges all around the perimeter.

In a cup, mix remaining egg with 2 tablespoons of water (the resultant mixture is called in French *la dorure,* which translates precisely as glazing but by implication also means "golden" or "gilded"). Brush the exposed dough with this glazing mixture. If you have no brush, simply use the corner of a paper napkin. Almost invariably, you will have a few scraps of excess dough. Roll them out again until they are flat, then cut into some artistic shape of your own choosing —hearts, flower petals, leaves—and place on top of the crust. Glaze your artwork.

Place the *pâté en croûte* in a preheated oven and bake for 45 minutes at 350°. Let cool.

One of the most chic ways to present this pâté is to garnish it with frosted grapes (see page 158 for directions).

Most Americans are familiar with the culinary term "mousse," as in chocolate mousse or salmon mousse. And, quite rightly, there is an aura of elegance attached to mousse dishes. Here is a gourmet dish you can make starting with only a couple of cups of leftover ham: *mousseline de jambon.* One might define any mousseline dish as a first cousin of mousse; it is somewhat lighter and also, because it uses egg whites, is related to the soufflé. My way of serving ham mousseline is with a Madeira sauce.

Ham Mousseline with Madeira Sauce

Serves 4–6

2 cups cooked ground ham
2 cups heavy cream, whipped
3 egg whites, beaten stiff
1 teaspoon paprika
Pepper and salt

In a mixing bowl gently fold together ham, whipped cream, egg whites, paprika, and pepper and salt to taste (light on the salt, because of the ham).

Butter a 1/2-quart charlotte mold and pour the mixture into it. In an oven pan large enough to hold your charlotte mold pour 1 1/2 to 2 inches of water, then set in it the filled mold. Bake for 40 minutes at 350°. When baking, your mousseline will puff slightly. Remove from the oven and let stand for 5 minutes or so before unmolding. To serve, turn the charlotte mold upside down and release onto a warm serving platter.

To make the Madeira sauce, you will need:

2 tablespoons butter
2 tablespoons flour
1 tablespoon prepared mustard
1/2 cup light cream
1/2 cup Madeira wine
Pepper and salt

Melt the butter in a saucepan, stir in the flour, and cook for a few minutes. Add gradually the mustard, cream, and wine. Stir. Season to taste.

NOTE: If your sauce comes out too liquid, remove a bit of it, blend in a teaspoon of flour, then pour the mixture back into the saucepan and simmer for another minute or so. If it comes out too thick, add a little more cream or wine until the desired consistency is obtained. Cover mousseline with sauce and serve.

Another light delicacy that can be made from only a cup or two of leftover ham is *poufs au jambon*—puffs stuffed with ham. The "puff" part of this dish is the same as you would use for cream puffs. Ideal for a large party or buffet, this can also be served, with a green salad, as a main course for a lunch. I recommend serving the puffs warm.

Puffs Stuffed with Ham

Serves 8–10
1 cup water
1 stick butter
1 cup flour
4 eggs

In a saucepan heat the water and butter, and bring to a boil over low flame. (The reason for the low flame is to allow the butter fully to melt; if the water is brought to a fast boil, the butter may not have melted completely.) Turn off the flame. All at once, pour in the flour, stirring vigorously to make a thick paste. Add the eggs one at a time, while continuing to stir until all are incorporated. Now, using a teaspoon, scoop out dough and drop onto a cookie sheet about an inch apart. Bake in a preheated 375° oven for 30 to 40 minutes (the length of time will vary slightly from oven to oven; when the dough has puffed and turned golden, your puffs are done, no matter what the clock may say). While your puffs are cooking, prepare your filling:

1–2 cups ground cooked ham
8-ounce package cream cheese
½ cup whipped cream
3–4 eggs, hard-boiled and mashed
½ teaspoon paprika
½ teaspoon cayenne
2 tablespoons brandy
Chopped parsley

In a bowl, mix all the ingredients except parsley until smooth. When your puffs are done, remove from the oven and cut off the tops, about half an inch from the top. You may be surprised to see that beneath this golden crown you have a hidden hollow. (If perchance the "lining" is still slightly wet and doughy, don't despair: simply scoop this out with a teaspoon and discard.) Fill the hollows of your puffs with the filling, sprinkle with parsley, replace the tops, and serve.

NOTE: The above quantity should give you 40 to 50 puffs about 2 inches plus in diameter. If you need or prefer bite-size puffs, only half fill your teaspoon: you'll have a hundred or so smaller ones, ideal for cocktails, but be forewarned: it takes twice as long to fill the mini puffs.

So much for light leftovers. If you're in the mood for something substantial, you may want to try *pain de nouilles au jambon au gratin:*

Noodloff with Ham Gratin

I baptized this in English "Noodle Loaf," but my family, as usual making fun of my accent, soon abbreviated it to "noodloff" and claims despite my denials that it has to be of Russian origin. It isn't. To the best of my knowledge it's French. Anyway, here is another way to turn a handful of leftover ham into a full—and copious—meal.

Serves 4–5

½ pound wide noodles
1 stick butter
1 onion, finely chopped
3 eggs, lightly beaten
½ cup sour cream
1 cup or so diced cooked ham
½ cup finely chopped parsley
Pepper and salt
¼ cup bread crumbs

In a kettle, bring 2 quarts of salty water to a boil. Cook the noodles for 10 minutes. Drain.

In a skillet, heat half the butter and sauté the onion until golden. In a bowl, mix the eggs and sour cream, and add the cooked noodles and onion, the remaining butter, ham, parsley, and pepper and salt to taste. Stir until well mixed, then transfer into a buttered, ovenproof dish. Sprinkle with bread crumbs. Bake at 350° for 45 minutes. At time of serving, loosen the edges with a knife and unmold onto a warm serving platter. Slice to serve, as with any loaf.

Another delectable and copious meal that can be made starting with only a few scraps of leftover ham is *croustade florentine,* which in English does not sound nearly as exotic: ham and spinach pie. Still, the taste is just as good.

Ham and Spinach Pie

Serves 5–6

Dough for 9-inch pie crust
  (see page 39)
1 package frozen chopped
  spinach
2 sticks butter
1 tablespoon olive oil
1 onion, finely chopped
1–2 cups ground cooked ham
½ cup ground beef
2 tablespoons heavy cream
1 tablespoon flour
1 cup grated Parmesan cheese
Pepper and salt
½ teaspoon nutmeg

Prepare dough and put in refrigerator to chill. Cook spinach according to directions on the package. Drain. Add ½ stick of butter.

In a skillet melt the oil and one stick of butter over a medium flame. Sauté the onion for 5 minutes. Add the ham and beef, and cook for another 5 minutes. Add the cream, flour, cheese, and pepper and salt to taste, and continue cooking for 5 more minutes. By the time this filling has finished cooking, it will be fairly firm.

While the filling is cooling, roll out the dough onto a floured board and line a 9-inch pie mold. Spread the meat filling over the uncooked pie crust, as evenly as possible, then on top spread the spinach. Dot with the remaining butter, sprinkle with nutmeg, and bake for 35 minutes at 350°. Serve.

If all you have left from your ham is a few scarcely presentable scraps, you might want to turn them into deviled ham, for a luncheon sandwich spread.

Deviled Ham

Makes 1½ cups

- 1 cup cooked ham scraps
- 1 hard-boiled egg, mashed
- 2 tablespoons sour cream
- 1 tablespoon mayonnaise
- 1 teaspoon prepared mustard
- Pepper and salt

In a blender, purée all the ingredients until smooth. Store in a covered bowl if not for immediate use. It will take you all of 2 to 3 minutes to make your deviled ham spread, and as with most homemade creations you will not only save considerable money but it will taste better than any canned variety.

VEAL

Veal roast is relatively common in many European countries, but far less so in the United States, for whatever reasons. Moreover, veal roast has a tendency to shrink by about a third when cooking, so your chances of having much left over are relatively slim. Still, if you are among the happy few who have enjoyed the culinary delights that roast veal can offer, here are a couple of recipes to dress up your leftovers in a style commensurate with its marvelous taste.

The first is a Normandy dish—*veau à la normande*—which immediately implies calvados, apples, or cream. This variation uses cream.

Leftover Veal Normandy Style

Serves 4–5

- 1 onion, finely chopped
- 1 stick butter
- 1–2 cups diced cooked veal
- 1 tablespoon sugar
- 8-ounce can boiled onions, drained
- 1 bay leaf
- ½ teaspoon rosemary
- ½ teaspoon thyme
- ¼ teaspoon nutmeg
- 1 cup white wine
- ½ pound mushrooms, cleaned and sliced
- 1 cup heavy cream
- Salt and pepper
- ½ cup finely chopped parsley

In a skillet, over a medium flame, sauté the chopped onion in half the butter until golden. Add veal and cook gently for 8 minutes. Turn off flame. In a saucepan, melt the remaining butter, add sugar and the boiled onions, and cook, stirring constantly, until the onions are caramelized (you can tell that they are caramelized when they are covered with a light layer of brown glaze—a candied effect). Transfer the onions to the meat skillet, and add bay leaf, rosemary, thyme, nutmeg, wine, mushrooms, cream, and salt and pepper to taste. Simmer for 5 minutes, stirring constantly. Sprinkle with parsley and serve.

NOTE: If you want to make it more "Normandy," you can add a jigger of apple brandy—calvados.

If you like cooked endives, you'll surely enjoy *tranches de veau à l'estragon et aux endives:*

Veal with Braised Endives and Tarragon

Serves 4

- 6 Belgian endives
- 1 stick butter
- Juice of ½ lemon
- Pepper and salt
- 4–5 slices veal roast
- ⅓ cup heavy cream
- 1 tablespoon dry tarragon

Discard the outer leaves of the endives, if damaged; wash and cook endives in boiling water for 10 minutes. In a skillet, melt two-thirds of the butter and sauté the endives for 8 to 10 minutes, turning gently. Add the lemon juice and pepper and salt to taste, cover, and simmer for 30 minutes. In a separate skillet, melt the remaining butter and cook the veal for 5 minutes, turning once. Add the cream and tarragon. Serve, surrounding the meat slices with the braised endives.

Whenever I'm stuck for an idea and have no immediate brainstorm when facing a few bits or slices of any meat or fowl, I think of a casserole. And whenever you do, remember the varieties with pasta—noodles, spaghetti, macaroni—cheese, and mushrooms. Here's an Italian dish employing all these.

Veal Italian Style

Serves 4–5

¼ pound noodles
4 tablespoons butter
1 cup mushrooms, cleaned and sliced
¼ teaspoon nutmeg
2 tablespoons sherry or white wine

Pepper and salt
3 tablespoons flour
1 cup chicken stock
1–1½ cups cooked, diced veal
⅓ cup heavy cream
½ cup grated Parmesan cheese

In a quart of salty water, boil the noodles for 10 minutes. Drain. In a skillet, melt the butter and sauté the mushrooms for 5 minutes. Add nutmeg, wine, and pepper and salt to taste. Add flour and stock, stirring to form a medium-thick sauce.

In an ovenproof casserole mix the noodles with the veal, cream, and contents of the skillet. Sprinkle with cheese and bake 15 minutes, or until top is crisp. Serve.

POULTRY

Poultry offers a whole spectrum of culinary possibilities for leftovers, the possibilities depending quite naturally on the kind of fowl. Turkey, because of its very size, is the prime candidate for second servings, as well as third, fourth, and even fifth, as all cooks remember from their post-Thanksgiving experiences. When one cooks a turkey one knows automatically that leftovers must inevitably follow. Ducks, on the contrary, which have an impressive protective layer of fat which melts away during cooking, lose as much as a third of their weight prior to reaching the table, as does the goose: therefore, chances are you won't have too much of a leftover problem with either. In the case of chicken, the sheer frequency with which it is served means that the question of what to make of chicken the second time around will arise sooner or later—and probably sooner. The rest of the poultry family—squab, quail, partridge, pheasant, and the like—are generally small and often are served individually; thus they will rarely become candidates for this chapter.

Turkey: "The turkey," wrote Brillat-Savarin, "is certainly one of the most beautiful presents the New World made to the Old." It is, indeed; and it is not by chance that it is connected with so many festive occasions. Less common in France than in America, the turkey—which in French is called *dinde* or *dindon,* short for *coq d'Inde* or *poule d'Inde,* stemming from the early discoverers' belief that the land they had reached was India—makes its appearance mostly at Christmas and at wedding receptions. If we can believe Brillat-Savarin, however, in earlier times at least, the turkey was a fairly common—and always festive—dish guaranteed to prove to the invited guest that the host was offering a very special celebration:

> When our vine-dressers and our farmers wish to regale themselves in the long winter evenings, what do we see roasting at the brilliant fire of the kitchen where the table is spread? A turkey.
>
> When a useful mechanic, when a laborious artist, assembles a few friends to enjoy some relaxation, which is the more prized because it is so rare, what is the dish which, as a matter of course, he sets before them? A turkey stuffed with sausages or Lyons chestnuts. . . .
>
> And my "Secret Memoirs" tell me that the turkey's restorative juices have more than once lighted up diplomatic faces.

There are enough recipes for leftover turkey to make a book in itself. Beyond the few standard recipes such as turkey pie, creamed turkey, turkey croquettes, and such, I have developed a few of my own that are less standard and have the virtue, I think, of being simple and savory. One is:

Turkey Florentine

Serves 6

- 2 packages frozen spinach
- 6–8 slices cooked turkey
- 2 cups white cream sauce (see page 46)
- ½ teaspoon nutmeg
- ½ cup grated Swiss cheese
- ½ stick butter
- Pepper and salt

Cook the spinach according to the directions on the package. Drain well. Line a buttered casserole dish with the turkey slices. Place the spinach over the turkey. Season the white sauce with nutmeg, pepper and salt and pour over the spinach. Cover with a layer of grated cheese, and dot with butter. Bake in a preheated oven for 20 minutes at 350°. Serve.

As an accompanying dish, I suggest thin spaghetti.

If you want to make a very fancy presentation for very little effort, try:

Truffled Turkey with Madeira Sauce on Toast

Serves 6

- 1 stick butter
- 6–8 slices bread
- 6–8 slices cooked turkey
- 1 tablespoon flour
- ½ cup broth
- 1 cup Madeira wine
- 1 tablespoon tarragon
- Pepper and salt
- 1 truffle, sliced (or 4 mushroom caps, sliced)

In a skillet, melt half the butter and fry the bread on both sides until crisp. Remove bread and place on a warm serving platter. In the same skillet, sauté the turkey in the remaining butter for 2 minutes on each side. Add the flour and blend in the broth and wine. Add tarragon and pepper and salt to taste. Add the sliced truffle (or mushrooms).

On each piece of bread, place a slice of meat, and top with a slice or two of truffle. Pour the Madeira sauce over each "canapé" and serve at once.

The style of this main dish lends itself to endive salad afterward, but any green salad will do.

NOTE: If you don't have any Madeira wine, sherry will substitute nicely, as will white wine.

Similar to but somewhat richer than Turkey Florentine is:

Turkey with Broccoli and Asparagus in a Dry Vermouth Sauce

Serves 6

- 1 bunch broccoli
- 8 stalks asparagus
- 1 tablespoon melted butter
- 3 tablespoons grated Parmesan cheese
- ½ cup dry vermouth
- 6 slices cooked turkey
- 1½ cups white cream sauce (see page 46)
- 2 egg yolks, lightly beaten
- ½ cup whipped cream
- ½ teaspoon nutmeg
- Pepper and salt

Separate the broccoli, then wash and cook it in one quart of salty water for 12 minutes. At the same time, in another saucepan containing a like amount of salty water, cook the asparagus for 10 minutes. Drain both vegetables. Line an ovenproof dish with the vegetables, pour the melted butter over, sprinkle one tablespoon of the cheese on top, and add 2 tablespoons of the vermouth.

Over the vegetables place the turkey slices, then sprinkle a second tablespoon of cheese and add another 2 tablespoons of vermouth. To the cream sauce add the egg yolks, and fold in the whipped cream. Now sprinkle in the nutmeg, and add the remaining dry vermouth and pepper and salt to taste.

Cover the turkey with this sauce, using all of it. Top with the remaining cheese. Bake for 12 minutes, until top is light brown. Serve at once, preferably with noodles or boiled rice as the side dish.

If you're almost down to the bone with your turkey and you're tempted to put the remaining meat in your kettle to make stock, don't: there's more than meets the eye on a turkey, and even when it looks almost stripped you can, by careful prospecting, usually come up with at least two to three cups of meat. And with that quantity you can make *mousse de volaille, sauce aux champignons et aux amandes*. By the time you've reached this last-vestige stage, you may have reached the end of your tolerance for turkey—even disguised in the form of a *mousse*. In this case, simply save the meat you have collected and freeze it until your desire for turkey has been rekindled.

Turkey Mousse with a Mushroom and Almond Sauce

Serves 5–6

3 cups cooked turkey meat
4 eggs
1 cup heavy cream
½ cup sour cream
Pepper and salt
2 tablespoons butter

¼ pound mushrooms, cleaned and sliced
1 cup white cream sauce (see page 46)
Juice of ½ lemon
½ cup sliced almonds

In a blender, or a meat grinder, grind the turkey. If you use a blender, remember to put in a handful of meat at a time, no more; otherwise it won't blend. If you have neither instrument, chop turkey by hand as finely as you can. In a bowl, mix the ground meat with the eggs. Add the heavy cream, the sour cream, and pepper and salt to taste. Pour into a baking dish—or, if you have them, several small ramequins or individual soufflé dishes—and place in a roasting pan filled with an inch of water. Bake in a preheated oven for 30 minutes at 375°.

While the mousse is baking, melt the butter in a saucepan. Sauté the mushrooms for 3 to 4 minutes, add the cream sauce, stir, then pour in the lemon juice and stir in the almonds. Season to taste. Serve the sauce in a gravy bowl, for individual use.

When you've exhausted the meat supply on your turkey, you have nowhere to go but to a broth (or stock). Even if you make turkey broth, you'll undoubtedly not eat it all, since an average-size turkey will make from 5 to 6 quarts. Save whatever you do not use, store in plastic (not glass) containers, preferably the 16-ounce size, label and date, and freeze.

Turkey Broth

Makes 6 quarts
1 turkey carcass
1 large onion, pricked with 3 cloves
1 bunch parsley
2–3 stalks celery
2 carrots, cleaned
1 turnip (optional)
2 bay leaves
Pepper and salt

Put all the ingredients in a deep kettle filled to within 2 or 3 inches of the top with water. Bring to a boil, cover, and reduce flame. Simmer for at least an hour to an hour and a half.

There are two ways of serving the soup: the first is to strain it; the second is to purée all the cooked vegetables and return them to the broth. The basic taste will be the same, but the latter will have slightly more consistency.

If your purpose is not to make soup but stock for subsequent cooking, follow the preceding directions, but all you really need are the cloved onion, bay leaves, pepper, and salt. Strain and freeze.

Chicken: Chicken is one of the most popular and appetizing main courses available to any cook. Not so long ago it was considered a relatively special dish, reserved for the rites of Sunday dinner. Over the past couple of decades the price of chicken has made it more accessible as weekday fare, but I still think of it as special.

Chicken lends itself to an infinite variety of "gourmet" possibilities. I will limit myself to a few that are among my particular favorites and with which you may not be as familiar as you probably are with such standards as chicken pie, chicken fricassee, and creamed chicken. And they can all without exception be made quite quickly and simply. I might note, too, that all the following recipes can be applied to turkey as well.

If you have served as your initial presentation roast chicken, you should remember that you can offer a repeat performance with equal pleasure. Since obviously you'll probably not want to offer it two days in succession (!) you can wrap it in foil and refrigerate, but no longer than two or three days. To re-serve, preheat your oven to 350°, place the chicken in an ovenproof dish (if by chance you have stored your chicken in a Pyrex dish, do *not* transfer directly from the refrigerator to the oven; I have known Pyrex to burst when subjected to drastic changes of temperature). Keep covered with foil for the first 10 minutes or so of reheating, to prevent dryness, then remove foil and continue cooking for another 10 minutes to regain crispness. During the cooking, baste two or three times.

Roast chicken can, of course, be served a second time around cold, with a variety of cold dishes such as salads. One I've often served is leeks.

Cold Roast Chicken with Leeks Vinaigrette

Serves 4

4 leeks
Cooked cold chicken, cut into 3-inch chunks
½ head lettuce
2 hard-boiled eggs, sliced
½ cup black olives
4-ounce can pimientos, drained and diced
½ cup finely chopped parsley
Pepper and salt
1 cup vinaigrette (see page 46)

Leeks grow underground, and therefore tend to be very sandy. To get rid of the sand, make two or three incisions at the bottom of the leek, running upward to the leaves, which will open up the leek and allow the water to reach the leaf folds where the sand tends to hide. Under running water, wash thoroughly, fingering the leaves until absolutely smooth. Trim by cutting off the top couple of inches of the leeks, and the bottom "beard," and let leeks soak for a few minutes in a bowl of cold water.

In a kettle of boiling salty water cook the leeks for 15 minutes. Drain. (You may want to help the draining process by squeezing the leeks lightly.) Cut into 3- to 4-inch pieces. On a platter, place the chicken on a bed of lettuce leaves. Surround it with the leeks and egg slices. Dot with black olives. Sprinkle the entire platter with pimiento, parsley, pepper, and salt. Pour the vinaigrette sauce over the eggs and leeks. Serve.

If you want to dress up your cold chicken with a marvelously sinful sauce—I rank it close to *pesto* in the sin department, because of its caloric content—here is a Middle Eastern sauce that will quickly turn your chicken into an exotic specialty.

Cold Chicken with Walnut Sauce

Serves 4

Cooked chicken pieces
Lettuce leaves
1½ cups shelled walnuts
1 medium-sized onion, quartered
1 large piece French bread
    (or 4 slices American bread)
1 teaspoon paprika
1 teaspoon salt
1½ cups broth (or 1½ cups water and 2 bouillon cubes)

Arrange the chicken pieces on a bed of lettuce. Blend remaining ingredients until puréed, and pour over the chicken. Decorate with a little additional paprika and serve.

NOTE: If you find the above sauce too sharp for your taste, add 3 tablespoons of sour cream.

A chicken salad is, of course, always a good way of serving leftover chicken cold. Here is one of the ways they may serve it in the south of France, known as *salade de poulet méridionale*:

Chicken Salad, Southern French Style

Serves 4

Cooked chicken, cubed
3 tomatoes, washed and sliced
2 green peppers, washed and cut in strips
1 cup black olives, pitted
1 bunch watercress, washed and separated
4 tablespoons olive oil
1 tablespoon wine vinegar
Juice of 1 lemon
Pepper and salt

Mix and serve.

If you prefer your leftover chicken warm rather than cold, here are two French recipes varying the traditional fricassee—which comes from the French verb *fricasser,* meaning "to cut up and fry." The first, from the southwestern French province of Gascony, is *fricassée de poulet à la Gasconne:*

Fricasseed Chicken Gascony Style

Serves 4–5

- 2 cups cooked chicken, cut in 1-inch pieces
- 2 slices ham, diced
- 2 tablespoons olive oil
- 2 onions, minced
- 1 clove garlic, minced
- 1 bay leaf, crumbled
- 1 teaspoon thyme
- ½ cup finely chopped parsley
- Pepper and salt
- ¼ cup brandy
- 4 tomatoes, peeled and quartered (or 15-ounce can whole tomatoes)

In a Dutch oven, sauté the chicken and ham in the olive oil for about 5 minutes. Add onions and garlic, and cook until light brown. Add bay leaf, thyme, parsley, and pepper and salt to taste. Pour in the brandy, and ignite. When the flames have subsided, add the tomatoes, stir, and cook for another 5 minutes. Transfer to a warm serving platter.

If, predictably, the preceding recipe from the south of France contains garlic and onion, another fricasseed dish from central France relies essentially on dairy products: *fricassée de poulet berrichonne:*

Fricasseed Chicken Berri Style

Serves 6

- ½ stick butter
- 8 carrots, peeled and cut lengthwise in sticks
- 2 cups cooked, diced chicken
- 1 onion, finely chopped
- 1½ tablespoons flour
- 1 cup chicken stock
- Pepper and salt
- 2 egg yolks
- 1 tablespoon wine vinegar
- 1 cup heavy cream

In a Dutch oven, heat the butter and sauté the carrots over a low flame for about 5 minutes. Add the chicken and onion, and sprinkle in the flour. Dilute with stock, stir well, and simmer for 15 minutes. Season to taste.

In a bowl, mix the egg yolks, vinegar, and cream, and pour into the Dutch oven. Place in an oven preheated to 250° (low temperature so that the egg won't cake), and cook for 10 minutes. Serve.

If you are a paella buff but haven't the time, money, or inclination to invest in the lobster and shrimp that are part of the classic paella recipe, here's a way of approximating the dish using only your leftover chicken. For this you will need at least half a leftover chicken, and preferably a bit more.

Poor-Cousin Paella

Serves 4–5

- 1 cup rice
- 2 tablespoons olive oil
- 1 tablespoon lard
- 2 onions, chopped
- 1 clove garlic, minced
- 2 green peppers, cut into 1-inch pieces
- 1 chorizo or Spanish sausage, sliced (optional)
- 1 cup chicken broth
- Pepper and salt
- ½ cooked chicken, cut into small pieces
- 2 slices cooked ham, diced
- 3 tomatoes, peeled and diced
- 2 large artichoke bottoms, sliced (or 1 package frozen artichoke hearts)
- 1 package frozen green peas

Cook the rice in 2 cups of salty water, in a covered saucepan, for about 10 minutes or until water is gone. In a skillet, melt the oil and the lard, and sauté the onions and garlic until golden. Add green peppers and sausage, and cook over a low flame for 5 minutes. Stir in the cooked rice, add the broth and pepper and salt to taste and transfer to a casserole dish. Add the chicken pieces, ham, tomatoes, artichokes, and peas (still unthawed—straight from the freezer to the casserole dish). In a preheated oven, cook at 350° for 25 minutes. Serve.

With only a couple of cups of leftover chicken and one truffle you can make a good lavish meal: *soufflé de poulet aux truffes dans un turban de riz*. The only expensive item, of course, is the truffle, and if this poses a problem you can eliminate the truffle; if you do, replace it with a quarter-pound of mushrooms.

Chicken and Truffle Soufflé in a Turban of Rice

Serves 4–5

- 2 cups cooked, chopped chicken meat
- ½ cup heavy cream
- 3 egg yolks
- ½ teaspoon rosemary
- ½ teaspoon tarragon
- 1 tablespoon brandy
- Parsley (minced)
- Pepper and salt
- 3 egg whites, beaten stiff
- 1 truffle, diced

In the blender purée the chicken with the cream, egg yolks, rosemary, tarragon, brandy, parsley and pepper and salt to taste. (Reminder: never fill your blender with more than a cupful at a time.) Pour contents of the blender into a mixing bowl, and fold in egg whites. Pour this mixture into a buttered charlotte mold. Spread the diced truffle evenly through the purée, then set the mold in a roasting pan containing about an inch of water. Bake at 350° for 30 minutes.

While the soufflé is baking, make your turban of rice:

- 1 tablespoon butter
- 1½ cups rice
- 3 cups cold water
- 1½ teaspoons salt
- ½ cup grated Swiss cheese
- Pepper
- ½ cup chopped parsley

In a saucepan melt the butter and sauté the rice until translucent. Add the water and the salt, bring to a boil, reduce flame, cover, and cook for 15 minutes. Pour cooked rice into a buttered ring mold, mix in the cheese and pepper to taste, place next to the charlotte mold (in the same roasting pan), and cook for 10 minutes.

Unmold the turban onto a warm serving platter. Now unmold the chicken and truffle mixture into the center (don't be shy about fitting the chicken mixture into the center of the ring mold by using your hands; it may need a little adjusting, and any good cook, like a good artisan, is a master fitter).

Sprinkle with parsley and serve.

One of the true "miracles" of the French cuisine is quenelles. These little oblong-shaped delicacies come in four basic varieties: *quenelles de volaille* (poultry), *quenelles de brochet* (pike), *quenelles de veau* (veal), and *quenelles de moelle* (marrow). The contradictory characteristic of quenelles is that they are simultaneously firm and light—they have a mousselike quality to them.

In France, you can find them in most charcuteries, where they are made fresh daily. The French cook will generally buy them and make his or her own sauce. Good restaurants also feature them, and each chef prides himself on his own secret formula.

We are so fond of them that I have made it a custom of making my own quenelles at least once or twice a month and freezing what we don't eat immediately. I feel about quenelles the same kind of proselytizing zeal I have for *rillettes*. Through the years I have managed through experimentation to simplify quenelle making, to the point where anyone can compete with the professional chefs in this department. Below is my recipe for *quenelles de volaille*.

Chicken Quenelles with a Cream and Nutmeg Sauce

Serves 4–6

1 cup chopped cooked chicken
2 egg yolks
1 whole egg
½ stick butter
1 teaspoon nutmeg

Pepper and salt
4 slices stale white bread
½ cup hot milk
2 quarts salty water
½ cup flour

In the blender purée the chicken, egg yolks, whole egg, butter, nutmeg, and pepper and salt to taste. Soften the bread with the hot milk, then blend milk and bread. All the blending should be done a cupful at a time, transferring successively to a mixing bowl as blended. Refrigerate for a little while, which means from an hour to a whole day depending on your schedule. (The reason for this—and I cannot stress too strongly the importance of this culinary "secret"—is that any batter or dough, be it crêpe batter, cream puff dough, or fritter batter, will benefit from a resting period, preferably chilled. In this instance, the eggs have a chance to "bind" the quenelles blend, and at the same time the result will be lighter, not only for quenelles but for your puff paste, crêpe batter, or whatever.)

Heat the salty water. Remove the chilled quenelles mixture from the refrigerator. The classic form of quenelles is long and thin, roughly the form of a miniature French bread. I form them with my hands, by flouring my hands, then scooping up some of the mixture and rolling until I have a long cylinder. When you pick up the mixture it will be rather soft (not liquid, but soft); be reassured, that's its proper consistency. And the flour will hold it together. If you prefer a spoon, dip a tablespoonful of the mixture into the flour, then set your floured "mound" on a plate or board. Repeat until all the quenelles are shaped. The quenelles won't have the cylinder (traditional) shape, but the taste will be as good.

When the water is boiling briskly, gently put the quenelles—no more than 8 to 10 at a time, since they need room to rise to the surface—into the kettle. When they surface, reduce flame to low and let simmer for 10 minutes. With a slotted spoon remove and drain. Set aside. Repeat process until all quenelles are cooked. Set the quenelles side by side in an ovenproof dish. If you're serving your quenelles as a main dish, the above quantities should suffice for from 8–10 guests. If you're serving them as an hors d'oeuvre—as I often do—you'll have about twice the quantity you will need. Those you don't serve can be frozen for a future feast.

Now make the sauce:

Serves 4–6
½ stick butter
3 tablespoons flour
3 cups milk
1 teaspoon nutmeg
Pepper and salt

In a saucepan melt the butter over a medium flame, stir in the flour, then pour the milk gradually, stirring until the mixture thickens. (If at this stage there are still lumps, remove and blend until smooth.) Season with nutmeg and pepper and salt to taste. The sauce should be fairly liquid, more or less like a pancake batter; if you find yours is a bit too thick or firm, add a bit of milk or cream.

Pour the sauce over the quenelles. Bake for 10 to 12 minutes at 350°. Serve.

NOTE: You may if you like, before baking, sprinkle a cup of freshly grated Swiss cheese over the quenelles and cream sauce.

Two suggestions: as indicated, quenelles can be frozen. I store them in quantities of about 10 quenelles to a package, so that I need only defrost the quantity I will be serving. Second, I recommend, for extra effect, investing in eight or ten individual-size ovenproof dishes to bake and serve them bubbling hot.

If you have literally nothing less than scraps—and I am sometimes amazed by how much meat one can glean from a seemingly bare carcass—you still have the potential for a meal or two. One possibility, of Austrian origin, is chicken dumplings which when added to your broth will not only dress it up but make a lunch in itself.

The only way to get the scraps from the chicken carcass is to ferret them out with your fingertips. The following advice may seem so self-evident as to appear plain silly, but I offer it nonetheless: make sure, before probing, that after washing your hands you rinse thoroughly to eliminate any semblance of soap; otherwise your fingers could taint the chicken meat.

Chicken Broth with Dumplings

Serves 4–5
Chicken giblets ⎫ to make ½ cup
Chicken scraps ⎭ or less
3 slices stale bread, soaked in milk
⅓ stick butter
2 eggs
½ cup finely chopped parsley
1 tablespoon tarragon
Pepper and salt
½ cup flour
2 quarts chicken broth

In a mixing bowl, put the giblets and scraps (with or without skin, as you prefer). Add the bread, butter, eggs, parsley, tarragon, and pepper and salt to taste). Purée in blender, a cupful at a time.

I am assuming that you have just made, from the chicken carcass, a broth. Now, bring the broth to a boil. Again, as with the quenelles (see preceding recipe), you can either form the dumplings into little balls with your floured hands, or use a floured teaspoon. In either case, drop the dumplings into the broth, reduce flame, and simmer for 10 minutes. Serve.

Another possibility if you have only scraps from roast or boiled chicken is to make a chicken spread for sandwiches or canapés.

Chicken Spread

Makes 1 cup
½ cup cooked chicken scraps
2 tablespoons mayonnaise
1 tablespoon sour cream
Pepper and salt

Purée in blender and refrigerate.

Duck: As I've indicated, your chances of having much leftover duck are slim (because the duck is fat). Nonetheless, it can happen that you have had six people to dinner and have served two to three ducks. And from that quantity you may well have two or three cups of leftover duck, enough for the following gourmet recipes. Save the drippings and store in the refrigerator.

If you have one large chunk of leftover duck (as opposed to

having to pick over the duck to collect two or three cups), I suggest you freeze it for a future cassoulet. When you've collected two or three such pieces, you have the basis for a cassoulet sufficient to feed six to eight. Or, you can use your single piece to make a cassoulet for three or four.

As is the case with *boeuf bourguignon,* this classic regional dish from Languedoc—the name for it, cassoulet, derives from the regional term for the earthenware recipient in which the dish is cooked: *cassolo*—is now part of the standard fare not only in France but abroad as well. The dish varies to some degree according to its precise geographical point of origin. The best known is *cassoulet toulousain*—from Toulouse—in which duck, or goose, is the dominant meat, together with the distinctive Toulouse sausage. The Carcassonne variety utilizes young lamb and partridge, while a third classic variety, from Castelnaudary, emphasizes breast of lamb and pork.

The time to think of an eventual cassoulet is when you're serving duck. And when you think ahead to cassoulet, remember to save as well if you can any of the other prime ingredients it contains, such as a bit of lamb, a leftover pork chop or two, some knockwurst. However, by far the most important ingredient is the duck itself, and by far the most expensive; thus if you must you can easily purchase the others.

Remember, too, that if you don't finish the cassoulet, it can be kept (refrigerated) for up to several days. In fact, it actually improves a second or even a third time around, if it should come to that.

Cassoulet, Toulouse Style

Serves 4–6

- 3 tablespoons duck fat (drippings)
- 1 pork cutlet, cubed in 1-inch pieces
- 1 lamb chop, cubed in 1-inch pieces
- 2–3 pieces roast duck (about half a duck)
- 2 knockwurst, sliced
- 1 onion, halved and pricked with 2 cloves
- 1 teaspoon thyme
- 1 teaspoon tarragon
- ½ cup finely chopped parsley
- 1 clove garlic, minced
- 3 slices bacon
- 2 20-ounce cans white beans, rinsed and drained
- Pepper and salt
- ½ cup bread crumbs
- Minced parsley for garnish

In your original roasting of the duck(s), you have collected and stored the fat—drippings. In a skillet heat the duck fat, brown the pork, and cook for 10 minutes. Add the lamb and cook for 5 minutes. Transfer the meat, drippings, and all the other ingredients (except bread crumbs and garnish) into an ovenproof dish. Top neatly with bread crumbs (not just for looks: the bread crumbs will absorb the fat). Bake at 350° for 35 minutes, by which time the top will be crisp and golden brown. Sprinkle with parsley and serve.

Two exotic ways of re-serving leftover duck dip into Far Eastern cuisine. Both in India and in China duck is often used as a basic ingredient in a number of recipes. Here are two I have made and liked. The first is *canard à l'indienne*.

Duck Indian Style

Serves 4

2 tablespoons duck fat (drippings)
1 large piece cooked duck, diced
1 onion, finely chopped
1 apple, peeled and diced
½ cup broth
1 teaspoon chili powder
1 teaspoon curry powder
½ cup finely chopped parsley
Pepper and salt
4 cups hot cooked rice
½ stick butter
1 cup peanuts, chopped
1 banana, sliced

In a skillet melt the duck fat and sauté the diced duck for 5 minutes. Add the onion, and cook until light brown. Add apple, stir; add broth, chili, curry, parsley, and pepper and salt to taste. Cook for another 3 minutes.

Into the rice mix butter, peanuts, and sliced banana, and heat gently. Serve with the spiced duck: either have the duck in the center surrounded by the rice, or serve in two separate platters, as you prefer.

The second of these dishes is: *canard à la chinoise*.

Duck Chinese Style

Serves 4

- 1½–2 cups cooked, diced duck
- 1 cup duck broth (made with the duck bones)
- 1 tablespoon cooking oil
- 1 cup bamboo shoots
- 1 cup mushrooms, cleaned and sliced
- 1 tablespoon soy sauce
- 1 teaspoon cornstarch
- ¼ cup water
- Pepper and salt

Put the duck in a saucepan, cover with the broth, and simmer for 15 minutes.

In a skillet, heat the oil and sauté the bamboo shoots and the mushrooms for 5 minutes. Pour the contents of the saucepan into the skillet, cover, and cook for 20 minutes. Add the soy sauce. In a cup, mix the cornstarch with the water, pepper, and salt, and pour into the skillet. Stir for an additional 2 minutes, and serve.

With a bit of leftover duck and some help from other poultry, you can quickly make a marvelous *pâté de volaille*. Sorry, but "poultry pâté" just will not do, so I'm calling this:

Pâté de Volaille

Serves 8

- 2 tablespoons duck fat (drippings)
- 2 chicken breasts, boned
- 3 chicken livers
- 1 cup cooked duck meat
- 1 egg
- 1 tablespoon heavy cream
- 2 slices stale bread
- 2 tablespoons brandy
- 1 teaspoon rosemary
- 1 teaspoon tarragon
- 1 teaspoon thyme
- Pepper and salt
- 6 slices bacon
- Parsley sprigs (optional)

In a skillet heat the duck fat, sauté chicken 5 minutes on each side over medium flame, add the livers, and cook for 1 more minute. Blend chicken, duck, and liver, a cupful at a time. In a bowl, mix the blended meat with all the other ingredients except the bacon and parsley. Line a mold of your choice (I prefer rectangular, such as a bread loaf, for my pâtés) with most of the bacon slices, letting them overhang the sides of the mold. Fill mold with the mixture, fold over the bottom bacon slices, then top with the remaining bacon slices. Cover tightly with foil and bake at 350° for one hour. Cool and refrigerate, at least from morning to evening and preferably overnight. In order to acquire its "pâté" consistency, it must cool for several hours after baking. If the mold in which you have made your pâté is attractive, you can serve it directly. Otherwise, unmold, decorate with sprigs of parsley, and serve with French bread or melba toast.

NOTE: Don't serve directly from the refrigerator. Let pâté come to room temperature for an hour or so before serving to attain full flavor. Also: if you have a specialty shop available that sells imported French cornichons, they are an ideal accompaniment for your pâté. Some may feel cornichons—small gherkins in vinegar—a frivolity; perhaps so. But when it comes to pâté I think of them as a frivolous necessity.

FISH

A little leftover fish will enable any inventive cook to go a long way. With only half a cup of leftover fish—blue, bass, sole, halibut, salmon, or whatever—plus a few other ingredients, you can, for example, make a *salade niçoise,* which in France is served as either an hors d'oeuvre or a main course.

Mediterranean Salad

Serves 4

- 1 cup cooked green beans
- 2 potatoes, cooked and sliced
- 1 onion, finely chopped
- 1 teaspoon basil
- ⅔ cup vinaigrette with lemon juice (see page 46)
- Pepper and salt
- ½ cup cooked fish
- 2 hard-boiled eggs, quartered
- 2 tomatoes, washed and quartered

Mix together the beans, potatoes, and onion with the basil and vinaigrette. Season to taste. Crown the top of the salad with the fish, eggs, and tomatoes.

This next recipe is a perfect summer dish, or ideal for buffet or any elegant lunch: *poisson froid, sauce mousseline vert-pré.* The mousseline sauce can be made ahead and kept cold.

Cold Fish with Mousseline Sauce Vert-Pré

Serves 4
Cooked fish
2 tomatoes, sliced
2 hard-boiled eggs, quartered
½ pound cooked asparagus
2 potatoes, cooked and sliced
3 egg yolks
1 stick butter
Juice of 1 lemon
½ cup cooked spinach
½ cup watercress
½ cup parsley
3 egg whites, beaten stiff
Pepper and salt

On a pretty serving platter, arrange the fish, tomatoes, hard-boiled eggs, asparagus, and potatoes in any decorative pattern you prefer.

In a double boiler (or, if you don't have one, in an ovenproof mixing bowl set in a frying pan containing an inch or so of water) put the egg yolks, butter, and lemon juice. Turn on your flame to medium, allow water to bubble gently, then beat contents of double boiler with a wire whisk or a fork until of custard consistency. Turn off the flame, and remove.

In the blender, purée the spinach, watercress, and parsley. Mix this green purée with contents of the double boiler, then fold in egg whites. Season to taste. Chill. Spread the sauce generously over the contents of the serving platter. If there is any remaining sauce, serve it in a separate bowl.

It's always fun to serve seafood on a seashell. The shells, by the way, are scallop shells, which you can buy inexpensively almost anywhere and wash and reuse just like plates. Here is a fine appetizer which can also be served as a luncheon main course: *coquilles de poisson froid, sauce à l'anchois.*

Cold Fish on the Half Shell with Anchovy Sauce

Serves 3–4
1 cup mayonnaise
½ tube anchovy paste
Pepper
Juice of ½ lemon
1 cup cooked fish, cut into 1-inch pieces
6½-ounce can minced clams, drained
2 scallions, finely chopped
1 potato, cooked and cubed
6–8 lettuce leaves, washed and dried

In a bowl, mix thoroughly the mayonnaise, anchovy paste, pepper (no salt, because anchovy paste and clams are salty), and lemon juice. Add fish, clams, scallions, and potatoes, and mix well. Line 3 or 4 scallop shells with the lettuce leaves, and fill each shell with the cold fish cocktail. Serve chilled.

But leftover fish does not have to be served cold. There are many appetizing ways of disguising your original fish. Here are a few of my favorites. The first is *timbales de poisson*. A "timbale" is a tall circular mold, ranging from individual small size to one large enough to serve 10 to 12 people. It generally implies a crust, either on top or on both top and bottom.

Fish in a Deep Dish

Serves 6–8

- 1/2 stick butter
- 1 cup mushrooms, cleaned and sliced
- Juice of 1/2 lemon
- 1 cup cooked fish
- 1 cup cooked macaroni
- 1/2 cup tomato sauce
- 1 teaspoon capers
- 1/2 cup heavy cream
- 1/2 cup finely chopped parsley
- Pepper and salt
- Dough for 9-inch crust (see page 39)
- 1 egg mixed with 1 tablespoon water

In a skillet melt the butter, and cook the mushrooms for 5 minutes, stirring with a wooden spoon. Add the lemon juice.

In a bowl mix the fish, macaroni, tomato sauce, capers, cream, mushrooms, parsley, and pepper and salt to taste. If you are using individual deep dishes—and I heartily recommend that you invest in a dozen individual ovenproof deep dishes—the above quantities should be enough to serve from six to eight. Apportion the fish mixture among your buttered timbales; if you are using a large one, transfer contents of bowl to the oven-proof dish.

Roll out your dough onto a floured board. Cut the rolled dough into circles large enough to fit the top of the deep dishes. Prick the dough (or make small crisscrosses with a knife point), to allow the steam to escape without bursting the crust, and fit each "cover" onto a deep dish. Brush egg and water mixture over each cover, to glaze. Bake in the oven at 350° for 30 minutes.

This dish is as amusing as it is delicious; it's always a joy to see seemingly heavy little balls magically turn into something light and fluffy. Such is the fate of *croquettes de poisson soufflées*.

Souffléed Fish Puffs

Serves 6
½ cup milk
½ cup water
1 stick butter
1 cup flour
6 eggs
1 cup cooked fish
4 medium-sized potatoes, boiled and mashed
1 teaspoon nutmeg
Pepper and salt
1–2 quarts cooking oil

In a saucepan bring the milk, water, and butter to a boil. Add the flour all at once, turn off the flame, and add four eggs, one at a time, stirring vigorously.

In the mixer, whip the fish, potatoes, nutmeg, and pepper and salt to taste. Add the two remaining eggs, and mix with the contents of the saucepan. Refrigerate for at least 2 hours.

Half an hour or so before supper, remove the mixture from the refrigerator. Begin heating the oil in a deep fryer. From the fish and egg mixture form little balls an inch or so in diameter. When your oil is hot—and to ascertain whether or not it is drop in a smidgen of your mixture; if it sizzles, the oil is hot enough—drop the balls into it one by one. After the initial sizzling, reduce flame to medium, then cook for 3 to 5 minutes, gently turning the balls with a fork so that they become golden brown on all sides. Drain on a paper towel. Keep warm in the oven, and serve.

If you like dishes with a crust, try *croustade de poisson forestière*. *Croustade* is a French culinary term which contains the word "crust" and refers to a meat or fish preparation, prepared for individual portions, either fried or baked. The term *forestière* always implies the presence of mushrooms and herbs.

Little Fish Turnovers Forestière

For the crust:

Serves 6–8
2 cups flour
1½ sticks butter
½ teaspoon salt
1 tablespoon cooking oil
1 egg yolk
½ cup ice water

In a mixing bowl knead all the ingredients with your fingers, working until you obtain a smooth, elastic ball of dough. Refrigerate for half an hour.

While the dough is chilling, proceed to the filling.

½ stick butter
¼ pound mushrooms, cleaned and diced
2 shallots, finely chopped
1 tablespoon flour
½ cup white wine
1 cup finely chopped parsley

2 tablespoons tarragon
1 tablespoon capers
1–1½ cups cooked flaked fish
4 anchovies mashed with 2 tablespoons sweet butter
Pepper and salt
½ cup grated Swiss cheese

In a skillet, melt the butter and cook the mushrooms for 5 minutes. Add the shallots and cook until they turn golden brown. Add the flour, and blend in the wine, stirring with a wooden spoon. Add parsley, tarragon, and capers, and simmer for 5 minutes. It should now have a creamy consistency. Stir in the fish and the anchovy and butter mixture, and add pepper and a little salt to taste.

Remove your dough from the refrigerator. Roll out onto a floured board until dough is about ¼ inch thick. If you own small oblong pie molds, line them with the dough. If you do not, roll the dough into a long rectangle and cut it into smaller rectangles roughly 3 by 5 inches. With the scraps of dough, roll out again and cut long thin ribbons of dough with which you will make a border on all four sides, thus:

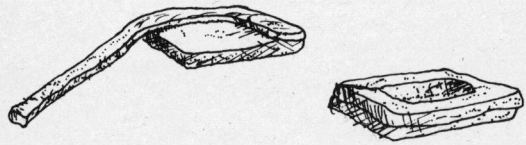

On each rectangle place two or three dried beans (or small washed stones from the beach or garden, which will do the trick nicely), to prevent the crust from "popping" as it bakes without a filling. Bake these rectangles (or pie molds) in an oven preheated to 350° for 15 minutes. Remove. Now fill each baked croustade with the fish mixture, sprinkle a layer of grated cheese, and bake for 8 minutes until tops are golden brown. Serve.

If you serve this as an hors d'oeuvre, follow it with a roast or grilled meat—in any case a light main course—since the croustade itself is rather rich. If offered as a main dish for lunch, accompany with a lettuce salad in a lemon and oil dressing.

Casserole dishes are always to be borne in mind when thinking of leftovers. So you may want to try *casserole de poisson à l'espagnole*.

Fish Casserole Spanish Style

Serves 5

- ¼ cup olive oil
- 2 onions, sliced
- 2 cloves garlic, minced
- 2 green peppers, washed and diced
- 2 tomatoes, peeled and sliced
- 1 tablespoon flour
- ½ cup white wine
- 1 cup finely chopped parsley
- 1 teaspoon thyme
- 1 bay leaf
- Pepper and salt
- 1 cup (or more) cooked fish, cut into 1-inch pieces
- 4 medium-sized potatoes, boiled and sliced
- ½ cup bread crumbs
- 2 tablespoons butter

In a skillet heat the oil, sauté the onions until golden brown, then add the garlic, peppers, and tomatoes. Cook for 5 minutes. Add the flour, and stir in the white wine until mixture has a creamy consistency. Add parsley, thyme, bay leaf, and salt and pepper to taste. Transfer the contents of the skillet into a casserole dish. Add the fish, spreading throughout, then the potatoes. Top with bread crumbs, dot with butter, and bake in a preheated 350° oven for 20 minutes. Serve.

Here is another good stretcher for leftover fish.

Fish Croquettes

Serves 5

- ½ stick butter
- ½ cup mushrooms, cleaned
- 1 cup cooked fish
- 1 cup white cream sauce (see page 46)
- 2 eggs
- Pepper and salt
- 1 quart deep-frying oil
- ½ cup bread crumbs
- 1 bunch parsley, washed and dried
- 1 lemon, quartered

In a skillet melt the butter and sauté the mushrooms for 5 minutes.

In the blender, combine and purée the fish, cream sauce, one egg, sautéed mushrooms, and salt and pepper to taste. Transfer to a mixing bowl and refrigerate for 30 minutes at least.

A few minutes before removing mixture from the refrigerator, start heating oil in the deep fryer. Remove the mixture and shape into small, oblong patties. Into a bowl break the second egg, and beat lightly. Dip the patties in the egg, then in the bread crumbs. Deep fry them until golden on all sides (no more than 4 or 5 minutes in all). Remove and drain on a paper towel. Place on a serving platter. Deep fry the sprigs of parsley for a few seconds until crisp. Drain and use to decorate your platter, alternating with lemon quarters. Serve.

If, like my family, you have a weakness for crêpes, one of the nicest ways to bring back fish in a new and enticing form is *crêpes farcies au poisson*.

Crêpes Stuffed with Fish

Serves 8

Crêpe batter (see page 76)
1 cup cooked fish, flaked
1 cup mushrooms, cleaned and sliced
1 cup finely chopped parsley
1 cup grated Swiss cheese
½ teaspoon paprika
2 cups white cream sauce (see page 46)
Pepper and salt
½ teaspoon nutmeg

Make the crêpe batter, and cook a pile of 10 to 12 crêpes.

In a bowl, mix the fish, mushrooms, parsley, ½ cup cheese, paprika, 1 cup cream sauce, and pepper and salt to taste. Fill the center of each crêpe with 2 tablespoons of this filling, and roll. Place the rolled crêpes side by side in an ovenproof dish. Cover with the remaining cream sauce, top with the remaining cheese, sprinkle with nutmeg, and bake in a preheated 350° oven for 15 minutes. Serve.

EGGS

Leftover eggs, cooked or uncooked, are tempting candidates to be dispensed with forthwith. But even here there are a number of possible ways you can use them again.

Take French toast: inevitably there is a spoonful or two left of the egg-milk mixture in the bottom of the bowl, sometimes more. It's an irritatingly small quantity, yet can be put to fun use. For example, if I am preparing a soup, I trickle it into the soup, which gives an egg-drop effect. Or I store it, covered, for use as a future glaze for one of my baking uses—bread, brioches, crusts, and so on.

Leftover scrambled eggs can always be added to any stuffing, or become part of a cold salad. I often dice them and add them to any existing soup.

An omelet can also be used as above, or can be used, with mayonnaise, for sandwiches.

In all probability the leftover items you have to deal with most frequently—because they are used in so many meals—are the starches: potatoes, rice, and pasta. Potatoes being the most common of all, let's start with them.

POTATOES

What to do with a few leftover potatoes—be they boiled, mashed, baked, or sautéed? Keep them, no matter what. You can store them safely for two or three days in the refrigerator (no longer!), by which time some inspiration will surely strike. Here is one idea: *pommes de terre forestière,* which in itself will serve as a main course for any lunch, or as a side dish with grilled meat for a dinner.

Potatoes Forestière

Serves 4

1 stick butter
1 tablespoon cooking oil
1 piece slab bacon, cut into 1-inch squares (or 3–4 slices regular bacon, similarly cut)
3 onions, quartered
½ pound mushrooms, cleaned and sliced
Juice of ½ lemon
5–6 cooked potatoes, quartered
1 cup stock
1 cup finely chopped parsley
Pepper and salt

In a skillet, melt the butter and oil, and cook the bacon and onions until translucent. Add the mushrooms and lemon juice; stir and cook for another 5 minutes. Add potatoes and reduce flame, allowing the potatoes to turn golden. Add the stock, cover, and cook for 10 minutes, or until the liquid has evaporated. Mix in parsley and salt and pepper to taste. Serve.

Tourte comtoise is a French regional specialty from the eastern province of Franche-Comté, known for its dairy products. Its well-known cheeses include l'Emmenthal, an excellent blue cheese, and Comté, which is very similar in looks and taste to Swiss cheese—the Comté province lying not far from Switzerland. This is a rather rich dish, and I recommend you serve it with nothing except a crisp green salad.

Pie, Besançon Style

For the crust:

Serves 4
2 cups flour
1 egg
1 stick butter
½ teaspoon salt

In a bowl, knead the ingredients with your fingers until smooth. Refrigerate for half an hour, then make your filling as follows:

4 eggs
½ cup milk
½ cup heavy cream
½ teaspoon nutmeg
Pepper and salt
3 boiled potatoes, sliced
2 slices ham, ground or chopped very finely
1 cup grated Swiss cheese

In a bowl, beat the eggs with the milk, cream, nutmeg, pepper, and salt (light on the salt because the ham and cheese are already salty). If you have no heavy cream handy, you can use evaporated milk in its place.

Remove the dough from the refrigerator, roll out onto a floured board, and line a buttered 9-inch pie mold. (If you can, invest in a French pie mold: it's the one whose center you can lift out after baking, giving you a fluted crust perfect in looks.) On the dough, form first a layer of potatoes, then a layer of ham, then finally a layer of cheese, reserving ⅓ cup of the cheese for topping. Pour the contents of the bowl over pie, and top with remaining cheese. In a preheated 350° oven bake for 45 minutes. Unmold and serve.

Pommes de terres surprises will, as the name suggests, surprise and delight. I defy anyone served these potato puffs to even dream that they began with three leftover boiled potatoes.

Potato Puffs

Serves 5–6
1 cup water
Salt
1 stick butter
1 cup flour

4 eggs
4 boiled potatoes, mashed with ½ stick butter
1–2 quarts deep-frying oil

In a saucepan, bring the water, salt, and butter to a boil. Turn off flame and add the flour all at once. Stir vigorously for one minute until you have a thick, smooth paste. Add the eggs one at a time, then the mashed potatoes. Work together until all ingredients are properly blended. Refrigerate for at least half an hour. (Like so many recipes in this book, this one can be done in advance. This first stage of making potato puffs can, for instance, be done in a very few minutes in the morning, before you leave for work. The all-day refrigeration will be all to the good.)

Remove the saucepan from the refrigerator. Roll the dough into small balls roughly the size of Ping-Pong balls.

In a deep fryer, heat the oil until it's sizzling hot. Immerse enough of the potato balls to cover the surface of the deep fryer—probably ten to a dozen. When they become puffy and golden on one side, which will be a matter of a minute or so, turn them gently for another minute on the opposite side. Remove and drain. Repeat process until all the "puffs" are cooked.

Ideally, the potato puffs should be served as they come out of the deep fryer. However, to do so would defy one of my cardinal culinary principles, which is to avoid being absent from the table, slaving over a hot stove while the others are eating. Therefore, I make *all* my puffs before serving, transferring them into a casserole dish and keeping them warm, at 300°, for 15 minutes, or until the first course is finished. They may lose a fraction of their crispness, but the difference, if any, is as nothing compared to the advantages the cook will gain from this method.

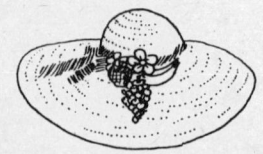

Leftover potatoes are always a prime candidate for a ragoût—or stew. Here is *pommes de terre en ragoût,* a hearty peasant dish which on lean days will make a substantial meal in itself.

Potatoes Bourguignonne

Serves 3–4
½ stick butter
2 onions, finely chopped
3 slices bacon, cut in 1-inch pieces
1 tablespoon flour
½ cup stock
½ cup red wine
1 tablespoon vinegar
1 bay leaf
1 teaspoon thyme
1 cup finely chopped parsley
4–5 cooked potatoes, quartered
Salt and pepper

In a Dutch oven heat the butter, and sauté the onions and bacon until translucent Stir in the flour and dilute gradually with the stock and wine. (NOTE: If you have no stock on hand, remember that you can improvise some with a bouillon cube and half a cup of hot water.) Add vinegar, bay leaf, thyme, parsley, and potatoes. Season to taste. Cover and simmer for 15 minutes. Serve.

The Italian dish gnocchi can be made from a number of ingredients: semolina, Cream of Wheat, farina. This tasty pasta dish can also be made with potatoes. Rich and filling, it can be served as a main course in itself, or if you prefer as the side dish for a grilled meat.

Potato Gnocchi

Serves 4
3–4 cooked potatoes
1 whole egg
1 egg yolk
⅔ cup flour
½ teaspoon nutmeg
Pepper and salt
1 cup grated Swiss cheese
½ stick butter

Beat all the ingredients except cheese and butter with a mixer until smooth. With your hands, form little balls about an inch or two in diameter, drop them into boiling salty water, and simmer for 5 minutes. Remove with a slotted spoon and place in an ovenproof dish. Smother with the grated cheese, dot with butter, and bake in a preheated 350° oven for 15 minutes. Serve.

Most people wouldn't dream of making any form of mashed potatoes with only cold leftover potatoes as a basis. But you can. Here's how, with several variations offered. The first is *purée de pommes de terre et de cerfeuil*.

Chervil and Potato Purée

Serves 4

- 1 quart salty water
- 2 cups chopped chervil (if unavailable, flat-leafed parsley will do fine)
- 4–6 cooked potatoes
- ½ cup heavy cream
- 1 stick butter
- Pepper and salt

In a kettle, bring the water to a boil. Drop in the chervil (or parsley) and cook for 5 minutes. Add the potatoes and cook for 2 minutes (just long enough to make them hot and tender again). Drain over a colander.

With a mixer, whip the contents of the colander with the cream, butter, and pepper and salt to taste. Transfer to a saucepan and heat for a couple of minutes, stirring with a wooden spoon. Serve.

While potatoes don't automatically evoke an image of "delicacy," here's a purée, reminiscent of *céleri rémoulade,* that qualifies for that term: *purée de pommes de terre et de céleri-rave, mayonnaise.*

Purée of Celeriac and Potatoes in a Mayonnaise Sauce

Serves 4–5

- 1 pound celeriac (celery root), peeled and cubed
- 1 quart salty water
- 3–4 cooked potatoes
- 1 hard-boiled egg
- 1 cup mayonnaise (see page 46), made with lemon juice
- 2 tablespoons Dijon mustard
- Pepper and salt
- Truffles (optional)

In a kettle, cook the celeriac in boiling water for 15 minutes. Drain.

With a mixer, whip the potatoes, celeriac, hard-boiled egg, mayonnaise, mustard, and pepper and salt to taste, until fluffy and smooth. If you have any truffles among your staples, open a can, mince, and mix into the purée. Heat gently and serve.

NOTE: You can also serve this dish cold. If you do, serve on a bed of lettuce leaves, and squeeze over it a few drops of lemon juice.

Also in the purée family are the following two recipes. The first is *purée rose.*

Rose Purée

Serves 3–5
6–8 carrots, peeled
1 quart salty water
3–4 cooked potatoes
½ cup heavy cream
1 stick butter
1 teaspoon nutmeg
Pepper and salt

In a saucepan, boil the carrots in salty water for 15 minutes. Drain. With a mixer, whip the cooked carrots, potatoes, cream, butter, nutmeg, and pepper and salt to taste, until fluffy. Serve.

NOTE: You may if you wish keep this dish warm in a casserole at low temperature—about 250°—for as much as 45 minutes prior to dinner time.

The second is *purée verte:*

Green Purée

This is identical to the preceding recipe for *rose purée* with the exception that instead of carrots you utilize a pound of green beans (2 cups cooked).

Here are two more leftover potato dishes which I make because they're fun, savory, and marvelously mask the fact that they began as not very appetizing cold potatoes fresh from the refrigerator.

Potatoes Marquise

Serves 4
4–5 cooked potatoes
1 stick butter
3 egg yolks
6-ounce can tomato purée
Pepper and salt
½ cup grated Swiss cheese

In a bowl mix all the ingredients except the cheese. (Use your electric mixer if you have one; otherwise a fork will do.) Form little balls the size of a nut. Roll them in the cheese. Arrange on a buttered cookie sheet and bake in a preheated 350° oven for 30 minutes.

Souffléed Potato Puffs with Ham

Serves 4

- 1 slice ham
- 4 cooked potatoes
- 1 stick butter
- ½ cup milk
- ½ cup water
- 1 cup flour
- 6 eggs
- 1 teaspoon nutmeg
- Pepper and salt
- 1–2 quarts cooking oil
- Chopped parsley

In a blender purée the ham, potatoes, and half the butter. If you have no blender, chop ham as finely as possible, then mix with potatoes and butter in a mixer or with a fork.

In a saucepan, bring the milk, water, and remaining butter to a boil. Turn off the flame, pour in the flour all at once, and add the eggs one by one, stirring vigorously. Add ham and potato mixture, nutmeg, some pepper, and a little salt.

Form little balls the size of a walnut. Heat up the oil in your deep fryer to medium hot (if you see that it smokes, reduce flame and wait a minute or two), and put in as many balls as the circumference will accommodate. Let the balls cook until golden, then remove and drain. This first-stage operation compares to the French method of making *frites* or *pommes soufflédevelopmentes;* it can, if you like— and I often do—be done in the morning, or well in advance of your serving time. It's the second stage that will make the balls puff. For this second stage, heat the oil to very hot, and drop in the balls. They will puff in a matter of a minute or two. Remove, drain on a paper towel, and sprinkle with parsley. Serve.

Charlotte renaissance sounds somewhat pretentious, but don't let it discourage you: first of all, potatoes were virtually unknown in

Europe during the Renaissance and did not begin to be widely used until Parmentier went to work on the problem in France in the eighteenth century—all of which would indicate that the "Renaissance" description of the dish is historically inaccurate. Be that as it may, although it requires a baking time of 45 minutes, this dish—which can serve as either a main course or a side dish according to the culinary situation—takes only a few minutes to prepare.

Charlotte Renaissance

Serves 4–5
- 5–6 cooked potatoes
- 3 egg yolks
- ½ stick butter
- ½ cup heavy cream
- 1 slice ham, diced
- Pepper and salt
- 3 egg whites, beaten stiff
- ½ cup finely chopped parsley

With a mixer, whip the potatoes, egg yolks, butter, cream, ham, and pepper and salt to taste. Fold in the whites, then pour this mixture into a buttered charlotte mold. Set the mold in a roasting pan filled with an inch of water, and bake in a preheated 350° oven for 45 minutes. Unmold onto a warm serving platter. Sprinkle with parsley, and serve.

Every region and country has its own special way—and often several—of offering potatoes. *Pommes de terre lyonnaise* utilizes onions, or onions and mushrooms, to revitalize your leftover potatoes.

Potatoes Lyons Style

Serves 4
- ½ stick butter
- 1 onion, finely chopped
- 4–5 cooked potatoes, diced
- Pepper and salt
- 2 tablespoons stock
- ½ cup finely chopped parsley

In a skillet melt the butter and cook the onion for 5 minutes. Add the potatoes and pepper and salt to taste, and stir. Pour in the stock. Reduce flame to low, and cook until the bottoms of the potatoes and onions are brown and crisp. (The whole point is not to touch the contents of the skillet till then; if you do, you'll end up with hash brown potatoes rather than an omeletlike texture.) Fold, as you would an omelet, garnish with parsley, and serve.

Pommes de terre à l'italienne features green pepper and cheese.

Potatoes Italian Style

Serves 4

- 1 large green pepper, minced
- 4–5 cooked potatoes, cubed
- Pepper and salt
- 1 egg, slightly beaten with $2/3$ cup milk
- 1/2 cup grated Parmesan cheese
- 2 tablespoons butter

Cook the minced green pepper in boiling water for 5 minutes, and drain. In a buttered casserole dish put the potatoes and the cooked green pepper. Sprinkle on pepper and salt. Pour in the egg and milk mixture, sprinkle with a layer of cheese, dot with butter, and bake for 10 minutes in the oven at 400°. Serve.

Salade de Grenoble is a very substantial dish, ideal for a lunch, buffet, or picnic.

Salad Grenoble Style

Serves 3–4

- 4 cooked potatoes, sliced
- 1 cup white wine
- 3 tablespoons olive oil
- Juice of 1 lemon
- 1 head Boston lettuce, washed and cut finely
- 1/2 cooked sausage (Polish or garlic), sliced
- 1 slice ham, diced
- 1/2 cup green olives, pitted
- 1/2 cup finely chopped parsley
- Pepper and salt

In a saucepan boil a cup or so of water, and add the potatoes to warm them slightly—one minute ought to suffice—and render them porous so that they can absorb the dressing. Drain. Transfer to a salad bowl. While the potatoes are still warm, pour the wine over them, and add oil and lemon juice. Then add the remaining ingredients, toss, and serve.

Thus far I've assumed you may have had three to six leftover potatoes. Suppose you have only one or two? Remember that you can always use them to thicken any soup or broth. This you do by adding a few tablespoons of the existing soup to the potatoes, mashing, then returning to the soup kettle.

You can also use them to add substance to an omelet.

Potato Omelet

Serves 4

½ stick butter
1 onion, finely chopped, or
    4 scallions, finely chopped
1–2 cooked potatoes, sliced

5 eggs
¼ cup milk
Pepper and salt
½ cup finely chopped parsley

In a skillet melt the butter and sauté the onion until pale brown. Add the potatoes, cook 2 minutes, remove from the skillet, and set aside.

In a bowl, beat the eggs with the milk, and season to taste with pepper and salt. Pour into the skillet, reduce flame to low, and cook without disturbing for a minute or two. With a fork gently lift the outer edges and peek to see if the bottom has set. Tilt the frying pan to allow more of the liquid omelet to reach the bottom of the skillet. While the center of the omelet is still wet, distribute the potatoes, onion, and half the parsley on it. With a spatula, fold the omelet in half, slide onto a serving platter, garnish with parsley, and serve.

N O T E : Omelets are good warm or cold.

RICE

Rice, almost as widely used as potatoes, is equally versatile. And, like potatoes, if you have a cup or two of leftover rice, you can always put it to good use.

Rice with Mushrooms

Serves 6

1 stick butter
Juice of ½ lemon
¼ pound mushrooms, cleaned
    and sliced

1½ cups cooked rice
Pepper and salt
½ cup finely chopped parsley

In a skillet melt the butter. Pour the lemon juice over the mushrooms, and sauté them for 5 minutes. Mix in the rice, add pepper and salt to taste, and stir for another 5 minutes or so. Transfer to a serving platter, sprinkle with parsley, and serve.

A very old, and very rich, French recipe is *riz au gras*, also known as *riz à la moelle*. It is the marrow that makes it rich—and gives it its exquisite taste.

Rich Rice

Serves 3–4

4 marrow bones, rinsed
1 stick butter
3 shallots, finely chopped
1½–2 cups cooked rice
½ cup grated Swiss cheese
½ cup stock
Pepper and salt

In a saucepan bring a quart of salty water to a boil. Immerse the marrow bones and cook for 10 minutes. Remove and drain bones. With a teaspoon, scoop out the marrow from inside the bones. Discard the bones. In a skillet, melt the butter, sauté the shallots until golden brown, and add the marrow, rice, cheese, stock, and pepper and salt to taste. Stir. Cook over a low flame for 5 minutes or so, until the rice is hot. Serve.

Brillat-Savarin calls the truffle "the diamond of the kitchen." He was doubtless referring to their qualities rather than their price, but the fact is that truffles are abominably expensive, particularly the French ones. The Italian truffle, however, a grayish white variety as opposed to the French black, is considerably less expensive and still a great delicacy.

One of the bases of my leftover mentality, however, is that because of the obvious economies I am achieving by using leftovers, I often feel that I can indulge in extra frivolities. And how pleasurable to see a savory gourmet dish arrive on the table—and only you are aware of its modest origins. Such a dish is *riz à la Torino*.

Rice à la Torino

Serves 6

1½–2 cups cooked rice
1 can Italian truffles, minced
1 cup grated Parmesan cheese
½ cup tomato purée
Pepper and salt
½ stick butter

Mix all the ingredients except butter in a casserole dish, dot with butter, and bake for 15 minutes at 350°. Serve.

Cream cheese is usually part of a cook's refrigerated staples, which gives you the possibility of making *croquettes au riz et au fromage blanc*—only one of many creations using cream cheese and rice as bases.

Rice and Cream Cheese Croquettes

Serves 4–5

1½ cups cooked rice
2 eggs
8-ounce package cream cheese
1 cup finely chopped parsley
½ cup grated Parmesan cheese
Pepper and salt
½ cup flour
1 egg, slightly beaten
½ cup bread crumbs
1 stick butter
½ cup cooking oil
1 whole bunch parsley sprigs, washed

In a blender, purée the rice, the two eggs, and cream cheese. Add the chopped parsley, Parmesan cheese, and pepper and salt to taste. Form little balls. In three different bowls put your flour, beaten egg, and bread crumbs. Roll the balls in the flour, then in the egg, and finally in the bread crumbs.

In a skillet, heat the butter and the oil. Fry the rice balls, flattening them slightly with a fork or spatula, for about 5 minutes on each side, until they become light brown and crisp. Remove and drain on paper towels. Transfer to warm serving platter.

In the same skillet, fry the parsley sprigs for 2 to 3 minutes in the remaining butter and oil. Drain on paper towel. Garnish the serving platter with the parsley sprigs. Serve.

Rice can also be served to good advantage with all kinds of other vegetables: rice and mushrooms, rice and peas, rice with almonds, and so on. Here is a combination rice and vegetable dish quick to prepare and guaranteed to enhance your leftover rice: *jardinière de légumes au riz.*

Rice with Mixed Vegetables

Serves 4

- 1 stick butter
- 1 onion, peeled and quartered
- 1 cup (or more) cooked rice
- 16-ounce can mixed vegetables, drained and rinsed
- 1 cup finely chopped parsley
- 1 teaspoon thyme
- 2 tablespoons stock
- Pepper and salt

In a skillet, melt the butter, and sauté the onion until translucent. Add the remaining ingredients. Stir for 5 minutes over a low flame, and serve.

Another, very different dish combines mixed vegetables (of a different kind) and shrimp: *charlotte de riz à la haitienne.*

Charlotte of Rice Haitian Style

Serves 4

- 5 tablespoons olive oil
- 2 large onions, finely chopped
- 2 cloves garlic, minced
- 8-ounce can tiny shrimp, drained and rinsed
- 2 tablespoons flour
- 1/3 cup water
- 1–1½ cups cooked rice
- 1 green pepper, washed and minced
- 4-ounce can red pimientos, minced
- 1 teaspoon hot crushed peppers
- Pepper and salt

In a Dutch oven heat the oil and sauté the onion and garlic until light brown. Add the shrimp, and stir for one minute. Add the flour, then stir in the water. Now add the rice, green pepper, pimientos, hot peppers, and pepper and salt to taste. Mix well. Turn off flame.

Butter a charlotte mold and pack in the mixture very tightly. In an oven preheated to 350° bake for 15 minutes. Remove, unmold onto a warm platter, and serve.

Instead of a charlotte mold, try if you like a ring mold. This will give you a very appetizing ring or crown, inside of which you may feel free to add fricasseed chicken, stew, or any other meat. Here is *couronne de riz au poulet.*

Ring of Rice, Chicken in Sauce

Serves 4–5

- 1–1½ cups cooked rice
- 1 cup milk
- 4 tablespoons butter, melted
- 1 onion, finely chopped
- 1 egg
- ½ cup grated Swiss (or cheddar) cheese
- ½ teaspoon paprika
- ½ cup finely chopped parsley
- Pepper and salt

In a bowl, mix all the ingredients. Transfer into a buttered ring mold. In an oven preheated to 350° bake for 45 minutes. Unmold onto a warm serving platter, and fill the center with fricasseed chicken.

For the fricasseed chicken you will need:

- 2 breasts of chicken
- 1 quart water
- 1 small onion, pricked with two cloves
- 1 bay leaf
- Pepper and salt

Put chicken in a kettle, cover with water, add the onion, bay leaf, pepper, and salt, and boil for about 35 minutes. Remove the chicken, bone, and cube.

For the sauce:

- 1 stick butter
- 2 tablespoons flour
- 1 cup milk
- 1 tablespoon Worcestershire sauce
- Juice of ½ lemon

In a Dutch oven, melt the butter, then add the flour. Stir in the milk, Worcestershire sauce, and lemon juice. Stir until smooth and thick (if by chance it looks too thick, add a little more milk). Mix in cubed chicken, stir for 5 minutes, and serve in the center of the ring of rice.

Rice is also an ideal ingredient for a stuffed dish. For example, the Armenians stuff mussels with rice mixed with seafood; Russian and Middle European cuisines feature stuffed cabbage, which usually means cabbage leaves rolled around cooked rice or a combination of rice and meat. The French very often include rice in a stuffing of cold tomatoes, as in *tomates farcies au riz et au jambon*.

Tomatoes Stuffed with Rice and Ham in a Mayonnaise Sauce

Serves 4–5

6–7 small tomatoes, washed	1 cup mayonnaise (see page 46), made with lemon juice
1–1½ cups cooked rice	
1 slice ham, diced	Pepper and salt

Cut off tomato tops and scoop out the insides, reserving the pulp for a later soup. Mix rice, ham, and mayonnaise, season to taste, and fill hollowed-out tomatoes with this mixture. Replace "hats" on top of tomatoes and serve chilled.

This can serve as a luncheon main course, or is recommended as part of a buffet.

Another cold rice dish is *salade de riz*. There are literally dozens of rice salads, each with its own virtue. Here is one I often make.

Rice Salad

Serves 4–5

2 cups cooked rice	1 small onion, finely chopped
1 tomato, cubed	4 tablespoons olive oil
2 green peppers, diced	Juice of 1 lemon
2 tablespoons Dijon (or other prepared) mustard	1 tablespoon tarragon
	½ cup finely chopped parsley
1 cup black olives, pitted	Pepper and salt

In a salad bowl, mix all the ingredients. Chill and serve.

NOTE: Any other odd meat, vegetable, or cooked egg leftovers you may have in your refrigerator can be diced and added to this salad, to create your own variation. If you do add ingredients, check your seasoning, and if necessary add lemon juice or oil to taste.

Rice, of course, is also used as a basic ingredient for all manner of desserts. If you have your meal planned and have no place in it for a salad or vegetable, perhaps you'd like to utilize that forlorn cup of leftover rice to make a dessert. Here's one that's almost instant and is a close cousin of rice pudding. The French call it *gâteau de riz d'urgence*:

Instant Rice Cake

Serves 4
- 1 tablespoon cornstarch
- ½ cup milk
- Grated rind of 1 lemon
- 3 tablespoons sugar
- 1 tablespoon vanilla extract
- 1 cup cooked rice
- ½ jar currant (or raspberry) jelly, warmed

In a cup, blend the cornstarch with a tablespoon of the milk. In a saucepan, heat remaining milk with lemon rind, sugar, and vanilla. Add the cornstarch, and stir with a wooden spoon until mixture thickens. Mix in the rice. Pour into a bowl or a mold and refrigerate. Unmold onto a serving platter, and smother with warm jelly. Serve.

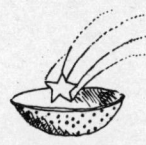

PASTA

Pasta is the Italian term for the paste made with flour and water or flour and eggs, and sometimes other ingredients that becomes spaghetti, macaroni, noodles, and so forth. An infinite variety of pastas, however they vary in precise composition and shape, derives essentially from the same principle of dough.

Pasta is so integral a part of the Italian daily culinary tradition that it appears almost automatically as a first or second course (after soup). The innocent and unsuspecting tourist is liable to think, after finishing a copious dish of ravioli or lasagna, that he is ready for salad or dessert. But no: inevitably, he is offered a *real* main course of meat or fish. In this country, however, pasta is very often a main course in itself.

The Italians, and connoisseurs of Italian food, will claim that pasta should be eaten only when freshly cooked. They are right. But it is often hard to anticipate accurately just how much pasta to prepare; therefore, you will often find yourself with some left over. Realizing that I am risking the disapproval of the guardians of *haute cuisine,* I nonetheless give in to my thrifty nature: I keep my leftover pasta. Here are a few uses I put it to.

In the summer, or for a buffet dinner, go salad. As is the case with rice salad, everyone has his or her own recipe for pasta salad. Here is one of mine:

Macaroni Salad

Serves 4–5

- 2 cups cooked macaroni (or any other cooked pasta)
- 1 cup mayonnaise
- 1 green pepper, diced
- 1 onion, finely chopped
- 1 carrot, peeled and thinly sliced
- 1 slice ham, diced (optional)
- Juice of 1 lemon
- 2 tablespoons olive oil
- Pepper and salt

In a salad bowl thoroughly mix all the ingredients. Chill and serve.

The following recipe may seem a contradiction of terms—for pasta implies heaviness and mousse implies lightness—but *mousse de macaroni* defies the laws of gravity.

Macaroni Mousse

Serves 4–5

- 1 cup cooked macaroni (or other pasta)
- 2 eggs
- 1½ cups hot milk
- ½ stick butter
- 1 small onion, quartered
- 1 cup bread crumbs
- ½ teaspoon nutmeg
- Pepper and salt
- ½ cup grated Swiss cheese
- 1 green pepper, minced

In a blender, purée the macaroni, eggs, milk, butter, onion, half the bread crumbs, nutmeg, and pepper and salt to taste. Pour the contents of the blender into a buttered charlotte mold. Add cheese and pepper, and cover with remaining bread crumbs. Set the mold in a roasting pan with an inch of water, and bake in a preheated 350° oven for 45 minutes. Unmold onto a platter. Serve.

I often serve this mousse with a tomato sauce which I make as follows:

- ⅓ stick butter
- 1 onion, minced
- 8-ounce can tomato sauce
- 1 cup mushrooms, cleaned and minced (optional)

In a saucepan, melt the butter and sauté the onion until golden brown. Pour in tomato sauce, add mushrooms if you like, and stir over low flame for a few minutes, until hot.

You can also deep-fry your leftover pasta to good advantage. Here is a fun side dish: *nouilles frites.*

Fried Noodles

Serves 4–5

- 1–2 quarts cooking oil
- 1–2 cups cooked noodles (or other pasta)
- 1 bunch fresh parsley, washed and dried
- Salt

In your deep fryer, heat the oil until it is sizzling hot. Drop in the noodles, limiting each frying operation to the amount that will cover the surface of the oil: probably a cup will be the most you can fry at a time. Fry until golden and crisp. Drain on a paper towel. When you've finished frying all the noodles, fry the parsley for a minute or so until crisp. Remove and drain. Place the fried noodles on a platter, and use the parsley to decorate as crown. Sprinkle with salt and serve.

In Normandy, they make a macaroni loaf rich in cream and eggs: *pain de macaroni Normandie,* a meal in itself. Don't be fazed by this long list: preparation time, including the sauce, will take only minutes.

Macaroni Loaf, Normandy Style

Serves 5–6

- 2 cups cooked macaroni (or other pasta)
- 6 egg yolks
- ½ cup grated Swiss cheese
- ½ cup grated Parmesan cheese
- 2 slices ham, diced
- 1 teaspoon nutmeg
- ¼ pound mushrooms, cleaned and sliced
- Pepper and salt
- 6 egg whites, beaten stiff
- ½ stick butter
- 1 cup heavy cream
- 1 tablespoon flour
- ½ cup sour cream

In a bowl, mix the macaroni, egg yolks, cheeses, ham, half the nutmeg, half the mushrooms, and pepper and salt to taste. Fold in the egg whites, and pour mixture into a buttered charlotte mold. Set mold in a roasting pan containing an inch of water and bake in a preheated 375° oven for one hour.

Now make the sauce: In a saucepan, melt the butter and sauté the remaining mushrooms for 5 minutes. Add the heavy cream and flour. Stir for 5 minutes over a low flame. Add the sour cream, the remaining nutmeg, and pepper and salt to taste. (NOTE: If the sauce should thicken too much, add a teaspoon or so of milk.)

Unmold the charlotte onto a warm serving platter. Pour the sauce over the loaf, and serve.

This next recipe contains more or less the same ingredients as the preceding two, but the outcome is quite different: *croquettes italiennes*. Whether or not this is a truly authentic Italian dish I don't know; but that at least is the title given to the dish by the French.

Croquettes Italian Style

Serves 4–5

- 1 cup cooked noodles (or any other pasta)
- 1 cup grated Swiss cheese
- 2 egg yolks
- 1 whole egg
- 1 cup diced ham
- Pepper and salt
- 2 egg whites
- 1 cup bread crumbs
- ½ cup cooking oil

In a bowl, mix noodles with the cheese, egg yolks, the whole egg, ham, and pepper and salt to taste. With your hands, form balls, then flatten slightly. Dip them in the egg whites, then in the bread crumbs.

In a skillet, heat the oil until hot. Fry the croquettes until golden and crisp on each side. Drain. Sprinkle with salt. Serve.

Another Italian dish using leftover pasta and served as a casserole is:

Baked Macaroni Italian Style

Serves 4–5

- 2 cups cooked macaroni (or any other pasta)
- 1 cup cottage cheese
- 1½ cups sour cream
- 2 tablespoons oregano
- 1 teaspoon basil
- 8-ounce can tomato sauce
- 1 cup finely chopped parsley
- 1 onion, minced
- 1 clove garlic, minced
- Pepper and salt
- ¼ cup grated Parmesan cheese
- ¼ cup bread crumbs
- 1 tablespoon butter

In an ovenproof dish, mix all ingredients except Parmesan cheese, bread crumbs, and butter. Mix cheese and crumbs, and top the casserole. Dot with butter. Bake in a preheated 350° oven for 20 minutes. Serve.

Galantine in French indicates a preparation of ground meat or poultry formed in a loaf with various spices (depending on the region or the recipe), baked slowly in an oven, but served cold. Here is a recipe in the same tradition, but using only vegetables and some leftover pasta: *galantine du vegetarien*.

Vegetarian Galantine

Serves 4–5

1 stick butter
3 onions, finely chopped
1 cup cooked macaroni (or any other pasta)
1 cup white beans
1 cup tomato purée
½ cup green beans, cut small
1 hard-boiled egg
1 egg, lightly beaten
1 cup finely chopped parsley
1 tablespoon tarragon
1 teaspoon thyme
Pepper and salt
1 bay leaf
Parsley sprigs

In a skillet, melt half the butter and sauté the onions until golden brown. Place in a bowl and mix well with all but the bay leaf and parsley sprigs, seasoning to taste.

With a wooden spoon, scoop the contents of the bowl into a buttered ovenproof dish. Top with the bay leaf. Bake in a preheated 375° oven for 20 minutes, then reduce to 325° for half an hour. Remove, let cool to room temperature, then cool in the refrigerator. (It's best to make your galantine the night or the day before serving; as with pâtés, it will have had a chance to set properly.) Unmold onto a platter. Decorate with sprigs of parsley. Serve.

Galantine can be served as a main dish with a green salad, or as an accompanying dish with cold meat.

BREAD

I always save *all* bread, as you doubtless have gathered by now. That includes leftover buttered toast from breakfast, rolls from lunch or dinner—anything that has been served and comes back to the kitchen untouched. All this staff of life goes automatically into my "bread bag." My family makes fun of me; but I have the last laugh when they are obviously enjoying some dish I have concocted from my "bread bag."

Here are but a few:

Family Meat Loaf

Serves 5-6

- 1-1½ pounds ground beef
- 1 egg
- 4-5 slices stale bread, soaked in water and squeezed
- ½ teaspoon thyme
- ½ teaspoon tarragon
- 1 onion, finely chopped
- 1 tablespoon bacon fat
- ½ cup finely chopped parsley
- Pepper and salt

In a bowl, mix with your fingers all ingredients until they are well integrated. Scoop into an ovenproof dish and bake at 325° for about an hour.

NOTE: This same recipe works very well for making small meatballs for party canapés.

Pâté

Any pâté will benefit from the presence of leftover bread soaked in milk or water. For exact quantity, see page 159.

Stuffing

Virtually all stuffings contain bread as a basic ingredient. Some stuffings consist solely of bread and spices. *A propos* stuffing, you needn't wait for Thanksgiving or Christmas to stuff a turkey or chicken. Any small chicken will not only go further when it is stuffed, but will add a festive touch to an everyday family dinner. Stuffing takes but a few minutes to prepare, and is well worth the effort. At Thanksgiving or Christmas, the enjoyment of that added element—the stuffing—was clearly such that I saw no reason to limit it. Here again, most cooks develop their own favorite stuffing. Here is a simple bread stuffing I like. The following recipe will suffice for a 3–4-pound chicken.

Bread Stuffing

1 stick butter
1 onion, finely chopped
5 slices stale bread, cubed
1 garlic clove, minced (optional)
2 tablespoons tarragon
½ teaspoon thyme
½ cup finely chopped parsley
Pepper and salt
¼ cup hot milk

In a skillet, melt the butter and cook the onion for 5 minutes, until light brown. Add the bread cubes, toasting them as well. In mixing bowl, combine remaining ingredients, and pour over them the contents of the skillet. Mash thoroughly with your fingers. Stuff your chicken, and roast as you normally would. Preparing this stuffing will take only 10 worthwhile minutes.

If I find a soup too thin, I blend a piece or two of stale bread and a cup of the existing soup, then add the blended mixture to the soup kettle.

In fact, if I have almost nothing in the house and have to whip up a hot soup in a few minutes, my "bread bag" may save the situation. It can produce what is called a *panade*—a bread and liquid mixture normally used as a basis for various recipes, including quenelles, pâtés, and stuffing. But you can also make:

Panade Soup

Serves 6
½ stick butter
1 onion, minced
2 cloves garlic, minced
6 slices American bread (or half a loaf French bread), soaked in water
2 cups water
1 bouillon cube
Salt and pepper

In a skillet, melt the butter and brown the onion and garlic. Squeeze the water out of the bread, then put the bread in the blender, together with the water and the bouillon cube. (If it seems contradictory to squeeze out the water and then add water to the bread, remember simply that the water added is a specific quantity.) Transfer to the kettle. Add the contents of the skillet. Stir with a wooden spoon. Season to taste.

NOTE: To give this soup an added zest, you may if you like add the juice of half a lemon, a bit of finely chopped parsley—from a tablespoon to half a cup—and a dot or two of fresh butter. However you do it, though, panade soup will be one of the most inexpensive soups you can make.

In Austria, I was introduced to a marvelous dish which often accompanies a roast or poultry, or is served as a main dish with sauerkraut. Horrible for the waistline, it is nonetheless delectable for the soul.

Bread Dumplings

Serves 4

½ stick butter
1 onion, finely chopped
3 cups stale bread, cubed
½ cup flour
½ cup finely chopped parsley

½ teaspoon nutmeg
1 tablespoon tarragon
Salt and pepper
¼ cup milk
Chopped parsley for garnish

In a skillet, melt the butter and cook the onion until it becomes pale brown. Add the bread cubes, stirring to keep the onion from burning, until they too are light brown. Transfer the contents of the skillet to a large bowl, and add the flour, parsley, nutmeg, tarragon, and salt and pepper to taste. Pour in the milk.

With your fingers, knead as you would any dough. When the mixture is well integrated, form two long "loaves" about 10 to 12 inches in length. Put them on a plate and refrigerate for 30 minutes.

Put two quarts of water in a kettle large enough to accommodate your loaves. When the water is boiling, slip in the loaves, reduce flame, and cook for 20 minutes. Drain. Slice and sprinkle with chopped parsley.

If you're serving the bread dumplings as a main dish, place them on the center of the platter and surround with sauerkraut. If you're serving them as an accompaniment, arrange them around the roast.

Other dried-bread uses you should bear in mind: bread will act as one of the best firming agents for any number of things. For example:

Pesto (*pistou* in French) : if when making my *pesto* I find it too short, or too liquid, I sneak in a few pieces of bread to firm it.

The same holds true for: eggplant caviar (see page 194), guacamole (see page 100), and all puréed vegetables, such as: broccoli purée, carrot purée, green bean purée, turnip purée. Being watery vegetables, they all need a firming agent. Bread will do the trick. How much? For a turnip purée made from eight turnips, for instance, I would begin by adding two or three slices of stale bread. You may find you need still more, in which case add another slice, or part of a slice.

VEGETABLES

After almost every meal we all have some vegetables left over, usually one of those maddening spoonfuls or two but sometimes more. However tempted you may be to throw them away, resist the temptation. Most of us do suffer to some degree from the "squirrel complex," and I have a number of friends who do save these awkward vegetable remains. Too frequently, though, once having taken the step of keeping them, they really don't know why they've kept them, and a week or two later they'll end up throwing them out, mold and all. Here are a few concrete suggestions for your leftover vegetables; using them may lead you to thoughts of your own.

Artichokes: remove the leaves and beard of any artichokes you may find yourself with after a dinner. Discard the beard but save the leaves; they will come in handy the following day or two (no more!) as a handy appetizer with a vinaigrette sauce for a luncheon. As for the hearts, freeze them for a later luxurious side dish (sautéed in butter and lemon juice) for any meat course. What I do is accumulate frozen artichoke hearts until I have enough to make my full garnish. Thus even if I have only one left over, I save it. But if you prefer to put your artichoke hearts to good use immediately, here's a delicacy you can make with only a couple to start with: *riz aux artichauts*.

Rice with Artichokes

Serves 4
½ stick butter
1 onion, finely chopped
1–2 artichoke hearts, cubed
1 tomato, cubed
2 cups cooked rice
½ cup finely chopped parsley
Pepper and salt

In a skillet, melt the butter and cook the onion until blond. Add the artichokes and tomato cubes, stir for a minute, then add rice, parsley, and pepper and salt to taste. Stir over a low flame for 5 minutes. Serve.

Asparagus: haven't you noticed that no matter how much asparagus you serve there are inevitably two or three stalks that remain? Doubtless your polite guests—or family—don't want to serve themselves the last stalks. What they don't know is that they are doing you an enormous favor: those stalks will embellish any soup, either minced or blended. They will also be a welcome addition to any mixed cold salad. Diced and sautéed in butter, they will form the basis for an asparagus omelet.

Beans (green): if you have only a spoonful or two, there are two immediate possibilities that come to mind: (1) chop coarsely and add to whatever soup you're making; (2) add, as is, to your salad. If you have somewhat more, say a cup or two, improvise a:

Green Bean Purée

Serves 4–5
1–2 cups cooked green beans
4 slices stale bread, soaked in milk
1 stick butter
Pepper and salt
½ cup blanched almonds

In a blender, purée the beans, bread, butter, and pepper and salt to taste. Transfer contents to a casserole dish. Cover with the almonds. Bake in a preheated 350° oven for 20 to 25 minutes. Serve. Recommended with lamb, but good with any meat.

If you have accumulated enough leftover artichoke hearts for a dinner of four or six, you can combine the artichoke and green bean leftovers and make a really *haute cuisine* garnish by simply sautéeing the artichoke hearts in butter for 5 minutes and filling them with the bean purée. Dot these little "boats" with chopped parsley, and serve.

With a couple of cups you can also make a green bean salad. To dress it up, combine with a couple of shallots, minced; a potato or two, sliced; and a vinegar and oil dressing.

Beans (*cooked, white*): almost inevitably, I think salad, unless I don't have enough, in which case I add them to (almost any) soup. They will enhance any salad, but here's one in which white beans form the nucleus: *salade de haricots blancs*.

White Bean Salad

Serves 4

2 cups white beans	2 tablespoons wine vinegar
1 onion, finely chopped	5 tablespoons olive oil
1 green pepper, diced	½ cup finely chopped parsley
1 tomato, cubed	1 tablespoon prepared mustard
1 clove garlic, minced	Pepper and salt

Mix well in a salad bowl, and serve.

Beets: think salad or soup. If you have less than a cup, mix in a vinaigrette sauce with a couple of endives, cut up into one-inch pieces, and serve as a salad. If you have two cups, you can whip up an instant appetizer by adding one onion finely chopped, half a cup finely chopped parsley, and a vinaigrette sauce.

The soup possibility is "poor-man's borscht" (see page 122).

Broccoli: salad or soup.

Cabbage: leftover cabbage is leftover cabbage. You can't use it for salad, but you can add it to soup to make it more hearty. But with a scant two cups, I make my adaptation of Russian cabbage piroshki, a Russian pie with filling. The filling can also be, in addition to cabbage, either meat (see page 226) or fish.

Russian Cabbage Pie

Serves 4–6

2 cups cooked cabbage	1 teaspoon dill
4 hard-boiled eggs, mashed	Pepper and salt
½ stick butter	Pinch of sugar

In a bowl, mix all the ingredients. Now, for the dough, I use:

1½ sticks butter	2 egg yolks
1 cup sour cream	1 whole egg beaten with a
3 cups flour	tablespoon of water

In a bowl, mix the butter, cream, flour, and yolks with your fingers. Form a ball and refrigerate for 30 minutes. (If you make this in the morning, you can of course store it in the refrigerator for the day. In which case you may want to wait until evening to make your filling. Or, after the initial half-hour chilling, you can actually roll out your dough, insert the cabbage filling in the piroshki, and store uncooked until baking time. Or, finally, you can of course complete the baking in one step, refrigerate the baked piroshki, then simply heat it up at 350° for no more than 20 minutes just prior to serving.) Whatever your baking preference, here is what you do: divide your dough in two. On a floured surface roll it out, making two rectangles roughly the size of the casserole dish you are using (*plus a couple of inches extra on all sides for depth, for one of the two rectangles*). Line the buttered casserole dish with one rectangle of dough. Fill with the cabbage mixture. Before placing the second, smaller rectangle on top, prick it or crisscross with the point of a knife. Seal the edges of the top and bottom rectangles with your fingers. Flute the edges with a fork, for beauty's sake. Should you have dough scraps left over, you can further beautify by using them to make any inventive shape, to decorate the top. Brush the exposed dough with the egg and water mixture. In a preheated oven bake at 375° for 30 minutes. Serve warm.

Carrots: a cup of leftover carrots can be puréed with a potato or two and turned into my *purée rose*—pink purée (see page 269). Also, diced, carrots can be added to soups.

If you have two cups, however, you might want to try this carrot pudding, which will add a colorful note to any meat dish.

Carrot Pudding

Serves 4
2 cups cooked carrots
1 onion, minced
1 cup milk
1 egg
1 teaspoon nutmeg
1 teaspoon sugar
Pepper and salt
½ cup bread crumbs
½ stick butter

In a bowl, mix all the ingredients except for the bread crumbs and half the butter. (You can also use your blender; or, lacking both blender and mixer, you can mash with a fork.) Pour into a buttered casserole dish. Melt the remaining butter and pour over. Top with bread crumbs. Bake in a preheated oven at 350° for 35 minutes.

Cauliflower: if your original cauliflower was served gratin, as it often is, your only route is to the soup. If plain, it's marvelous cold in a vinaigrette sauce as either an appetizer or a salad. Or you can make:

Cauliflower Croquettes

Serves 4
1 cup cooked cauliflower
1 whole egg
1 egg yolk
½ cup grated Swiss cheese
½ stick butter or margarine
⅓ cup flour
⅓ cup milk
Pepper and salt
1 egg white
1 cup bread crumbs

In a bowl, mash all ingredients except half the butter, the egg white and bread crumbs. Form patties, dip them in egg white, then in bread crumbs, and fry in remaining butter or margarine. Drain and serve.

Celery: raw celery has many re-uses, from salads to stuffings. To maintain crispness, remember to keep your raw celery in a jar of water in the refrigerator. Diced, it can be added to any soup.

Corn: leftover corn has a variety of uses. Cut the kernels from whatever number of ears you have left, and add to soups. Cold corn can be served in salads. Or, mixed with peas or lima beans, it can, of course, make succotash.

Cucumber: any cucumbers remaining from your cucumber salad can be used as a basis for Greek soup (see page 78). If you've served them first time around in a vinaigrette sauce, don't let the fact that they may appear limp and weary deter you. They're still fine. Gazpacho is another prime candidate for them.

Eggplant: even if you have only a couple of tablespoons left over of any form of cooked eggplant, you can always use them to good advantage to enhance any spaghetti sauce. Also use to add variety to your homemade pizza.

Mushrooms: this delicate, savory vegetable will be a happy addition to any soup (not only cooked; even if its original preparation was in a vinaigrette sauce in salad). The same applies to stuffings. Even a tablespoon or so can be used to dot your quiche. If you have a cupful or more, you can make a mushroom-cream sauce and store in the freezer, until needed to add a gourmet touch to a meat such as veal, or to poultry. Or, it can be one of your several side sauces for a meat fondue. Or, over toast, you have a light and tasty lunch.

With a cupful or more, try making this delectable regional French mushroom and snail dish: *cassolettes forestière*. Cassolettes are individual-sized earthenware ovenproof dishes common in the south of France. I have served this both as a first course—it is a rich opener, so it should be followed by a light main course—and as a main dish. If the latter, have warm, crisp French bread to go with it, followed by a green salad and cheese.

Cassolettes Foreștière

Serves 6–8

2 tablespoons olive oil	1 teaspoon nutmeg
1 cup cooked mushrooms	3 shallots, finely chopped
1 can (24) snails	2 cloves garlic, minced
Pepper and salt	1 generous cup very finely chopped parsley
2 sticks butter	

In a skillet, heat the oil, stir in mushrooms and snails, and cook over a low flame for 5 minutes. Add pepper and salt to taste.

Apportion among 6 to 8 earthenware cassolettes.

Now prepare your *beurre d'escargot* as follows: in a bowl, mix the butter, nutmeg, shallots, garlic, half the parsley, pepper and salt, until well combined. Divide and cover the top of each dish with this *beurre d'escargot*. If possible, leave your cassolettes overnight in the refrigerator (not only will you have made your preparation ahead of time, but also the *beurre d'escargot* will act as a marinade).

When ready for baking, place the dishes in a roasting pan (no water required; the reason I do this is simply for ease in removing the individual dishes from the oven. Not only is there an economy of movement, but also you lessen the chances of spilling and burning). Cook for 8 minutes, sprinkle with remaining parsley, and serve.

Onions: add leftover cooked onions to a soup—cream and all if that's how they were served originally. Or to virtually any casserole dish. Or to a meat pie.

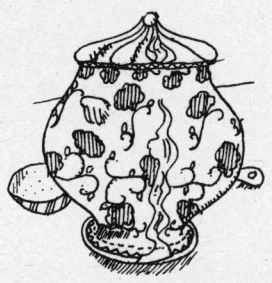

Peas: again, add to soups. Or, as additional ingredients for casseroles and meat pies. If you have a cupful or so, you can mix mayonnaise and lemon juice and use to stuff a hollowed-out raw tomato. Mixed with cooked rice, meat stock, salt, and pepper, peas become a perfectly respectable accompaniment for poultry.

Peppers: green or red, many salads will profit from peppers. Or make gazpacho.

Salad: no one with any normal culinary instincts would dream of saving leftover salad, which has already been subjected to a dressing and by the end of a meal looks forlorn and wilted. But remember: looks aren't everything. I save even the most jaded salad, for I know that it can play its part in an upcoming gazpacho.

The preceding applies to already prepared salad soaked in dressing. But suppose you've bought lettuce on Monday and for some reason you've not had a chance to use it, or forgotten it in your refrigerator: by Friday it looks practically irretrievable. Maybe it is; but first try to revive it in cold water. You'll be surprised how often a goodly inner portion will spring back and within an hour's time be fresh and crisp and ready for your vinaigrette. But even if it doesn't, there are a couple of ideas on how to put it to use: one is *pain de salade à l'ancienne.*

Old-Fashioned Salad Loaf

Serves 4

4 limp heads Boston lettuce (or equivalent)
3 eggs
1 cup white cream sauce (see page 46)
1 teaspoon nutmeg
1 pinch sugar
½ stick butter
3 slices stale bread
Pepper and salt

In a kettle, cook the washed lettuce in boiling water for 10 minutes. Drain. Purée in blender with the remaining ingredients. Pour contents of the blender into a buttered ovenproof dish and bake at 350° for 45 minutes. Cut as you would a cake or loaf of bread, and serve.

Braised Lettuce

Serves 4

1 stick butter
1 limp head lettuce
Juice of ½ lemon
½ cup stock
1 teaspoon sugar
Pepper and salt

In a Dutch oven melt the butter, and sauté the lettuce over a low flame for 5 minutes. Pour in lemon juice and stock; add sugar and pepper and salt to taste. Cover, and cook over low flame for 30 minutes. Serve.

Tomatoes (cooked): can be used in tomato sauce and in soup—any soup, not just tomato. Can also be added to your homemade pizza, or served over meat loaf.

Tomatoes (in salad): save both tomatoes *and* vinaigrette. Both will go into your gazpacho. You may also drain the vinaigrette and make the tomatoes part of the next day's luncheon sandwiches.

CHEESES

Blue cheese: any member of the blue cheese family—Roquefort, gorgonzola, and so on—can be mixed with mayonnaise, sour cream, salt, and pepper and blended in a matter of seconds into a creamy salad dressing. Or simply crumbled over a salad that has an oil and vinegar dressing. Not to mention its use as one of the ingredients of my homemade cheeses (see pages 68, 80, 161).

Cheddar: a chunk always goes into my homemade cheese. Shaved or grated, can be added to scrambled eggs, omelets, and cream sauces.

Camembert: what can you do with half a Camembert which is by now dry, ammonia-smelling, and totally unappetizing? You'd doubtless throw it out. Don't. First, cheese is quite expensive, and Camembert especially so. Half a Camembert, no matter how hard, represents a hard dollar. Therefore remove the skin and whip or mash with a 4-ounce cream cheese and a half-pint of whipped cream, which will produce a soft, mild cheese that you can shape or mold for presentation (see pages 68 and 80). A skinned half Camembert can also be used to make the delicious Hungarian cheese called Liptauer (see page 170).

Another way to solve the dilemma of the leftover Camembert is to soak it for 24 hours in enough white wine to cover it. (That takes care of the wine once and for all; even with all my admonitions for thriftiness, here is where I draw the line.) Drain off the wine. Peel the softened skin, then cream the cheese with half a stick of sweet butter (remember to use sweet butter; the elder Camembert will tend to be very salty in itself). Mold into a ball, then roll it in 2 or 3 ounces of crushed walnuts. Refrigerate until time of serving.

The same possibilities exist for the other soft-centered cheeses such as Brie, Coulommiers, and such.

ODDS AND ENDS

If you thought that odds and ends had been the subject of this entire chapter up to now, here are some real odds and ends impossible—or embarrassing—to fit into any recognizable classification. Such as:

Cake: keep any leftover pieces in your refrigerator, even for several days. They may look hopeless, but with a little ingenuity you can metamorphose them into a "cake pudding"—which is Marie Antoinette's equivalent of bread pudding. Add 3 eggs slightly beaten, 1 cup milk, 2 teaspoons vanilla, to 2 cups dried-out cake. Bake in the oven at 350° for 45 minutes. Serve with a vanilla sauce.

Chocolate candies: hard, stale, inedible. Yet they were a gift, and you hate to throw them out. Put them into a saucepan and heat over a very low flame—or in the top of the double boiler—until melted. Add a tablespoon of brandy or Grand Marnier or coffee. The resulting chocolate syrup can be refrigerated and stored for future topping and frosting.

Cookies: however dried, crumbled, or even soggy, save them in a sealed jar. Why? Because cookie crumbs can be used to line the crust of any fruit pie. Fruit tends to render liquid when cooked; the cookie crumbs will absorb the excess liquid and give you a crisper, fresher pie.

Gravy: save *any* gravy. Whenever I've suggested this to my friends, or when they've seen me storing leftover gravies after a meal, I've almost inevitably had some comment such as: "Why save that? There's so little of it, and it's so fatty!" Any gravies—even roast beef—do tend to be fatty, true. But to me that's no excuse to throw them out. When chilled, any gravy will coalesce its fats, which will rise to the surface; they can then be easily spooned off. What remains may be preserved under refrigeration for the next two to three days. Use it to flavor rice, noodles, green vegetables, and above all soups. If you can foresee no immediate use for your gravy during the next two to three days, freeze it. And make sure you label it properly. Here are some uses to which you can put it later on: As one of your several sauces for a meat fondue, by simply adding it to a finely chopped sautéed onion, stirring in a tablespoon of flour, and seasoning to taste (tarragon and parsley, fresh or dry depending on the season). You can if you like add a touch of sherry. Any casserole requires a cream sauce, to bind it. Adding one of your leftover meat stocks to the cream sauce will greatly enhance its flavor. Meat pies in themselves are often leftovers to begin with, as the reader of this chapter can readily attest. But if you depend only on the gravy of the meat you are using for your pie, you may find yourself short. At which point one of your well-labeled frozen gravy jars will be a godsend.

Lemon, semisqueezed: it's almost time to discard this, but not quite. If there is a soup in progress, cut lemon into halves and stir it into the soup. Or place the halves as little *chapeaux* on top of any poultry or roast, during roasting time. Either way, the lemon does its aromatic bit.

Wine: almost inevitably, some wine is left over after a dinner or dinner party. Too little to recork, but too much to discard. I pour it into a jar and store in my refrigerator for a future marinade or sauce.

NOTE: Do the same with beer. Yes, beer. Added to sharp cheddar cheese, a dash of Worcestershire sauce, mustard, pepper and salt, it becomes Welsh rarebit.

The point to constantly bear in mind about leftovers is that they represent a daily challenge to the creative cook. Not only can virtually everything be put to some good use, but often it will be to a truly gourmet use. Whenever you bring a still-bubbling casserole dish or soufflé, or a steaming soup, to the table, the appreciation of your family or guests is reward in itself. But when these dishes—as only you, your stove, and cupboard know—have sprung in whole or in part from the humble beginnings of leftovers, the pleasure is even greater. At least mine has always been. For not only have you been culinarily creative in the most meaningful, and fun, sense of the term; you have also exhibited the quality of thrift. And you have cleaned out your fridge.

WINE TIPS

Let me state my position straight off: I am not, nor do I fancy myself, an expert on the subject of wine. But I do enjoy and appreciate wine, and today I would find it hard to conceive of a dinner without wine. Doubtless this is due in part to the fact that I married a French girl and spent several years in France, where wine is drunk with every meal except breakfast (and there are some Frenchmen who fail even to make that exception); also, there can be no question but that wine, an end and a pleasure in itself whose bounties have been amply noted since the beginning of recorded history, enhances the taste of fine food. In fact, I have always found that wine enhances the taste of almost any food and adds a festive note to any meal.

Ever since my salad days in Paris, when daily I would perform the ritual of carefully rinsing the liter bottle that had housed the previous day's nectar and take it down to the local wine merchant to have it refilled with *le gros rouge* at a cost of about twenty-five cents a bottle, I have pursued the elusive goal of finding the "magic" wine—that is, one whose excellence is matched by its reasonable price. A few years ago this "game" was played far more easily than it is today, when inflation, speculation, and wine investment have forced prices, especially of the *grands crus* or "classed growth" Bordeaux wines, to virtually unreachable heights.* It wasn't all that long ago

---

* As of this writing, some Bordeaux wines have come down slightly from their lofty peaks, due partly to market conditions and partly to the economy. But most of the great "name" wines still remain beyond the reach of all but the lucky few and it is among the lesser-known vineyards that one must go prospecting.

that I found it possible to buy, not on a daily basis of course but for some slightly special occasion, a good vintage Château Lascombes, Château Talbot, or Château Calon-Ségur. I managed to lay down a few cases of some of them, but to my undying shame I confess we drank some of them before they had reached full maturity.

In the many years we have made it a practice to have wine with dinner, we have experimented, made some mistakes, discovered a few gems (by which I mean wines without a world-renowned name or reputation that turned out nonetheless to possess the characteristics of the *grands crus*), and perhaps most important of all, had a lot of fun.

In talking to friends, I have found that very often they are slightly intimidated by the subject, not only by the cult and mystique of wine but also by the bewildering number of wines from which to choose. As for the "cult," it is only natural, since wine making and wine drinking have a very long history, that certain customs and habits have been passed down through the centuries. One can, as one's interest in the subject grows, explore it more fully, but if there is one worthwhile piece of advice I can offer it is that an appreciation of wine requires no arcane knowledge or long education. It does require a normal curiosity, a basic interest in good food, and a palate you learn to trust. As for the hundreds if not thousands of wines from a dozen or more countries available to you, I would suggest that if you are a relative neophyte you rely on known labels, be they domestic or foreign, and on the advice of your wine merchant. You may soon discover that your tastes and his don't agree, but I have generally found that once he knows your budget and what you're looking for he can be most helpful. For one thing, when it comes to vintage wines, he will steer you away from poor or mediocre years. As for the question of budget, it's been our experience that it spoils the enjoyment to spend more for wine than you can really afford, however great the temptation.

Compared to Europe, the United States and Great Britain can hardly be called "wine-drinking" countries, although the latter has been importing Bordeaux wines since the twelfth century, when the former province of Gascony in southwestern France was a British colony.* In France, for example, the per capita consumption of wine is rated, depending on which expert or statistics you consult, as between 150 and 180 bottles per year, whereas Americans drink less than one-tenth that amount and the British consume only about

---

* The term "claret," still used in Britain to define Bordeaux red wine, derives from the French word *clairet*, for the Gascony wines were lighter than the other wines of southern France.

five bottles per capita. But in the United States especially, wine drinking and wine appreciation are growing—per capita consumption has doubled in the last decade, for example—and the American wine industry has also been developing rapidly. Today American wine production stands at about 200 million gallons per year, about 80 per cent of which is grown in California and virtually all of which is consumed domestically, though in the past few years more and more California wine has been exported to Europe.

Baron Philippe de Rothschild, a man of no little authority on the subject, several years ago visited California's vineyards and, rather pompously, came away proclaiming that its wines lacked character. "In California," he said, "everything is too perfect. The soil is too rich. The weather is too good. To develop character, great wines must go through hardship." Were the pun not so terrible, American winegrowers might well respond: "Sour grapes!" But the basic fact is that, over the past several years, California wines have won an increasing number of awards, and often proved their superiority, in blind tastings putting them against the best wines of the world, including the French. It may be that hardship is a prerequisite for forming the character of men and women, but the more even and predictable climate of California does not seem to have had any deleterious effect on its wine, Baron Philippe notwithstanding. If the results of the blind tastings are not evidence enough, perhaps the ultimate, and irrefutable, proof is the recent founding, in Napa Valley, of Domaine Chandon, a wholly-owned subsidiary of the French company Moët-Henessy, makers of the world-famous Moët & Chandon champagnes.

Whatever your source of wine, be it domestic or European, the question you will probably most often ask yourself is: what wine should I serve with the food I'm planning? Again let me emphasize that although there are traditions regarding what wines go with what foods, your own tastes and preferences ought to be the the final arbiter. Still, since traditions often do have a firm basis in logic, here are a few rules of thumb:

- *Red wines* go well with meats (steaks, roasts), poultry, game, omelettes, cheese.
- *White wines* go especially well with seafood or any fish dish, poultry, omelettes, desserts, and fruits.
- *Rosé wines* can be served with any of the dishes indicated for

white wines. They are also good with salads or any light meal, including lunches.

• *Champagne* goes well with almost any food, from hors d'oeuvres to desserts.

Let's assume now that you're giving a dinner party for eight and that your menu consists of the following:

> Soup
> Stuffed bass in brioche
> Green salad
> Cheese
> Plum tart

First, you should plan on at least four bottles of wine, that is, a half bottle per person. In times past in France, at least two and perhaps three different wines would have been served. A white or rosé wine, well chilled, would have been served initially because of the main course of fish (though the wine may have been poured at the start of the meal, it is not generally drunk with soup). A switch to red would have been made with the cheese, which has the ability to bring out the best in a red wine. And, with the plum tart, a sweet white wine would have been served.

Today one could follow that order, bearing in mind that if white wine is served initially it should be dry, not sweet. But in a day and age when few people have cellars in which to store any quantity of wine, chances are you will tend to serve only one wine with your meals, no matter what the menu. For the above menu, a rosé de Provence would be an excellent choice, since it would go well with all the courses. Or you might want to try a Greek wine we enjoy, Rodytis, which is also light and dry.

If, for the above menu, or any menu where a switch in wines would by strict protocol be called for, you opt to follow tradition, you might want to keep in mind these rules of thumb: in general, white should precede red, young should precede old, and dry should precede sweet.

The reasons for this are that, first, red wines are liable to have subtler flavors than white and the white will prepare the palate for them; second, there is a theory that one should "move up" when serving wines, and it is presumed that the older red wine will have a more delicate, more precious bouquet than the younger. Then, too, it is only logical that in any artistic endeavor, be it a novel, a play, or wine serving, you don't want the climax to come too soon. Anything served thereafter will seem tame and flat by comparison. If, indeed, your cellar (be it only a corner of your apartment closet) harbors a precious store of truly fine wines, the occasion for opening one can be both dramatic and festive. Not long ago friends of ours who visited us for the weekend brought with them a bottle of Château Talbot 1949. It was a wine that might well have reached its peak a few years before; what was more, it had endured a trip of several hours, which could have affected it. We did not drink it the first night, wanting to give it at least a fair rest. And when we did come to serve it, late in the meal the second night, after two decent but far lesser wines, there *was* drama as the bottle was opened, the first bit poured, the first sip taken. Not only was the wine still good, it was superb.

Finally, as for the rule of thumb regarding sweet versus dry, if you simply remember that sweet wines go best with desserts and fruits you'll have the one basic fact you need. This said, and at the risk of heresy, we rarely if ever serve any of the "sweet" white wines. But one of our favorites is Vouvray, which even in its youth has a tinge of sweetness, and we find often slightly *pétillant* (bubbly). Or, of course, Champagne, which goes just as well with desserts as it does elsewhere. The Champagne we like and drink is Brut, that is, the driest sort, and nothing less dry will do, even at the end of a meal, but you will have your own preferences.

As for the question "to chill or not to chill," the answer is: chill white and rosé wines but serve most red wines at room temperature. If you live in a house rather than an apartment and have the possibility of storing your wine in a real cellar, where ideally the temperature may be between 55 and 60 degrees, you'll want to bring your red wine upstairs for two to three hours at least before serving (some wine experts say to allow red Bordeaux to stand at room temperature for a good twenty-four hours, but I have never found this to be practical; in keeping with the principles of this book, however, one can think to bring up the anticipated number of bottles needed in the morning prior to the dinner party). Since red wine often has a sediment, the wines should be carried with care, to keep the sediment from mingling unnecessarily with the rest of the contents. You can see the sediment by holding the bottle up to the light. If there is a fair amount of it visible, many people advise decanting, that is, opening the bottle and pouring it slowly into a decanter. (A decanter, I might add, has another useful purpose: a handsome container in itself, it enhances the look if not the taste of ordinary wines and makes the wine presentation more elegant.)

The main purpose of decanting is to make sure that none of the deposit that has accumulated over the years slips into your guests' glasses, since you will stop pouring as soon as you see you've reached that part of the wine infiltrated by the sediment. But decanting is also espoused by many because it allows the wine to "breathe," that is, to make contact with the air. Once a bottle is corked, the only air in contact with the wine until it is opened is that bit trapped in the neck of the bottle—unless, of course, the cork is faulty or dries out, allowing air in and virtually condemning the contents (that, by the way, is why table wines are always stored on their sides: so that the wine will be in constant contact with the cork, thus keeping it moist and minimizing the possibility of its drying or crumbling). When red wine is not decanted, it is generally opened some time in advance of serving—an hour or two—again the amount of time depending on the personal experience of the host or hostess. The premise is that this "breathing" process is necessary to bring the wine to full maturation, to bring out its full flavor and bouquet. Since most wines, even the best, are drunk before they reach full maturity, "breathing" can and often does accomplish this end. But there have also been many cases of a wine's having been ruined by "breathing" too long before serving or by having been opened prematurely. In our own experience I don't think opening wine ahead of time makes much difference except in the case of the older, better wines. Even here, I have experimented with serving it both ways, and have had conflicting results. I know this too is heresy, but I suggest, after you've experimented a bit with wines, that you try both "breathing" your wine and opening it just prior to serving. See which tastes better, and let your palate be your guide.

For whites and rosés, if again you have a real cellar in which to keep your wines, they'll be reasonably chilled when you fetch them: forty-five minutes to an hour in the refrigerator will bring them down to optimum temperature for pleasant drinking. For apartment dwellers, you may need two to three hours' cooling. Wherever you live, I also think it's a good idea to have an ice bucket to keep your rosés and white wines chilled between servings. If you don't want to invest in a bucket, a large bowl half filled with cold water and two or three trays of ice cubes will substitute nicely.

As for laying down wine, be it in your cellar or your closet, the advantages are many. (Since we live in an apartment, we have "liberated" a piece of furniture originally intended to store our records—each record bin holds a case of wine, and the cabinet holds comfortably six to seven cases.) First, buying recent vintage wine is always considerably less expensive than buying a several-year-old bottle or case at the store. Second, by buying, when you first start exploring, two or three mixed cases of white, red, and rosé, you will have both the variety and quantity of wine you need to test your tastebuds. (There is nothing more frustrating than running out of wine in the course of a dinner party. Just having that extra bottle or two in reserve is worth the effort of having bought wine in advance.) And finally, wine should lie dormant for at least a week or so before you drink it, which is obviously impossible if you buy your wine just before a dinner party.

Just what you buy and how much will depend on both your dwelling and your pocketbook. What we have always done is experiment with a number of wines, and if and when we find one a cut above the ordinary for the price we try and stock up with a case—or several if we can. Finding a really good wine is too precious an event not to try and store up on it when you can.

Many people, especially in areas where the local merchants' selections are not the widest, are forming wine-tasting clubs. Several people get together, pool their talents and resources, and order a selection of wines, generally at relatively reduced prices, directly from shippers. Then, at regular intervals, they hold wine- and cheese-tasting parties, or take turns giving dinners at which the various wines are tasted, discussed, and rated. The discussions are often as zesty as the wines themselves. It's one of the best ways I know of learning about wine quite quickly.

Sometimes I have been asked to recommend a several-case cellar to a friend, and while I don't mind doing so, I think it's always better to begin by buying one or two mixed cases and, from tasting, lay down your own cellar. For starters, I would buy a half dozen or a dozen assorted French Bordeaux and Burgundies, all inexpensive: some of the minor château wines of Bordeaux can still be had at relatively reasonable prices; Côtes du Rhône, Beaujolais, Châteauneuf-du-Pape are all safe and solid wines. For contrast, try one or more of the Italian Chiantis, which we find somewhat harsh, but many people swear by and prefer to some of the medium-quality French wines. You might want to contrast your Burgundies with an Italian Piedmont such as Barolo (as of this writing a 1966 Barolo was still available for under three dollars a bottle). For rosés, we're partial to Provence and much prefer them to, say, the somewhat sweeter rosés from Anjou; try, too, the Greek Rodytis already mentioned. We drink relatively few white wines compared with red, but we are never without a basic stock which includes Vouvray, Muscadet (sometimes mistaken for a region of France, but actually a grape), Sancerre, Pouilly Fumé from Touraine and Pouilly Fuissé from Burgundy, and of the Alsatians, Riesling. Try, too, the Italian Soave from Veneto and, if you can find it, the Frecciarossa from Lombardy.

But above all, take advantage of the extraordinary flowering of California wines. Until fairly recently, many of the best West Coast wines were unavailable in the Middle West and East, where only the products of the largest wineries were widely sold. (Then too, many of the best West Coast wineries—the so-called boutique category—did not exist a decade ago.) Clearly, the late 70s and early 80s have seen a dramatic increase not only in new vineyards in California, but in a movement toward quality. The basic thing to remember when buying California wines is that there are two methods used to label them, generic and varietal. You'll see domestic wines labeled Burgundy and Claret and Chablis and Chianti, but in many cases the resemblance between them and their French or Italian counterparts may be nominal. Which is not to say that one is better than the other, merely different. Here, as always, let your palate be your guide. From my experience, however, I would strongly suggest that when buying domestic, you buy according to the varietal labeling, that is, where the type of grape used in making the wine is indicated: Cabernet Sauvignon, Pinot Noir, Gamay, Pinot Chardonnay, etc. The Cabernet Sauvignon grape is used to make the fine Bordeaux wines, so you might want to contrast the California varietal bearing that name with the French Bordeaux you have chosen. Similarly, contrast a domestic Gamay with a French Beaujolais.

Some of the best wine bargains in the 1980s, in my opinion, are to be found among the Spanish reds. For years I have drunk, and appreciated more bottles of Marques de Riscal than I care to remember. Ditto the Marques de Cacera red. And the Riojas.

Speaking of bargains—and by the term I do not mean simply inexpensive, but maximum quality for the price—don't overlook the jug wines you'll see in your wine shop. Just because the bottles are bigger, and perhaps not so elegantly corked or labeled as their smaller brethren, does not mean the contents are inferior. Many California wines come in jugs—which are generally 1.5, 3 or 4 liters in size, or the equivalent of 2, 6, or 8 "standard" bottles—both generic and varietal. The French once scorned the practice, but in the mid-1970s they yielded to the demands of the marketplace—and no doubt to skyrocketing prices—and began to market very decent jug wine in this country.

No wine chapter, however cursory, would be complete without some commentary on the most festive wine of all, Champagne. Most of us tend to think that this sparkling wine should be reserved for only Very Special Occasions, be they birthdays, weddings, anniversaries, or New Year's Eve. Maybe they should, and given the prices of the only true Champagnes, i.e., those emanating from the Champagne district of France, maybe they have to be. Nevertheless, we love a glass or two of champagne more frequently than that, and since the prices of Moët or Piper Hiedsieck or Mumms were beyond our reach, we began searching for worthy substitutes. Through the years we have found several. Many do not bear the name "Champagne," for in France sparkling wines made by the Champagne method, but coming from vineyards outside the Champagne region, cannot be so named. But, for less than half the price of "real" Champagne try, from France, Kriter or the Rothschild, both Sparkling Blanc de Blancs; from Spain, Freixenet, Cordon Negro; from Italy, Cordoniu. For a price not much above that of a bottle of still red or white wine, you can turn an otherwise mundane dinner into a really festive, romantic occasion.

As for opening and serving your wine, all you need is a simple corkscrew. You obviously must first remove the metal or wax seal, using a knife. Then, before pulling the cork, wipe the bottle clean to remove any dust or dirt that may have settled on the cork or rim of the bottle. Inevitably, although you will learn to minimize it, a fleck or two of cork may fall into the wine. That is the main reason the host pours himself the first partial glass, so that he rather than his guests will have the bits of cork if by chance there are any. Another reason the server pours himself the first taste is to make sure the wine is all right, that it is not "corky," or turned sour, in the bottle. If you open your wine ahead of time, as you well may, you can dispense with this "testing" operation, by tasting well before your guests arrive. I've been asked why in restaurants this ritual is performed, and the answer is of course that whereas at home you can select and open the wine ahead, in a restaurant the waiter has to open it on the spot, and therefore any advance verification is impossible.

As we have found through the years that an ordinary table wine is better than no wine at all with meals, so would I say that, in serving, it is preferable to have long-stemmed wine glasses, tulip-shaped if possible, but wine can be drunk in any glass. And, I'd add, better to drink wine in ordinary water glasses than forego the pleasure simply because you haven't the proper glasses. (In fact, since you should pour only half a glass or less of wine, a water glass is actually better than a very small wine glass, which one is almost obliged to fill.) A dozen long-stemmed, clear wine glasses, no smaller than six to nine ounces, are easy to find and quite inexpensive. Long-stemmed because, with chilled wines, ideally your hand should grasp the stem rather than the bowl; with fine Bordeaux you'll want to grasp the bowl, to warm the wine and further bring out the bouquet. And *clear* glass, the better to enjoy the full color of the wine.

Whether you have the proper glasses, the proper storage space in which to keep your wines, the proper decanter or serving basket (in most cases a pretension), the key is to explore, to rely increasingly on your own taste and inclinations. That, I have found, is the key to appreciating wine, as it is also the key to enjoying fine food.

RICHARD SEAVER

INDEX

almond (s)
  with fillets of sole, 98
  and mushroom sauce, 244
  and olive sauce, 117
  paste and butter filling, 44
  as staple, 25
  toasted, consommé topped with, 168
anchovy (ies)
  boats, 132
  canned, as staple, 20
  paste, as staple, 25
  sauce, 258
anise, general note on, 51–2
apple (s)
  flaming, 158
  sliced, leftover pork with, 228
  tart, 94
    caramelized, 175
applesauce, in Normandy tart, 173
apricot
  cream loaf, 161
  crescents, 121
  jam
    crêpes filled with, 75
    glaze, 151
    as staple, 25
  tart, 110
artichoke (s)
  bottoms, cream of, 172
  hearts
    beef croquettes with, 209

canned, as staple, 20
leftover, 287–8
with oil and lemon dressing, 111
rice with, 288
asparagus
  canned, as staple, 20
  leftover, 288
  turkey with broccoli and, 243
Austrian bacon dumplings, 233
avocado (s)
  in guacamole, 100
  sauce, veal in, 166

bacon
  dumplings, Austrian, 233
  slab, as staple, 25
baking powder, as staple, 20
banana (s)
in filling for melon, 116
  soufflés, little, 99
bashes, *see* cocktail parties
basic pie crust, my, 38
basil, general note on, 52
  in green sauce *(pesto)*, 164
Bavarian cream, *see* cream (s)
bay leaf, general note on, 52
beans, *see* black bean soup, green beans; white bean (s)
beef
  in *boeuf bourguignon,* 211

Index / iii

beef *(cont.)*
  boiled
    ground, pie, 215
    leftover, 214–16
    and vegetables, 152
    see also pot-au-feu
  casserole of, gratin, 208
  in a sort of chef's salad, 207
  in crêpes with meat filling, 210
  croquettes with artichoke hearts, 209
  filling, piroshki with, 216
  in goulash soup, 212
  leftover, 16, 199–216
  marinated, 71
  and mashed potatoes au gratin, 93
  in meat jelly, 206
  in meat omelet, 213
  roast
    cold, with (homemade) mayonnaise, 205
    leftover, 204–13
    sliced, 205
    sliced and baked, 205
  rolled stuffed, with cream and port wine, 208
  salad, Russian, 207
  steak
    cold, 203
    and cucumbers, in soy and lemon sauce, 202
    and kidney pie, 202
    leftover, 200–1
    pepper, 202
    sandwich, open, 200
    snow pea, 201
    tartar, 194
  stew, leftover, 212–13
  stroganoff, 200
  in whole stuffed cabbage, 226
beer, leftover, 297
beet(s)
  canned, sliced, as staple, 20
  and endive salad, 99
  leftover, 289
biscuits, hot, 70
black bean soup, canned, as staple, 20
blue cheese, leftover, 294
bluefish, baked, 104
boeuf bourguignon, 211
borscht, poor-man's, 122
bouillabaisse, chicken, with green sauce, 162
brandade de morue, 109

brandy, pear, pear sherbet with, 178
bread
  crumbs
    fried, ham dumplings with, 88
    as staple, 21
  dumplings, 286
  in family meat loaf, 284
  French, homemade, 36
  leftover, 283–7
  in panade soup, 285
  in pâté, 284
  in *pesto*, 287
  as staple, 25, 28
  stuffing, 285
  in stuffing, 284
Brie, leftover, 295
brik, 81
Brillat-Savarin
  on dining in New York, 8
  on turkey, 242
brioche(s)
  dough, 42
  frozen, as staple, 29
  general note on, 40–1
  individual, 41
  lamb and vegetables in, 224
  marrow-stuffed, 154
broccoli
  and asparagus, turkey with, 243
  leftover, 289
broth
  beef *(pot-au-feu)*, 152
  chicken, with dumplings, 253
  turkey, 245
butter
  and almond paste filling, 44
  Roquefort cheese mixed with, 89
  as staple, 25
  sweet, radishes with, 74

cabbage
  leftover, 289–90
  peasant style, 96
  pie, Russian, 290
  whole stuffed, 226
  see also sauerkraut
cake
  chocolate, thirty-minute, 118
  custard, plums in, 72
  leftover, 296
  Lily's, 85
  mocha, quick, 166
  raspberry soufflé, 108
  rice, instant, 279
calf's liver with shallots and herbs, 85

Camembert, leftover, 295
candied fruit soufflé with rum, 170
candies, leftover chocolate, 296
capers
    fried turnovers stuffed with herbs, egg, and, 81
    general note on, 52
caramel custard, 102
caramelized apple tart, 175
caraway seeds, general note on, 52
cardamom, general note on, 52–3
carrot(s)
    cream of, turnip, and potato soup, 84
    grated, with vinaigrette, 67
    leftover, 291
    and peas, canned, as staple, 20–1
    pudding, 291
    in rose purée, 269
    as staple, 25
casserole(s)
    of beef gratin, 208
    frozen, as staple, 28–9
cassolettes forestière, 292
cassoulet, Toulouse style, 254
cauliflower
    croquettes, 291
    au gratin, 85
    leftover, 291
caviar, eggplant, 194
celeriac (celery root)
    and potatoes in mayonnaise, purée of, 268
    with remoulade sauce, 93
    as staple, 25
celery
    hearts au gratin, 72
    leftover, 291
    marinated, 114
    as staple, 25
cereal, as staple, 21
charlotte Renaissance, 271
Cheddar, leftover, 295
cheese(s)
    cream, in basic pie dough, 38
    Greek-style, 68
    with herbs, 81
    Hungarian, 170
    leftover, 294–5
    pepper, 161
    souffléed omelet with ham and, 120
    as staple, 25–6
    with walnuts, 113
    see also names of individual cheeses
cherries, stewed, 113

chervil
    general note on, 53
    and potato purée, 268
chestnut purée, as staple, 21
chicken
    bouillabaisse with green sauce, 162
    broth with dumplings, 253
    cold, with walnut sauce, 247
    fricasseed
        Berri style, 248
        breasts, 277
        Gascony style, 248
    leftover, 245–53
    livers, in pâté, 139
    poached, with herb dumplings, 169
    in poor-cousin paella, 249
    quenelles with a cream and nutmeg sauce, 251
    roast, cold, with leeks vinaigrette, 246
    salad, southern French style, 247
    in sauce, ring of rice, 277
    sautéed, with herbs and cream, 115
    spread, 253
    and truffle soufflé in a turban of rice, 250
chickpea(s)
    canned, as staple, 21
    dip, 185
chilled melon, with mint leaves and lime juice, 123
chilled soup, Polish style, 156
Chinese pork
    snacks, cold, 229
    with water chestnuts and mushrooms, 231
chives, general note on, 53
chocolate
    cake, thirty-minute, 118
    candies, leftover, 296
    as staple, 21
cinnamon
    general note on, 53
    and sugar filling (for coffee cake), 44
clams, canned, as staple, 21, 22
cloves, general note on, 53
cocktail parties
    equipment for, 193
    finger food for, 193–5
    general notes on, 190–1, 196
    liquor for, 191–2
    mixes for, 193
codfish, whipped (*brandade de morue*), 109

coffee cake
  frozen, as staple, 29
  homemade, simplified, 42
cognac, mousse-pâté with, 138
compote: stewed cherries, 113
consommé, 177
  topped with toasted almonds, 168
cookies, leftover, 296
coriander, general note on, 54
corn
  canned creamed, as staple, 22
  leftover, 291
  meal, as staple, 22
cornichons
  with pâté, 139
  as staple, 26
Cornish game hens Quasimodo, 139
cornstarch, as staple, 22
Couloumiers, leftover, 295
cream (s)
  apricot, loaf, 161
  of artichoke bottoms, 172
  Bavarian, five-minute, 144
  of carrot, turnip, and potato soup, 84
  cheese and rice croquettes, 275
  heavy, as staple, 26
  and nutmeg sauce, chicken quenelles with, 251
  of parsley soup, 149
  and port wine, rolled stuffed beef with, 208
  sauce, leftover roast pork with, 228
  sauce, white, 46
  sautéed chicken with herbs and, 115
  wine, and mustard sauce, pork chops in, 67
  see also sour cream
cream puffs, mini, 164
crêpe (s)
  basic batter, 76
  filled with apricot jam, 75
  with meat filling, 210
  stuffed with creamed spinach, 90
  stuffed with fish, 263
  traditions, 75
croissants, 45
  apricot, 121
croquettes
  beef, with artichoke hearts, 209
  cauliflower, 291
  fish, 262
  Italian style, 282
  rice and cream cheese, 275
croutons, spinach salad with, 75

cucumber (s)
  leftover, 291-2
  salad with dill, 68
  steak and, in soy and lemon sauce, 202
cumin, general note on, 54
curried lamb, 225
curry, general note on, 54
custard
  cake, plums in, 72
  caramel, 102

deviled ham, *see* ham
dill
  cucumber salad with, 68
  general note on, 54
dinner (s)
  family
    general notes on, 63-6
    menus for, 67-124
  parties, large buffet, 188-90
  parties, small
    general notes on, 127-31
    menus for, 131-78
    ten preparatory steps for, 128-31
dip
  chickpea, 195
  Olivia's, 195
  plain, 195
dough (s)
  baking powder, 203
  basic (cream cheese), 35-45
  brioche, 42
  frozen, as staple, 29
  preparing in advance, 17
  puff pastry, 39
  for turnovers, 81
duck
  in cassoulet, Toulouse style, 254
  Chinese style, 256
  Indian style, 255
  leftover, 253-7
  Normandy style, 147
  in *pâté de volaille*, 256
dumplings, 223
  bacon, Austrian, 233
  bread, 286
  chicken broth with, 253
  ham, with fried bread crumbs, 88
  herb, poached chicken with, 169
  plain, 223

egg (s)
  baked stuffed, 171
  herbs and capers, fried turnovers stuffed with, 81

egg(s) *(cont.)*
   leftover, 263-4
   as staple, 26
   see also omelet(s); soufflé(s)
eggplant
   caviar, 194
   fried, with yogurt sauce, 107
   leftover, 292
   in moussaka I, 217
   in moussaka II, 218
endive(s)
   and beet salad, 99
   braised, and tarragon, veal with, 240
   salad, 150
entertaining, tips on, 179-84
equipment, 18-19
escargots (snails), canned, as staple, 26

family meals, importance of, 63-5
family meat loaf, 284
fennel, general note on, 54
filets mignons, 172
fillets of sole amandine, 98
filling(s)
   almond paste and butter, 44
   beef, piroshki with, 216
   meat, French pancakes with, 210
   sugar and cinnamon, 44
finger food, for large dinner parties and bashes, 193-4
fish
   casserole Spanish style, 262
   cold
      on the half shell with anchovy sauce, 258
      with mousseline sauce *vert-pré*, 258
   crêpes stuffed with, 263
   croquettes, 262
   in a deep dish, 259
   leftover, 257-63
   in Mediterranean salad, 257
   puffs, souffléed, 260
   see also names of individual fish
five-minute Bavarian cream, 144
flaming apples, 158
flaming pork roast, 143
flour, as staple, 22
French
   bread, 37
   fries, 101
   pancakes, *see crêpes*
fresh fruit basket, 69
fresh vegetables dipped in vinaigrette sauce, 142

fricasseed
   chicken Gascony style, 248
   chicken Berri style, 248
   definition, 248
fruit
   candied, soufflé with rum, 170
   fresh, basket, 69

galantine, vegetarian, 283
garlic
   in codfish *brandade*, 109
   general note on, 54-5
   as staple, 24
gazpacho from Sevilla, 87
gelatin, as staple, 22
gigot, see lamb, leg of
gin, tangerine, and ginger sauce, pork in, 230
ginger
   general note on, 55
   tangerine, and gin sauce, pork in, 230
gnocchi, potato, 268
goulash soup, 213
grapefruit soufflé, cold, 137
grapes, frosted, 158
grated carrots with vinaigrette, 67
gravy, leftover, 296
Greek soup, 78
Greek-style cheese, 68
green beans
   in green purée, 269
   leftover, 288-9
   in Mediterranean salad, 257
   purée, 288
   salad, Flemish style, 79
green peas, *see* peas
green pepper, *see* pepper(s)
green purée, 269
green sauce, 163
   bread in, 287
guacamole, 100

ham
   canned, as staple, 26
   and cheese, souffléed omelet with, 120
   deviled, 239
      as staple, 22
   dumplings with fried bread crumbs, 88
   fat, in dumplings, 233
   gratin, "noodloff" with, 238
   leftover, 16, 233-9
   mousseline with Madeira sauce, 236
   in pastry crust, 157

Index / vii

ham (cont.)
    slices with green olives and white wine sauce, 96
    souffléed omelet with, 120
    souffléed potato puffs with, 270
    and spinach pie, 238
    tomatoes stuffed with rice and, in a mayonnaise sauce, 278
    and veal pâté in pastry, 234
hazelnut (s)
    macaroons, 105
    soufflé, cold, 155
    as staple, 26
herbs
    cheese with, 80
    and spices, 50–60
    as staple, 24
    see also names of individual herbs
Hungarian cheese, homemade, 170

ice cream, vanilla, as staple, 29
instant rice cake, 279

jam, apricot
    crêpes stuffed with, 75
    as staple, 25
jelly, meat, beef in, 206
juniper berries, general note on, 55

kidney, steak and, pie, 202

lamb
    Burgundy style, 136
    in cassoulet, Toulouse style, 254
    curried, 225
    leftover, 216–27
    leg of
        cold, 217
        leftover, 216–26
        in moussaka I, 217
        in moussaka II, 218
        with Pernod, 175
    patties, surprise, 223
    pies, little, 220
    stew
        Middle Eastern style, 220
        in ramequins, 225
    in Transylvanian choucroute, 177
    with turnips, 221
    and vegetables in brioche, 224
    in whole stuffed cabbage, 226

lasagna, 112
laurel, *see* bay leaf
leeks
    peas, and salad leaves, vegetable soup with, 70
    vinaigrette, cold roast chicken with, 246
leftover (s)
    beef, 199–216
    bread, 283–7
    cheese, 294–5
    eggs, 263–4
    fish, 257–63
    ham, 233–9
    lamb, 216–27
    odds and ends, 296–7
    pasta, 279–83
    pork, 227–33
    poultry, 241–57
        see also names of individual poultry
    rice, 273–9
    veal, 239–41
    vegetables, 287–94
        see also names of individual vegetables
lemon (s)
    leftover, 297
    sauce
        for lamb, 222
        with roast veal, 160
    as staple, 26–7
    tartlets, 148
lettuce, braised, 294
Lily's cake, 85
lime juice, chilled melon with mint leaves and, 123
liquor
    for large dinner parties, 191–2
    see also wine (s)

macaroni
    baked, Italian style, 282
    loaf, Normandy style, 281
    mousse, 280
    salad, 280
    in vegetarian galantine, 283
macaroons, hazelnut, 105
mace, general note on, 55
Madeira sauce
    ham mousseline with, 236
    truffled turkey with, on toast, 243
margarine, as staple, 27
marinade, shrimp and green pepper, 165
marinated beef, 71
marinated celery, 114
marjoram, general note on, 55

marquise au chocolat, 140
mayonnaise, 46
  homemade, cold roast beef served with, 205
  sauce
    purée of celeriac and potatoes in, 268
    tomatoes stuffed with rice and ham in, 278
    as staple, 27
meat
  filling, crêpes with, 210
  jelly, beef in, 206
  loaf, family, 284
  omelet, 213
  see also names of individual meats
medallion of veal Provence style, 133
Mediterranean salad, 257
melon
  chilled, with mint leaves and lime juice, 123
  filled with mandarin oranges, bananas, and walnuts, 116
menus
  for family dinners, 67–124
  planning, 14–18
  for small dinner parties, 131–78
milk, evaporated, as staple, 22
mint
  general note on, 55
  leaves with chilled melon, 123
mocha cake, quick, 166
moussaka, to freeze, 219
moussaka I, 217
moussaka II, 218
mousse (s)
  macaroni, 280
  -pâté with cognac, 138
  turkey, with a mushroom and almond sauce, 244
mozzarella cheese Provence style, 30
mushroom (s)
  and almond sauce, 244
  in *cassolettes forestière,* 292
  Chinese pork with water chestnuts and, 231
  leftover, 292
  rice with, 273
  spinach salad with, 110
  and tomato sauce, 215
  with vinaigrette sauce, 120
mussels, steamed, in white wine and herbs, 82
mustard
  general note on, 55–6

sauce
  for roast pork, 228
  for pork chops, 67
  as staple, 22

noodles
  in croquettes, 282
  fried, 281
  in "noodloff," 238
noodloff with ham gratin, 238
Normandy tart, 173
nutmeg
  and cream sauce, 251
  general note on, 56

odds and ends, leftover, 296–7
oil, as staple, 22
old-fashioned salad loaf, 294
olive (s)
  and almond sauce, 117
  oil
    in salad dressings, 45–6
    as staple, 22
  and white wine sauce, 96
Olivia's dip, 195
omelet (s)
  meat, 213
  potato, 273
  souffléed, with ham and cheese, 120
onions
  canned, as staple, 22
  general note on, 56
  leftover, 293
  as staple, 24
open steak sandwich, 200
orange (s)
  juice
    "compromise," 27
    frozen, as staple, 29
  in filling for melon, 116
  as staple, 27
oregano, general note on, 56
oysters, smoked, as staple, 22

paella, poor-cousin, 249
panade soup, 285
pancakes, French
  filled with apricot jam, 75
  with meat filling, 210
  stuffed with creamed spinach, 90
  stuffed with fish, 263
  see also crêpe (s)

paprika, general note on, 56
parsley
  cream of, soup, 149
  general note on, 56, 149
  as staple, 27
pasta (s)
  leftover, 279–83
  as staple, 23
  see also names of individual pastas
pastry
  crust, ham in, 157
  veal and ham pâté in, 234
pâté feuilletée (puff paste), 39
pâté (s)
  bread in, 284
  frozen, as staple, 29
  mousse-, with cognac, 138
  pork, 145
  shrimp, with pistachios, 159
  veal and ham, in pastry, 234
  de volaille, 256
  paupiettes of beef, 208
peach (es)
  canned, as staple, 27
  melba, 91
  stewed with wine, 80
pear (s)
  brandy, syrup, 178
  canned, as staple, 27
  poached, with pineapple slices, 134
  sherbet with pear brandy, 178
  turnovers, 96
peas
  canned, as staple, 23
  green, French style, 160
  leftover, 293
  rice and, 140
  in vegetable soup (*Saint-Germain*), 70
pepper (s)
  cheese, my, 161
  general note on, 56–7
  green, shrimp and, marinade, 165
  steak, 202
Pernod, leg of lamb with, 175
pesto (pistou), 17, 169
pie (s)
  beef, ground boiled, 215
  Besançon style, 265
  cabbage, Russian, 290
  crust
    basic, my, 38
    sausages in, 78
  frozen, as staple, 29
  ham and spinach, 238
  lamb, little, 220

  steak and kidney, 202
  see also tarts; tartlets
pimiento, canned, as staple, 23
pineapple, sliced, poached pears with, 134
piroshki with beef filling, 216
pistachios, shrimp pâté with, 159
pizza dough, 39
plain dip, 195
plum (s)
  in custard cake, 72
  tart, 150
poor-cousin paella, 249
poor-man's borscht, 122
poppy seeds, general note on, 57
pork
  in cassoulet, Toulouse style, 254
  Chinese, with water chestnuts and
    mushrooms, 231
  chops in wine, mustard, and cream
    sauce, 67
  leftover, 227–33
  pâté, 145
  roast
    flaming, 143
    cold, 229
    leftover, with cream sauce, 228
    leftover, with mustard sauce, 228
    leftover, with sliced apples, 228
    leftover, with stewed prunes, 227
  with sauerkraut, 232
  snacks, Chinese cold, 229
  stuffed sliced, 232
  sweet and sour, 230
  in tangerine, ginger, and gin sauce, 230
  in Transylvanian choucroute, 177
Portuguese soup, 98
potato (es)
  baked, 68
  boiled, 105
  bourguignonne, 267
  in charlotte Renaissance, 271
  and chervil purée, 268
  cream of carrot, turnip, and, soup, 84
  gnocchi, 267
  in green purée, 269
  French fries, 101
  Italian style, 272
  leftover, 265–73
  Lyons style, 271
  marquis, 269
  mashed
    au gratin, 147
    beef and, au gratin, 93
  omelet, 273

potato(es) (cont.)
  puffs, 266
    with ham, souffléed, 270
  in pie, Besançon style, 265
  purée of celeriac and, in a mayonnaise sauce, 268
  in rose purée, 269
  in salad Grenoble style, 272
  as staple, 24
  in steak with French fries, 101
  steamed, 99
pot-au-feu
  cold
    sauce aïoli, 214
    sauce ravigote, 213
    sauce rémoulade, 213
  leftover, 213–16
  with watercress sauce, 214
poultry
  leftover, 241–57
  see also names of individual poultry
prunes, with leftover roast pork, 227
pudding, carrot, 291
puff paste, 39
puffs
  souffléed fish, 260
  stuffed with ham, 237
pumpkin soup, 103
purée(s)
  of celeriac and potatoes in a mayonnaise sauce, 268
  chervil and potato, 268
  green, 269
  green bean, 288
  rose, 269
  vegetable, bread in, 287

quenelles
  chicken, with a cream and nutmeg sauce, 251
  frozen, as staple, 29, 252
  ham (dumplings), 88
  herb, 169
quiches, frozen, as staple, 29
quick mocha cake, 166

radish(es)
  -leaf soup, 135
  served with sweet butter, 74
raspberry(ies)
  with Bavarian cream, 144
  soufflé cake, 108

syrup, as staple, 28
  with peach melba, 91
raw tomatoes with cooked mixed vegetables served cold, 206
rice
  with artichokes, 288
  cake, instant, 279
  charlotte of, Haitian style, 276
  and cream cheese croquettes, 275
  and ham, tomatoes stuffed with, in a mayonnaise sauce, 278
  leftover, 273–9
  with mixed vegetables, 276
  with mushrooms, 273
  and peas, 140
  rich, 274
  ring of, chicken in sauce, 277
  salad, 278
  as staple, 23
  à la Torino, 275
  turban of, 250
rich rice, 274
ring of rice, chicken in sauce, 277
Roquefort
  cheese mixed with butter, 89
  chunks, escarole salad with, 118
rosemary, general note on, 57
rose purée, 269
rum, candied fruit soufflé with, 170
Russian beef salad, 207
Russian cabbage pie, 290

saffron, general note on, 57
sage, general note on, 57
salad(s)
  beef, Russian, 207
  chef's, a sort of, 207
  chicken, southern French style, 247
  cucumber, with dill, 68
  dressing
    lemon, 46
    mayonnaise, 46
    preparation ahead, 17
    vinaigrette, 46
  endive, 150
  general discussion of, 47–50
  green bean, Flemish style, 79
  greens, as staple, 28
  Grenoble style, 272
  leaves
    stuffed, 150
    vegetable soup with peas, leeks, and, 70
  leftover, 293–4

Index / xi

salad(s) *(cont.)*
    loaf, old-fashioned, 294
    macaroni, 280
    Mediterranean, 257
    rice, 278
    spinach
        with croutons, 75
        with mushrooms, 110
    tomato, 106
    watercress, 115
    white bean, 289
salmis, 221
salmon
    canned, as staple, 23
    ring, with olive and almond sauce, 117
salt, as staple, 23
sandwich, open steak, 200
sangría, 192
sardines, canned, as staple, 23
sauce(s)
    aïoli, 214
    anchovy, 258
    avocado, veal in, 166
    basic, 45–7
    cream
        with leftover roast pork, 228
        and nutmeg, 251
        white, 46
    green *(pesto)*, 163
        chicken bouillabaisse with, 162
        spaghetti with, 123
    horseradish, 154
    lemon, roast veal with, 160
    Madeira
        ham mousseline with, 236
        truffled turkey with, 243
    mayonnaise, 46
        in purée of celeriac and potatoes, 268
        in stuffed tomatoes, 278
    mousseline vert-pré, 258
    mustard, 228
    in olive and almond sauce, 117
    ravigote, for cold pot-au-feu, 213
    rémoulade
        celeriac with, 93
        for cold pot-au-feu, 213
    tomato
        for macaroni mousse, 280
        and mushroom, 215
        as staple, 23
    vinaigrette, 46
    walnut, cold chicken with, 247
    watercress, 214
    yogurt, 107, 219

sauerkraut
    with Austrian bacon dumplings, 234
    pork with, 232
    in Transylvanian choucroute, 177
sausage(s)
    meat, 79
    in pie crust, 78
    in Transylvanian choucroute, 177
savory, general note on, 57
scallion(s)
    soup, 116
    as staple, 28
    and walnuts, lamb with, 222
seafood
    in chilled soup, Polish style, 156
    see also fish
Senegalese soup, 174
sesame seeds, general notes on, 57–8
shallots
    general note on, 58
    and herbs, calf's liver with, 85
    as staple, 24
shrimp
    and green pepper marinade, 165
    Olivia's dip, 195
    pâté with pistachios, 159
    in soup, Polish style, variant, 156
snails, canned, as staple, 26
snow pea steak, 201
sole, fillets of, amandine, 98
soufflé(s)
    banana, little, 99
    cake, raspberry, 108
    candied fruit, with rum, 170
    chicken and truffle, 250
    grapefruit, cold, 137
    hazelnut, cold, 155
souffléed fish puffs, 260
souffléed omelet with ham and cheese, 120
souffléed potato puffs with ham, 270
soup(s)
    black bean, canned, as staple, 20
    borscht, poor-man's, 122
    chilled, Polish style, 156
    chicken bouillabaisse broth, 163
    cream of carrot, turnip, and potato, 84
    cream of parsley, 149
    frozen, as staple, 17, 29
    gazpacho from Sevilla, 87
    goulash, 212
    Greek, 78
    panade, 285
    pot-au-feu broth, 153
    pumpkin, 103
    radish-leaf, 135

soup(s) *(cont.)*
  scallion, 116
  Senegalese, 174
  vegetable, with peas, leeks, and salad leaves, 70
  velvet, 90
  see also broth; consommé
sour cream
  five-minute Bavarian cream, 144
  as staple, 26
soy sauce, general note on, 58
spaghetti with green sauce, 123
spices
  herbs and, 50–60
  as staple, 24
  see also names of individual spices
spinach
  creamed, crêpes stuffed with, 91
  and ham pie, 238
  salad
    with croutons, 75
    with mushrooms, 110
  in turkey Florentine, 242
spread, chicken, 253
staples, 20–32
steak, *see* beef
stock, frozen, as staple, 29
stroganoff, beef, 200
stuffed baked tomatoes, 74
stuffed salad leaves, 150
stuffed sliced pork, 232
stuffed turnips, 136
stuffing
  bread, 285
  bread in, 284
sugar and cinnamon filling (for coffee cake), 44
surprise lamb patties, 223
sweet and sour pork, 230

Tabasco, general note on, 58
tangerine, ginger, and gin sauce, pork in, 230
tarragon
  general note on, 58
  veal with braised endives and, 240
tart(s)
  apple, 94
    caramelized, 175
  apricot, 110
  Normandy, 173
  plum, 150
  wine, 89
  see also pie(s); tartlets

tartar steak, 194
tartlets, lemon, 148
tea, as staple, 23
thirty-minute chocolate cake, 118
thyme, general note on, 59
toast, truffled turkey with Madeira sauce on, 243
tomato(es)
  leftover, 294
  and mushroom sauce, 215
  paste, as staple, 23
  in Portuguese soup, 98
  purée, as staple, 23
  raw, with cooked vegetables, 206
  salad, 106
  sauce
    for macaroni mousse, 280
    as staple, 23
  stuffed
    baked, 74
    with mixed vegetables, 205
    with rice and ham, 278
  whole, canned, as staple, 23
truffle(s)
  and chicken soufflé, 250
  as staple, 23
truffled turkey with Madeira sauce, 242
turkey
  with broccoli and asparagus, 243
  broth, 245
  Florentine, 242
  leftover, 242–5
  mousse with a mushroom and almond sauce, 244
  roll, frozen, as staple, 30
  truffled, with Madeira sauce on toast, 243
turmeric, general note on, 59
turnip(s)
  and carrot and potato soup, 84
  au gratin, 158
  lamb with, 221
  stuffed, 136
turnovers
  fried, stuffed with herbs, egg, and capers, 81
  little fish, *forestière*, 260
  pear, 96

vanilla, general note on, 59
veal
  in avocado sauce, 166
  with braised endives and tarragon, 240
  and ham pâté in pastry, 234

veal (*cont.*)
  Italian style, 241
  leftover, 239–41
    Normandy style, 240
  medallion of, Provence style, 133
  roast, with lemon sauce, 160
vegetable(s)
  boiled beef and, 152
  cooked mixed, raw tomatoes with, 206
  fresh, dipped in vinaigrette sauce, 142
  leftover, 287–94
  mixed, rice with, 276
  soup with peas, leeks, and salad leaves, 70
vegetarian galantine, 283
velvet soup, 90
vinaigrette, *see* sauce(s)
vinegar
  general note on, 59–60
  as staple, 24

walnut(s)
  homemade cheese with, 113
  lamb in lemon sauce with scallions and, 222
  in filled melon, 116
  sauce, 247
  as staple, 28

water chestnuts and mushrooms, Chinese pork with, 231
watercress
  salad, 115
  sauce, pot-au-feu with, 214
whipped codfish with olive oil and garlic (*brandade de morue*), 109
white bean(s)
  in cassoulet, Toulouse style, 254
  leftover, 289
  salad, 289
  as staple, 24
white cream sauce, 46
whole stuffed cabbage, 226
wine(s)
  leftover, 297
  port, with rolled stuffed beef, 208
  stewed peaches with, 80
  tart, 89
  tips on, 301–9
  white, and herbs, steamed mussels in, 82
Worcestershire sauce, 60

yeast, as staple, 28
yogurt, 107
  sauce, 219
    fried eggplant with, 107
  in soup, Polish style, 136

A NOTE ABOUT THE AUTHOR

Jeannette Seaver was born in Paris and studied at the Paris Conservatory and the Juilliard School of Music in New York. She was a concert violinist for many years and now is publisher of Seaver Books. The Seavers have three children—Natalie, who has illustrated *Jeannette's Secret Recipes,* Alexander, and Nicolas. Jeannette Seaver is also the author of another cookbook, entitled *Soups.*